The Pocket Guide to
French Food and Wine

"Une aimable et pratique encyclopédie gourmande pour les amoureux d'une France aux mille parfums de bonne table."

Michel Guérard

THE POCKET GUIDE TO
French Food and Wine

Tessa Youell & George Kimball

THE CARBERY PRESS

British Library Cataloguing in Publication Data

Youell, Tessa, *1953–*
 The pocket guide to French food and wine.
 I. Title II. Kimball, George, *1935–*
 641.0944.
 ISBN 0–9518714–0–4

First published by Xanadu Publications Ltd, London 1985

This edition (revised and updated) 1992
Published by The Carbery Press
Chilbolton, Stockbridge, Hampshire SO20 6BE

Distributed by Bookpoint Ltd
39 Milton Park, Abingdon, Oxon OX14 4TD

Typeset by Wyvern Typesetting Ltd, Bristol

Printed and bound in Great Britain by
Courier International Ltd
3 Colvilles Place, Kelvin, East Kilbride, Glasgow G75 0PZ

CONTENTS

SECTION ONE
Eating and Drinking in France Today

EATING AND DRINKING
IN FRANCE TODAY

> You first parents of the human race . . . who
> betrayed yourself for an apple—what
> might you not have done for a truffled turkey!
> —BRILLAT-SAVARIN

Only a Frenchman could have said that—and he could
only have been speaking about a French turkey, prepared
by a French chef in a French kitchen; which is what makes
France such a glorious country to visit.

Before setting off to test your conscience and constitution against the numberless temptations of French food
and wine, it is worth taking the time to at least cast a
glance over the practical information presented in this
first section of the book. It fills in much of the necessary
background, and helps avoid all sorts of uncertainties and
potential annoyances that might otherwise interfere with
the main task: enjoyment.

Section Two is a more leisurely tour of France's fourteen
different gastronomic regions, giving details of local cooking styles and specialities, together with information on
the wines, liqueurs and other drinks of each district, plus
local cheeses, meat, game, fish, mushrooms etc. Each
region has a map showing—in addition to the main
towns, rivers and autoroutes—places of particular
gastronomic interest, with the more prominent wines
keyed into the wine areas (shaded). This section has two
main purposes: to inspire you in planning your trip, and
to help you locate the good things once you're there.

The third section of the book is a dictionary of French
menu terms, and it is designed specifically to help you
read, understand and order from menus that can
sometimes confuse even the most experienced diner-out.
The names of the dishes on offer can be as complex as the
food itself, and to attempt to list each of them in full would
have made the book impossibly thick, and impractical to
use. Instead, it seemed more sensible to give all of the
principal foodstuffs (beef, cauliflower, garlic etc.) their
own identifying entries, and to list individually the
various *modes* in which these ingredients are prepared;
so to find out what *homard à la charantaise* might be you
would first look up *homard* (lobster), and then *charantaise, à la* (in a cream sauce blended with cognac and fresh
grape-juice, as far as lobster is concerned). This might
seem to involve a lot of page-turning, but in practice you'll
quickly learn (if you don't know them already) the names
of the main meats, fishes etc., and turn straight to the
mode part of the name, which tends to be more puzzling.

The order of the dictionary is strictly alphabetical, and
each French word or phrase is followed by a simple
phonetic equivalent, so that those with a less than fluent

command of the language can make themselves easily and quickly understood. The phonetic system is based upon ordinary spoken English, but in a few cases where the French sound has no English equivalent we have used special symbols: ө and ʀ. Otherwise, the letters are pretty much as English-speakers would pronounce them: the sound of the French word that emerges may not be perfect, but it will get the message across—and your efforts will probably be appreciated. A key to the phonetic symbols will be found in summary form (for convenience) on the back flap of the book-jacket, and spelled out in more detail at the beginning of the dictionary itself. But these symbols are used throughout the book, whenever it seemed helpful to include them.

To attempt a survey of a subject as huge and diverse as French food and wine within the scope of a pocket-sized book might seem ambitious, but it offers a great deal of information that isn't readily available elsewhere, and in a form that you can consult while you are on the move. We hope it's useful. *Bon voyage! Bon appetit!*

Guidebooks

For anyone going to France with a view to trying out different restaurants and hotels, the *Michelin* and *Gault-Millau* guides (published annually) contain invaluable information that can save you time, money and disappointment:

Guide Michelin (Red Guide) The most comprehensive guide (with maps), covering a vast selection of hotels and restaurants, which are classified alphabetically by town-name. A system of symbols gives you all the practical information you need—prices, times when closed, and available facilities, including any special provision for the physically handicapped or for children. In the Paris section there is a list of places where you can eat outside or late at night, and find ethnic food, fish or provincial specialities such as *bouillabaisse, cassoulet, choucroute, andouillettes* etc. The choice of restaurants ranges from places offering a fixed-price meal for under 70 francs to the eighteen establishments awarded three rosettes for excellence. Up to three house specialities are listed for restaurants having one or more rosettes.

Gault-Millau Primarily a restaurant guide, with highly informative and discerning observations on a wide selection of eating-places, giving entertaining and mouth-watering descriptions of the style, atmosphere and culinary expectations of each, whether it be of humble ambition or one of the rarefied twenty-nine to which four 'toques' (chef's hat symbols) have been awarded. Its selection of hotels is far smaller than that of *Michelin*, but a few well-aimed comments on details such as the view, the age of the building, its furniture and décor give you a vivid idea of what to expect from those it does cover.

Also of great use, though not an essential as *Michelin* and *Gault-Millau*, are:

Logis de France Annually-published directory of over 4000 inexpensive, family-run hotels in the country (none in Paris), many of which specialize in regional cooking; free from the French Government Tourist Office, 178 Piccadilly, London W1 (enclose 80 pence worth of stamps).

Guide des Relais Routiers Annually-published guide to good, inexpensive roadside restaurants (some with accommodation) throughout France.

Telephoning

pay phones French public pay phones (*cabines*) have been modernized in recent years and are now very easy to use. As with British and US systems you lift the receiver, insert the coins (½F, 1F, 5F, 10F), wait for the dial tone, then dial. For international calls dial 19, wait for the new tone then dial the country code followed by the number minus the initial 0. For calls within France, whether local or long distance (excepting to and from Paris), just dial the 8-digit number. If you are calling to Paris, you must dial 16-1 before the 8-digit number. If you are calling from Paris, dial 16 before the number.

Many pay phones now take phone cards (*Carte Téléphonique*) which you can buy from a post office (*PTT*) and larger *tabacs*. A blue logo of a ringing bell on some *cabines* means calls can be received there. You can also telephone from most *PTT* (see opening hours, p. 112). A clerk will direct you to a booth where he/she will connect your call which you pay for afterwards.

emergency numbers Police 17, Fire 18, Operator 13. First aid and medical advice is available from *pharmacies*, recognizable by a green cross.

Money

exchange When exchanging foreign currency or travellers' cheques for French francs, you will always get a better rate at a bank or an official exchange station (*bureau de change*). Most hotels, save the very smallest, will exchange money for you, but the rate will not be good. Some of the larger restaurants will also exchange money—but at an even worse rate.

credit cards Visa, Barclaycard and Carte Bleue have long been acepted credit cards. Equally acceptable now are Access/Mastercard (Eurocard)); less so, American Express and Diners' Club. Most hotels, except for the smallest, now honour at least Visa, but many restaurants—particularly those outside the major cities—still prefer to deal in cash, for purely practical reasons. All *Michelin* entries include a listing of the cards which are accepted.

Names of places where you can eat or drink

auberge, ho(s)tellerie or **relais** All originally meant a coaching-inn or hostelry; today, they are alternative names for 'restaurant' and may or may not have accommodation. An *auberge de jeunesse* is a youth hostel. See also *relais routier* below.

bar or **bar comptoir** Alcoholic drinks are served here and perhaps coffee, but usually no food. For adults, though children are permitted.

bistro Generally means a small, cheap, informal restaurant, but in Paris they can be *chic* and expensive.

boîte de nuit or **cabaret** Late-night spots where you can drink, eat and usually dance.

brasserie, café, bar-brasserie or **café-bar** Alcohol, soft drinks, hot beverages and usually ice-cream and snacks (including breakfast) will be available all day here.

buffet Self-service restaurant found in stations or airports.

cabaret—see *boîte de nuit*.

café—see *brasserie*.

dégustation The literal meaning is 'tasting', and the sign is often seen outside seafood or oyster bars. In wine-growing areas it indicates a place where you can taste and buy wine.

drugstore Only found in large city-centres; an expensive source of steaks, hamburgers, elaborate ice-creams and drinks as well as clothes, make-up, accessories and souvenirs.

hostellerie See *auberge*.

hôtel Not all hotels have restaurants, but those that do are open to non-residents. Large, city hotels generally have a public bar, but this is rarely the case in family-run, country establishments. *Hôtel de ville* means 'town-hall'.

libre-service Self-service cafeteria; found in city-centres, hypermarkets (usually on the outskirts) and on the autoroutes.

pizzeria An informal restaurant featuring pizzas, snacks, and often more substantial meals such as steaks or chops with potatoes, salads and desserts.

relais see *auberge* and *routier*.

restaurant Restaurant.

rôtisserie Steakhouse or grillroom.

routier or **relais routier** The literal meaning is 'transport café'. In practice, an excellent-value roadside restaurant frequented by businessmen, families and lorry-drivers alike. Some also have accommodation.

salon de thé Tea-room serving various kinds of teas, including herbal *infusions*, together with expensive little sandwiches and cakes.

Normal business hours

Allow for variations according to local custom, the season of the year, and the kind of establishment in question.

banks Open at 8:30 or 9:00, closing for lunch at 12:00 or 12:30, then open again from 14:00 or 14:30 to 17:00.

brasseries, snack bars etc. Open around 11:00, staying open continuously until 23:30 or later.

cafés and bars Licensing is based on local police regulations, and in theory a drink may legally be sold at any time of the day or night. In practice, normal licensing hours are run from 6:00 or 7:00 until midnight; late licensing until 1:00 or 2:00, or even later.

post office (PTT) Open at 8:00, closing for lunch at 12:00 or 12:30, then open again from 14:00 or 14:30 until 19:00.

restaurants Seating for lunch between 12:00 and 14:30; seating for dinner between 19:00 and 21:30 or 22:00; late-night restaurants stay open until 3:00 or 4:00.

shops selling food and drink (e.g. *alimentation, boucherie, boulangerie, charcuterie, épicerie, pâtisserie* etc.) Open around 7:00, closing for lunch at 12:00 or 12:30, open again from 14:30 or 15:00 until 18:00 or 19:00. Most open on Sunday mornings and close on Monday mornings.

tourist offices Open at 9:00 or 10:00, staying open until 17:00 or 18:00, although some close for lunch.

Meals and meal-times

breakfast The only important aspect of what is a diminutive repast in France is coffee, which is drunk freshly-ground, very strong (though sometimes with milk, at this hour), and in large quantities—French breakfast coffee-cups resemble small soup tureens! The 'continental breakfast' is typically eaten in private houses as well as hotels, but the range of cereals is limited and bran-eaters are advised to take their own supply.

snacks Mid-morning coffee with biscuits, 'brunch', and afternoon tea with cakes are not the institutions they are elsewhere. Nevertheless, cafés, brasseries and bars are open all day, serving hot beverages, soft drinks and alcohol. A fairly standard range of snacks (*casse-croûte*) is often available—look out for the sign *casse-croûte* (or *sandwichs*) *à toute heure*. *Charcuteries* are also an excellent source of take-away snacks, while for sweet pastries and cakes you should go to a *pâtisserie*. In Paris and other major cities there are *salons de thé*, which are formal (and expensive) tea-rooms—sometimes attached to *pâtisseries*—serving a variety of teas including herbal infusions or *tisanes*, as well as coffee and cakes. Here are some typical snacks:

croque-monsieur *(krok mǝ-syǝr)* Toasted cheese and ham sandwich.

croque-madame *(krok ma-dam)* Toasted cheese and ham sandwich with a fried egg.

assiette anglaise *(as-yet awн-glez)* Plate of mixed cold meats.

choucroute garnie *(shoo-kroot gar-nee)* Sauerkraut with pork, sausages, bacon and/or goose meat and potatoes.

crêpe *(kraip)* Pancake, either plain or filled.

frites *(freet)* French fries (UK: chips).

œuf *(ǝf)* Egg:
  à la coque *(. . .ah lah kok)* Boiled.
  dur *(. . .dǝǝr)* Hard-boiled.
  mollet *(. . .mo-lā)* Soft-boiled.
  sur le plat *(. . .sǝǝr lǝ pla)* Egg fried or baked in butter.

omelette *(om-let)* Omelette:
  aux champignons *(. . .ō shawн-peen-yawн)* With mushrooms.
  aux fines herbs *(. . .ō feen-zairb)* With herbs.
  au fromage *(. . .ō fro-mahzh)* With cheese.
  au jambon *(. . .ō zhawн-bawн)* With ham.
  nature *(na-tǝǝr)* Plain.

sandwich *(sawн-weesh)* Sandwich:
  au fromage *(. . .ō fro-mahzh)* Cheese.
  au pâté *(. . .ō pa-tā)* Pâté.
  au saucisson *(. . .ō sō-see-sawн)* Sausage, e.g. salami.

drinks The French spend a great deal of time in bars and cafés—chatting, reading, doing the crossword, staring into space or watching the world go by—and they often do so over a single drink, which may be anything from a tumbler of brandy to a tiny cup of coffee, according to whim rather than the time of day. The licensing hours are very liberal in France, and nobody minds if it takes you all day to finish one drink—as long as it isn't high season, with people queueing for tables. Useful phrases:

I/we would like an orangeade/lemonade
On voudrait une orangeade/limonade
(awн voo-dra ǝǝn or-awнzh-ad/lee-mo-nad)

a lemon/grapefruit/tomato/grape juice
un jus de citron/pamplemousse/tomate/raisin
(aн zhoo dǝ see-trawн/pam-plǝ-moos/to-mat/rā-zaн)

a freshly-squeezed lemon/orange juice
un/une citron/orange pressé(e)
(an/ǝǝn see-trawʀ/or-awʀzh pre-sā)

a coffee/hot chocolat
un café/chocolat chaud
(aʀ ka-fā/sho-ko-la shō)

an iced tea/coffee
un thé/café glacé
(aʀ tā/ka-fā gla-sā)

a bottle of fizzy/non-fizzy mineral water
une bouteille d'eau minérale gazeuze/non-gazeuze
(ǝǝn boo-tā dō mee-nā-ral ga-zǝz/nawʀ ga-zǝz)

a beer/draft beer
une bière/pression
(ǝǝn byair/prai-syawʀ)

a sherry/port/brandy
un xérès/porto/cognac
(aʀ ksā-res/por-tō/kon-yak)

a gin/vodka and tonic
un gin/vodka avec Schweppes
(aʀ jeen/vod-kah a-vek shweps)

a whisky with water/soda/ice
un whisky avec de l'eau/soda/glaçon
(aʀ wees-kee a-vek dǝ lō/sō-dah/gla-sawʀ)

lunch This is normally the main meal of the day, particularly in the provinces where, in both homes and restaurants, it may begin as early as 11:30 and last until after 14:00. In cities 12:30 to 14:00 is more usual. Quicker, lighter meals are served in most cafés and brasseries, and in motorway and hypermarket self-service restaurants. In big cities you can usually find sandwich bars and self-service cafeterias (*libre-services*), and hamburger and pizza restaurants and take-aways are on the increase. An enjoyable alternative is a picnic. *Charcuteries* and *traiteurs* (delicatessens) sell a wide range of suitable picnicking fare, and if there is a market in the area a picnic provides the perfect opportunity for sampling the local produce—pâté, cheese, French bread (*baguettes* are the classic long French loaves) and a bottle of wine are hard to beat for simplicity and style. Off the main roads, rural France is perfect picnicking country, and on the motorways there are large landscaped car-parks at regular intervals where you will find wooden tables and benches, lavatories and often telephones. The roads are noticeably empty during lunch so if you are in a hurry and not hungry it is a good time to be driving. Later, we'll have a good deal more to say about eating in restaurants, whether it is lunch or . . .

dinner In the provinces this is a lighter meal than lunch —theoretically. In practice, it is still substantial by most standards, and except in very simple village hotels and restaurants you will notice little difference between lunch and dinner menus. People eat early in the country—between 19:00 and 20:00, although 20:00 to 21:00 is more usual in the south. In big cities the restaurants are more flexible; many are open to the early hours and, in Paris, there are a few which never close their doors at all. As a general rule, few people go out on Sunday evenings, and some restaurants are closed from then until Tuesday lunchtime.

Sundays and holidays

Sundays Sunday lunch is the big gastronomic event of the week for French families and may last over three hours. Most restaurants will be full by 12:30 (if not, something is wrong) so to be sure of a table you should arrive by mid-day; even better, book in advance. The cheapest set meal is often unavailable on Sundays, as well as on public holidays (see below). On Sunday mornings, business is also brisk in most bakeries (*boulangeries*), pastry shops (*pâtisseries*) and delicatessens, where mouth-watering displays of ready-made delicacies can be an irresistible temptation to those contemplating a picnic.

weekly and seasonal closing Almost all restaurants take one—sometimes two—month-long holidays during the year (*fermeture annuelle*), as do many of the smaller hotels. The listings of restaurants and hotels in the *Guide Michelin* include their weekly and annual closing-times; a local *syndicat d'initiative* will inform you about others. Note, too, that restaurants and hotels in winter resort areas may close for all or most of the summer, although this practice is becoming less frequent. Restaurants and hotels in summer resort areas usually take their annual holidays in winter. There is, however, one exception to this rule which may disconcert those particularly interested in the best of French cuisine: certain very well-known restaurants (usually with three *Michelin* rosettes) will deliberately choose to close for the month of August, at the height of the tourist season, just because they don't want the trouble of dealing with crowds of foreigners: again, *Michelin* will list the closing dates. Gastronomes wanting to avoid disappointment may wish to keep this fact in mind when planning trips to France.

French public holidays In addition to Christmas, New Year, Easter, Ascension and Whitsun the French have holidays on the following days, and to eat out—especially at lunchtime—you will need to book anywhere from a week to several weeks ahead.

May Day:	1 May	Assumption Day	15 Aug
VE Day:	8 May	All Saints Day:	1 Nov
Bastille Day:	14 July	Remembrance Day:	11 Nov

French school summer holidays run from around the end of June to the first week in September.

IN THE RESTAURANT

Writing in the 1920s, the famous gastronome Curnonsky divided French cookery into four categories: *haute cuisine, cuisine bourgeoise, cuisine régionale* and *cuisine improvisée*. Since then these categories have undergone certain changes, but nevertheless anyone interested in food will probably recognize the following basic differences which still exist:

haute cuisine The grand opera of French cookery. It consists of a vast repertoire of rich and extravagant sauces and garnishes, developed over the last three centuries in order—according to some—to disguise the poor quality and staleness of the main ingredient. With the lavish use of butter, cream, alcohol, truffles, cockscombs and other exotica, *haute cuisine* is both incredibly expensive and—in the hands of brilliant cooks—pure hedonism! You still come across the real thing in France today, but thanks to modern methods of food production and preservation the quality of the main ingredient will now be *par excellence*. However, the fare that is presented in anonymous 'international French' restaurants all over the world is mere piped music in comparison with the original.

nouvelle cuisine Also called *cuisine inventive*, this is really *cuisine improvisée* given a new look by some of France's most talented chefs, in reaction against the rigidity and somewhat unhealthy excesses of traditional *haute cuisine*. In many people's view (including our own), it is food at its finest. Only absolutely fresh, top-quality ingredients are used, and these are carefully cooked to the minimum in order to retain their full flavour. Flour is regarded with disdain, and butter and cream with caution; sauces are light reductions designed to enhance rather than obscure the taste of the main ingredient. Food cooked in this way tastes fresh, pure, and simply of what it is: you always leave the table wanting more, although the modest size of the portions may have something to do with this!

cuisine minceur Unforeseen by Curnonsky, this is the most exquisitely delicious slimming food ever devised. It was invented by Michel Guérard and is very closely related to *nouvelle cuisine*, using only the freshest ingredients and emphasizing their natural qualities. Fats, sugar and carbohydrates are largely avoided by the ingenious use of *crème fraîche, fromage blanc*, vegetable purées, skimmed milk and artificial sweeteners.

cuisine bourgeoise Originally the food enjoyed by the well-off middle classes: superb but fairly straightforward casseroles of meat or game, often with wine, onions and mushrooms. Although the original *cuisine bourgeoise* lives on in such Burgundian classics as *coq au vin* and *bœuf à la bourguignonne*, this style of cooking tends to take the form of the reliable but unimaginative 'square meal' found in *relais* and middle-range restaurants everywhere; this is really 'meat-and-two-veg.' *à la française*, distinguishable from other versions only by presentation, a knowledgeable use of garlic and herbs, and the inimitable French *je ne sais quoi*.

cuisine régionale The type of cookery indigenous to each of France's fourteen geographical regions, which are described individually in Section Two. Traditionally it was based on the seasonal availability of locally-grown foodstuffs, employed by the inhabitants to suit their own particular needs and tastes—hence the heavy, hearty fare of the mountain regions, for example. Many of these dishes are becoming endangered species, for while they are still enjoyed in private homes, they have been ousted from most restaurant menus in favour of the more generally-acceptable *cuisine bourgeoise* described above. But you should still be able to find this rustic style of cooking in cafés and inns in small agricultural communities miles off the main roads, particularly in the less-frequented regions of central France.

The Menu

Menus, with prices, are displayed outside nearly every restaurant, providing a useful opportunity to peruse and translate at leisure, the only exceptions being in remote country places where you may simply be offered what is 'on' that day. But regardless of its style of cuisine, any restaurant will normally offer one or more fixed-price meals on its menu (called the *menu prix fixe*), along with a selection of *à la carte dishes*. The least expensive fixed-price meal (usually called the *menu conseillé*) will be the least interesting as regards both the number of courses and the choice of dishes within each course. More expensive *prix fixe* menus will offer more courses and a larger selection of dishes. But no matter which of a restaurant's fixed-price meals you decide on, it will always work out less expensive than an equivalent meal chosen from the *à la carte* menu.

Service compris (s.c.) written on a menu means that its price is inclusive of both value-added tax (TVA, in France) and a service charge, and that no additional tip is expected—though you may leave one if you wish. *Taxe comprise, service en sus* means only the tax is included and that a 12%–15% tip should be added. *Prix nets* on the bill indicates that tax and service have both been added already. If none of these notes appears on the menu —and they frequently don't—ask the waiter; simply say 'Taxe et service?' (*taks ā sair-vees*) in a questioning tone, and he will explain. When no note appears it usually means that both are included, but ask anyway.

Typical examples of a cheap menu and a more expensive one (sometimes called a *menu gastronomique*) from an average, middle-range restaurant are given overleaf, with an English translation on the facing page. The prices shown are 70f and 100f, but these are merely the sort of prices that you might find; the 70f list could be anywhere between 60f and 80f, and the 100f list anywhere between 90f and 110f, depending on the type and location of the restaurant and the time of year. Naturally, you will find regional variations: near the coast, fish feature more strongly, and in the south salads, vegetables and fruit play a larger role. During the hunting season (end-October to end-March) there will usually be a certain amount of game—roasted, or in pies and pâtés. *Garni(e)* (literally, 'garnished') usually means 'with french-fried potatoes' and perhaps a vegetable such as carrots, beans or peas. There may also be a choice of other vegetables and salads, for which you would pay extra. At this price-level the selection of puddings varies little.

Restaurants with higher aspirations such as those awarded *Michelin* 'rosettes' or *Gault-Millau* 'toques' are much harder to typify, since a chef gains recognition not just for his culinary skill and presentation, but also for his originality: of the 127 establishments awarded either three or four 'toques' in the Gault-Millau guide, only ten follow what the authors call *cuisine de tradition*. The *cuisine* of the other 117 is termed *particulièrement créative*, with gastronomic novelties that are often christened with equally novel titles that can baffle Frenchman and foreigner alike. The *carte* opposite should give you an idea of French food at its mouth-watering best; it is the creation of Michel Guérard, the inventor of *cuisine minceur*, whose culinary skills have long received the highest praise from both *Gault-Millau* and *Michelin*.

A *menu dégustation*, which you may have the luck to come across in one of the more expensive restaurants, especially one of the *nouvelle cuisine* school, is literally a 'tasting' or 'sampling' menu, consisting of five to eight fixed courses of two or three mouthfuls each. Half-way through you may be given a fruit sorbet to stimulate the appetite before continuing. Such a meal can titillate even the most jaded palate, and it has the advantage of removing any decision-making on your part. Michel Guérard has provided us with a delicious example, which is shown at the end of this chapter.

Carte Gourmande

Le melon au pamplemousse rafraîchi
au vin de Sauternes.[1]

Les escargots et les moules de bouchot
en pots aux croûtons.[2]

Le saumon frais mariné au citron, l'esturgeon
et les blinis à la pomme de terre.[3]

Le saumon fumé et les langoustines au
vert à la brouillade d'œuf au caviars.[4]

Le saumon cuit à l'étouffée en
marinière de legumes.[5]

Les langoustines grillées à l'huile vierge
et aux zestes de pomme.[6]

Le carré d'agneau rôti au four
parfumé au romarin.[7]

Le filet de bœuf poêlé ou grillé au beurre
de moutarde et de fines herbes.[8]

La mitonnée de lapereau, joue de cochon
et pieds d'agneau en cocotte.[9]

Les cabécous grillés à la fleur de citronnelle
et la salade aux noisettes rôties.[10]

La grande assiette de fruits et
sorbets du temps.[11]

Les crêpes fourrées de crème légère
au coulis de framboise.[12]

La feuillantine de poires caramélisées.[13]

---

1 A salad of melon and grapefruit flavoured with *Sauternes*.
2 A dish of snails and tiny mussels served with cubes of fried bread.
3 Fresh salmon marinated in lemon juice with sturgeon and little potato blinis (pancakes).
4 Smoked salmon and fresh crayfish with scrambled eggs and caviar.
5 Salmon gently steamed on a bed of vegetables.
6 Dublin Bay prawns grilled, flavoured with olive oil and the zest of apple.
7 Rack of lamb roasted and flavoured with rosemary.
8 Fillet of beef pot-roasted or grilled with mixed herbs and mustard butter.
9 Casserole of baby rabbit, pork cheek and lamb's trotters.
10 Little goat's cheeses grilled with lemon liqueur with a salad garnished with roast hazelnuts.
11 'The grand platter' of seasonal fruits and water-ices (sherbets).
12 Pancakes filled with lightly-whipped cream and served with a purée of raspberries.
13 Caramelized pears in puff pastry.

MENU

Menu à 70f

Crudités.
Salade de tomates.
Pâté de campagne.
Soupe à l'oignon.
Soupe de légumes.
Rillettes.
Assiette anglaise.
Omelette au choix
(jambon, fromage,
champignons, fines
herbes, nature).

———

Poulet rôti garni.
Grillade au choix garni.
Coq au vin.
Côte d'agneau.
Entrecôte garni.
Pintade rôtie garnie.
Andouillettes.

———

Fromage ou desserts
ou fruits.

Menu à 100f

Escargots à la
bourguignonne.
Jambon cru.
Saucissons secs.
Charcuterie assortie.
Terrine de foie de
volaille.
Bouchée à la reine.

———

Quenelles de brochet.
Cuisses de grenouilles.
Coquilles Saint-Jacques.
Moules à la marinière.
Truite meunière.

———

Escalope de veau.
Caille rôtie garnie.
Ris de veau.
Suprême de volaille.
Bifteck au poivre.
Carré d'agneau.

———

Le plateau de fromages.

———

Desserts au choix.

Les desserts

Glaces.
Sorbets (citron, cassis,
ananas, groseille,
fraise, framboise).
Crème caramel.
Pêche melba.

Pâtisserie maison.
Tarte aux pommes
(aux poires, aux
cerises).
Crêpes.
Corbeille de fruits.

Service compris – boissons en sus.

70 franc menu

Raw vegetables (grated or chopped) with mayonnais or other cold sauce.
Tomato salad with vinaigrette.
Pork or chicken pâté (usually).
Onion soup with cheese.
Vegetable soup.
Potted pork paste.
Plate of cold meats.
Choice of omelettes (ham, cheese, mushrooms, herbs, plain).

Roast chicken.
Choice of grilled meats.
Chicken cooked in wine with onions and mushrooms.
Lamb chop.
Entrecote steak.
Roast guinea-fowl.
Grilled sausages made of tripe and pork.

Cheese or dessert or fruit

100 franc menu

Snails in garlic and parsley butter.
Raw ham, thinly sliced.
Thin slices of some dried sausage such as salami.
Selection of cold, cooked pork preparations such as pâté, sausage, or brawn.
Coarse chicken-liver pâté.
Vol-au-vent with a savoury filling (often chicken and mushrooms).

Small pike mousses in a creamy white sauce.
Frogs' legs (usually in a garlic sauce).
Scallops in a creamy white wine sauce, browned under a grill.
Mussels cooked in white wine with shallots and parsley.
Fried trout served with brown butter, lemon juice and parsley.

Veal escalope, grilled or fried.
Roast quail.
Calf's sweetbreads
Chicken's breast (often in a cream sauce).
Steak covered in crushed peppercorns, sometimes in a brandy and cream sauce.
Loin of lamb.

Cheese board.

Your own choice of dessert.

Desserts

Ice-creams.
Water ices (lemon, blackcurrant, pineapple, gooseberry, strawberry, raspberry).
Cream caramel.
Peach Melba.

Home-made pastries.
Apple (pear, cherry) tart.
Pancakes.
Bowl of fresh fruit.

Service included – drinks extra

Practical information

Cooking is regarded as a very serious art in France and eating in a restaurant amounts to no less than live participation in a serious artistic performance.

children French children are taught gastronomic appreciation almost from birth, and by the time they are four or five years old they have usually developed the ability to sit quietly at the table and enjoy five or more courses. For this reason they are welcome in most restaurants, even at night. But a very dim view is taken of crying, running around and general naughtiness, so if your kids are likely to misbehave, leave them at home, or have a picnic instead.

etiquette If you have booked in advance, try to arrive promptly. If for some reason you can't get there, take a moment, if it is at all possible, to call or stop by and cancel; the courtesy will be appreciated—and remembered. When you do get there, don't under any circumstances call the waiter *garçon*. It will be taken as a deliberately belittling insult, despite what the textbooks say. *Monsieur* is the correct title always. A waitress is called *Madame* unless she is obviously young enough to be *Mademoiselle*; if in doubt, stick to *Madame*. Snapping fingers or clapping to get the waiter's attention are also taboo. Say either *Monsieur* (*Madame, Mademoiselle*) or *s'il vous plaît*.

apéritifs The French rarely have more than one drink before eating, and this will probably be wine, a wine-based aperitif such as vermouth or port, or a light pastis. There are good reasons for this, as alcohol—particularly strong spirits—tends to dull both the palate and the appetite. The following list includes only those drinks which are popular with the French but less well-known outside France; the more common drinks generally have the same name in French and English.

Brou de Noix A brown, sweet (almost treacly) aperitif made from walnuts, which is common in Périgord.

Chambéry A dry, refreshing vermouth made in Chambéry, Savoie. *Noilly Prat* is France's most famous dry vermouth.

liqueurs The following are some of the more popular herb-based liqueurs, which are often drunk with crushed ice as aperitifs; some are fairly bitter and most are either green or yellow, or come in both colours! *Trappistine, Vieille Cure, Raspail, Liqueur des Pins, Izarra, Chartreuse, Senancole,* and *Vervaine du Velay*.

Pastis, Pernod and Ricard Different brand names for an aniseed-flavoured drink—*anis* is the generic name. It is always mixed with water (which turns it cloudy), and vastly improves with ice. Quite alcoholic and refreshing.

Pineau des Charentes A delicious combination of Cognac and grape juice; produced in Cognac, but available elsewhere.

Suze A bitter-tasting, bright-yellow drink made from the gentian plant.

Vin blanc cassis or **Kir** Made by mixing a small quantity of *crème de cassis* (blackcurrant liqueur) with white wine.

Vins doux naturels (VDN) These are sweet, fortified wines made in S France, which include *Banyuls*, *Grenache*, *Maury*, and the *muscats* (*Beaumes de Venise*, *Frontignan*, *Lunel*, *Mireval* and *Rivesaltes*). Some taste not unlike port.

In more expensive restaurants, your aperitif may well be accompanied by a bowl of goodies—often tiny tarts with a filling of cheese or some other savoury mixture—to titillate the taste-buds as you contemplate the menu and the further delights in store.

ordering In many small, family-run, country hotels and restaurants there is no written menu at all; the single set meal will be made from whatever is good and fresh in the local market that day, and it may well be a dish that is traditional to that part of the country (Section Two tells you what to look out for). A verbal description will be given if you ask, but rural dialect delivered at speed bears little relation to standard French, so you should be feeling hungry and adventurous before trying this kind of meal, particularly as helpings tend to be large and the ingredients sometimes unfamiliar (see below). Usually the food will be beautifully prepared, and copious quantities of the local wine may well be included in the overall price: these are often the cheapest and best meals of all. However, in the vast majority of restaurants the selection of dishes and the wines to accompany them is yours.

Note that when you order you don't have to wrestle with the entire name of any dish, which in a smart restaurant could run to some length: simply ask for the salient ingredient. For example, *Poularde de Bresse au foie gras truffé accompagnée d'un sauce vin rouge et de champignons sauvages* can be reduced to *La poularde, s'il vous plaît*. The notes which follow might help in 'composing' a meal, after which we'll consider the complexities and delights of the wine-list.

Be adventurous! The dictionary at the end of the book will enable you to decipher all but the most obscure or innovatory menu terms, and perhaps to overcome the natural caution that you may feel when faced with unfamiliar food; the terror of inadvertently ordering something which, when it appears, is too appalling to eat forces many people to play it safe with steaks, omelettes and salads (many French waiters believe that foreigners eat nothing else), thereby missing out on many of the delights of French cuisine. The following list of 'confus-ables' may steer you clear of some potentially unpleasant surprises:

ail Garlic.
aile Bird's wing.

aiguillette Thin slice of meat.
anguillette Tiny eel.

animelle Testicle.
animal Animal.

brochet Pike.
brochette Food cooked on a skewer.

cervelas A type of sausage.
cervelle Brain.

chevreau Kid goat.
chevreuil Venison.

fraise des bois Wild strawberry.
fraise de veau Calf's mesentry.

fromage Cheese.
fromage de tête/porc Pig's head or brawn.

gras Fat.
gras double Tripe.

morue Salt cod.
mou Lung.

oreille Pig's or calf's ear.
oseille Sorrel.

ris Sweetbreads (pancreas).
riz Rice.

rognons Kidneys.
rognons blancs Testicles.

sauce tartare A mayonnaise sauce.
steak tartare Raw minced steak.

Composition and order of courses

The composition of a meal can vary considerably accord-ing to local tradition, the whim of the chef or the gastronomic status of the restaurant, and surprises are most likely to be encountered at the two extremes of the gastronomic scale, for both the humblest and the most exalted establishments are inclined to produce an unex-pected course: a steak when you were anticipating the cheese board, a sorbet when you had visions of tucking into a *carré d'agneau*, or perhaps a little bowl of soup when a starter of fish pâté seemed almost inevitable. 'Average' restaurants in the medium-price range, which constitute the vast majority of eating-places, tend to be far more conventional, although even here you will come across a few procedures that are unfamiliar to English-speakers, but common all over France. The following paragraphs are intended as a rough guide to the pattern of the French lunch or dinner; also included are various quirks you may meet with, and some pitfalls to avoid. Should you find yourself in a tricky situation that isn't covered here, the best policy is to do whatever your fellow-diners are doing.

Generally speaking, the first and second courses are comparatively substantial, and they may leave you wondering how you will cope with the next two or three; the main course, however, is usually relatively small. Having said this, you will find some restaurants—usually at the pricy end of the *nouvelle cuisine* school—where all the courses are equally minute, the intention being to send you away refreshed rather than refuelled, with a feeling of well-being rather than with the pains of over-indulgence. In less sophisticated places, the haunts of the hard-working farmhands, they appear to assume that you haven't eaten for weeks, and try to build you up with copious quantities of each course; friendly, but sometimes overwhelming.

The first course, starter or hors-d'œuvre At the most humble, no-menu end of the market the first course is very often soup: a steaming tureen filled with an aromatic concoction of vegetables and pieces of salt pork or garlicky sausage will be left on your table for you to help yourself.

Further up the price scale, there will be a choice of charcuterie such as *rillettes*, pâtés, terrines, *andouillettes*, smoked ham etc., as well as omelettes, *crudités* (raw vegetables in mayonnaise), soup and possibly snails or shellfish.

At the top of the gastronomic tree it would be misleading to specify any starter (or indeed any other course) as being typical, but whatever it is will be beautifully prepared and the exquisite presentation may belie the richness of the ingredients: meltingly light flaky-pastries filled with *foie-gras* and truffles, or perhaps mussels, lobster or some other shellfish in a cream sauce, delicate creamy soufflés or mousses of puréed vegetables or fish, little *croûtes* topped with quails' eggs set in *foie-gras* . . . and for those of failing appetite or frail constitution there will usually be a salad—a masterpiece of creativity in colour and texture.

In this sort of place you may be subjected to the initially puzzling experience of being served first of all—perhaps with your aperitif, as suggested earlier—with a little dish of something that bears absolutely no relation to the starter you thought you had ordered. However, everything is in order; this is simply the pre-starter that comes courtesy of those restaurants which want to make a particular effort to please you.

The second course, or entrée Most restaurants in the medium-to-top brackets will offer you one or two more expensive menus (*menus gourmands*), which include an additional course between the starter and the main course. The choice of dishes for the course will be orientated largely towards fish, which may be presented in a number of different ways: little fillets either deep-fried or poached, and served in a rich cream sauce; individual mousses, cold (*mousselines* or *biscuits*) or hot (*quenelles*); shellfish are generally present too, often hot as *gratins* (in a creamy sauce topped with breadcrumbs and browned), or cold in a mayonnaise or piquante dressing. Frogs' legs or snails may be also offered, and sometimes chicken or rabbit; these last two are usually cooked in a creamy sauce which is used as a filling for *vol-au-vents* or other kinds of pastry, or it can be made into *croquettes* and deep-fried.

You can always choose another starter as your *entrée*. Equally, there will be no raised eyebrows if you order an *entrée* or even a third starter for your main course.

In small, no-menu restaurants the chances of automatically being given an *entrée* are surprisingly high, and here lies a potential hazard: except in those places situated near the coast, this course will rarely consist of fish; an omelette with a rich mushroom, cheese or perhaps sausage filling is far more likely, or it might be some form of offal such as sweetbreads, kidneys, liver, or even brains in a spicy, garlicky sauce; or you may be served a generous slice of tart or pie filled with chicken or some other white meat or vegetable. From the humble appearance of the place and the substantial nature of the first course you may well have the impression (and the hope!) that you are now on to the main course: far from it! With a little careful observation you can normally establish which course you are on (since in these places you are frequently left to help yourself) by judging the size of helping taken by those around you, and you should be able to gauge how much there is to follow—but it is worth remembering that the French have prodigious appetites!

The main course This is traditionally the meat course, but you can choose fish; there are no rules. The choice will probably include red and white meat, poultry, offal and sometimes game (especially during the hunting season from October to March). The presentation and content of the dish can vary considerably according to the type of place you are in. One thing you will notice wherever you are is the absence on the menu of a selection of accompanying vegetables.

In an average, unpretentious sort of place such as a roadside *relais* or some other popular and reasonably-priced restaurant, the meat dish you order will usually be accompanied automatically by a pile of *frites* (french fries or chips) and an unassuming vegetable such as peas, string beans, carrots or haricot beans; these are sometimes indicated on the menu by the word *garni* after the name of the dish, but not always, and there won't often be much choice. Meat dishes typical of this sort of restaurant include lamb chops or cutlets (*côtes* or *côtelettes*); gammon steak; chicken fried or casseroled (*coq au vin*); grilled or fried veal escalopes; liver, tripe or some other kind of offal; or a steak, usually sirloin or rump. All these dishes will generally be beautifully but simply cooked with perhaps a hint of garlic, herbs and wine in the gravy but no rich creamy sauces with *foie-gras* and truffles: good food without frills would be an accurate description. By our standards the lamb will be a little pinkish and under-cooked, but you can always specify that you want it *bien cuit* (well done). As regards the cooking of steak, the French scale of very rare (*bleu*), rare (*saignant*), medium rare (*à point*) to well done (*bien cuit*) is perhaps one grade rarer than the rest of the world would have it. In fact, the Anglo-Saxon penchant for well-done meat is something of a standing joke among the French, for they have coined a fifth phrase to describe an extra degree of 'doneness' —*bien bien cuit* or BBC—expressly for the benefit of us crazy foreigners.

In both top-ranking and humble, no-menu restaurants you may well feel on rather less familiar ground when the main course arrives. In both cases there may be nothing on your plate except for the meat itself (Should you wait for the vegetables? Almost invariably not). In a rustic hostelry it will probably be a steak, lamb cutlet or leg of chicken, simply presented in its own juices or in a thickened wine sauce. At the top end of the scale it may be thin strips (*aiguillettes* or *éminces*) of game or poultry expertly sliced from the breast; or perhaps the breast left entire (*magret* of duck; *blanc* or *suprême* of chicken); or tender little *noisettes* of lamb or *filet mignons* of beef; or perhaps a ragoût of something with truffles in a creamy wine sauce . . . The possibilities are endless, but whatever you choose it may well sit in solitary splendour on the plate—a masterpiece to be admired and enjoyed without the distraction of heaps of vegetables (although there may be a little bouquet of tiny carrots and green beans to provide a little decoration and colour).

To refresh the palate, and possibly to make up for any previous lack of vitamin C, a green salad often appears immediately after the meat course, and this is especially likely in the humbler establishments.

Cheese Cheese, which always precedes the dessert course in France, is given a great deal of importance. A good cheese-board (and most *are* good) will contain a wide variety of goat's-, cow's- and possibly sheep's-milk cheeses. Most of them will be local and unfamiliar, since over 400 different cheeses are made in France and most of them are never seen outside the regions where they are made. Descriptions of all the principal regional cheeses are given in Section Two; meanwhile, here is a basic vocabularly of cheese terms:

Brebis (fromage de) Sheep's- or ewe's-milk cheese.

Cabécou Name for tiny goat's-milk cheeses (Rouergue, Quercy, Bordelais).

Cendré Cheese ripened in ashes (*cendres*).

Chèvre, (fromage de) Goat's-milk cheese.

Chevreton Name for goat's-milk cheeses (Burgundy, Auvergne, Lyonnaise).

Chevrotin Name for goat's-milk cheeses (Savoie).

Crottin Name for brown, dry goat's-milk cheeses in Berry (E Loire).

double-crème Double-cream cheese with 60% minimum fat content.

fromage frais Fresh, unripened cheese; soft, creamy and mild and often eaten with fruit and sugar. *Petit-Suisse* and *Demi-sel* are commercially-made versions.

fromage fondu Term for processed cheese with a minimum of 40% fat.

fromage laitier Factory or dairy-made cheese, as opposed to . . .

fromage fermier Farm-made cheese.

matière grasse Fat content.

noiseté The hazelnut taste characteristic of many goat's-milk cheeses.

Pélardon Name for goat's-milk cheeses in the Languedoc region.

persillé Description of the blue-veining in blue cheeses such as *Roquefort* and the goat's-milk cheeses of Savoie.

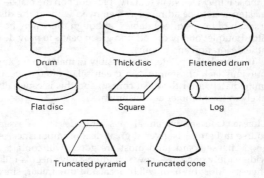

Drum   Thick disc   Flattened drum

Flat disc   Square   Log

Truncated pyramid   Truncated cone

Picodon Name for goat's milk cheeses in the Rhône and Languedoc areas.

Tomme Name for cheeses in the Alps and Provence, which are often made from goat's or sheep's milk.

triple-crème Triple-cream cheese with 75% minimum fat content.

vache Cow: the name *vachard* and *vacherin* denote cow's-milk cheese.

You can ask the waiter for small samples (*petits morceaux* or *bouchées*) of a number of different types, and he may advise you on the order (of strength) in which to eat them. Cheese is eaten either by itself in your fingers (with a knife and fork, if it is very soft) or with bread and perhaps butter, but rarely with biscuits. Red wine is the best accompaniment for most types, but see also 'What Wine with What Food?'.

The dessert course Desserts are given surprisingly little importance in most French restaurants—surprisingly, because the exceptional standard and choice of sweet pastries and cakes in the numerous *pâtisseries* indicates that the French have a high level of appreciation of things sweet. The list of desserts on the specimen menu given earlier is very typical of the average restaurant, and you will find little variation at or below this price bracket: most chefs seem to concentrate their skills on the savoury courses. However, in a top-calibre establishment, the dessert will be as exquisite as the rest of the meal: a *chariot* or trolley loaded with all sorts of pastries, mousses, soufflés, sorbets, fruit *compôtes* etc., plus a basket of fresh fruit, may be wheeled up to your table after you have finished with the cheese. Alternatively, you may be given a menu to select from. Note that hot puddings and pastries are often individually prepared for you, and these should be ordered right at the beginning; *à commander au début du repas*, or some similar instruction, will appear on the menu in such cases.

Finally, you will be served small cups of very strong black coffee, which in upmarket restaurants will be accompanied by a bowl of *petit-fours* (also called *friandises* or *mignardises*); these may be tiny biscuits, cakes, fruit tartlets or chocolates. There will also be a choice of brandy (*Cognac* or *Armagnac*), *marc*, fruit *eaux-de-vie* and liqueurs. Note that in France a 'liqueur' (or *ratafia*) is by definition sweet, as it is made from a syrup obtained by the maceration of fruit, nuts, flowers etc. with sugar, which is then mixed with a spirit, whereas an *eau-de-vie* is a bone-dry spirit produced by the distillation of wine (as in *Cognac, Armagnac, marc*), cider (as in *Calvados*) or of other fermented fruits; there is a list of these in the notes on Alsace in Section Two.

Useful phrases

S'il vous plaît (see *voo plā*), meaning 'please' is abbreviated to s.v.p. throughout.

I would like (to book) a table for two/three/four (people)
Je voudrais (réserver) une table pour deux/trois/quatre
(zhǝ voo-drā (rā-zair-vā) ǝǝn ta-blǝ poor dǝ/trwah/kat)

at seven/eight/nine o'clock, please
à sept/huit/neuf heures, s.v.p.
(ah set/weet/nǝf ǝr s.v.p.)

Need I book for lunch/dinner today?
Faut-il réserver pour déjeuner/dîner aujourd hui?
(fō teel rā-zair-vā poor dā-zhǝ-nā/dee-nā ō-zhoord-wee)

Waiter! Waitress!
Monsieur! Mademoiselle/Madame! Excusez-moi!
(mǝ-syǝr! mad-mwah-zel/ma-dam! eks-kǝǝ-zā mwah!)

We would like an aperitif, please
On voudrait des apéritifs, s.v.p.
(awʀ voo-drā dā za-pā-ree-teef s.v.p.)

I would like the 60/80/120 franc menu
Le menu à soixante/quatre-vingt/cent-vingt francs
(lǝ mǝ-nǝǝ ah swah-sawʀt/ka-trǝ vaʀ/sawʀ vaʀ frawʀ)

What do you recommend?
Qu'est-ce que vous recommendez?
(kes-kǝ voo rǝ-ko-mawʀ-dā)

What is this dish exactly?
En quoi consiste ce plat exactement?
(ahʀ kwa kon-seest sǝ pla eg-zak-tǝ-mawʀ)

We only want one course, please
On ne voudrait qu'un plat, merci
(awʀ nǝ voo-drā kaʀ pla mair-see)

No starter/entrée/cheese/dessert
Pas d'hors-d'œuvre/d'entrée/de fromage/de dessert
(pah dor-dǝv-rǝ/dawn-trā/dǝ fro-mahzh/dǝ dai-sair)

I would like salad with the main course
Je voudrais de la salade avec le plat principal
(zhǝ voo-drā dǝ lah sa-lad a-vek lǝ pla praʀ-see-pal)

I'd like my steak well done/medium-rare/rare/very rare
Je voudrais le steack bien cuit/à point/saignant/bleu
(zhǝ voo-drā lǝ stek b'yan kwee/ah pwaʀ/sen-yawʀ/blǝ)

I would like more . . . please
Encore de . . . s.v.p.
(awʀ-kor dǝ . . . s.v.p.)

I would like another . . . please
Un(e) autre . . . s.v.p.
(aʀ/əən ō-trə . . . s.v.p.)

It is/they are delicious (but I am full)
Il est/ils sont très bon (mais j'ai assez mangé)
(ee lā/eel zawʀ trā bawʀ (mā zhā a-sā mawʀ-zhā))

Where is the lavatory?
Où sont les toilettes s.v.p.?
(əə sawʀ lā twah-let s.v.p.?)

The bill, please
L'addition, s.v.p.
(la-dee-syawʀ s.v.p.)

Is service included?
Est-ce que le service est compris?
(es-kə lə sair-vees ā kom-pree?)

We enjoyed the meal very much, thank you
Nous avons très bien mangé, merci
(noo za-vawʀ trā byen mawʀ-zhā, mair-see)

Good day/ good evening/until the next time
Bonne journée/bonsoir/au revoir
(bon zhoor-nā/bawʀ-swahr/ō rə-vwahr)

The wine list (*la carte des vins*)

In France wine is considered an essential accompaniment to food and in most cases, though not all, the better the restaurant the better the range and quality of the wine-cellar. In areas where little or no wine is produced, a good wine-list will probably contain a fairly catholic selection from a number of different regions. However, in areas such as Bordeaux and Burgundy, where wine-making is a major industry, the range will be heavily biased towards their own produce, with only a token choice of wines from elsewhere. In more expensive restaurants, all the wines will be of *Appellation Contrôlée* standard unless there are any local vDQS wines of unusually high quality. Cheaper eating-places generally offer a limited selection of local wines only; these are almost always good value, and go well with the local food. *Vin ordinaire* can be ordered by the glass or *carafe*: anything better comes only by the bottle or half-bottle. Before the waiter opens your bottle it is a good idea to check on the label that the year and producer tally with what you ordered.

What wine with what food?

The table on the next two pages lists the main wines of each region alphabetically in broad categories, and shows what wine conventionally goes with what food. When

WHAT WINE GOES . . .

DRY WHITE

Alsace	*Riesling.*
Bordeaux	*Côtes de Blaye, Entre-Deux-Mers, Graves.*
Brittany	*Muscadet.*
Burgundy	*Chablis, Côte de Beaune, Côte de Nuits, Macon, Montagny, Pouilly-Fuissé, Pouilly-Fumé, Rully, St-Véran, Viré.*
Jura & the Alps	*Crépy, Seyssel.*
Loire	*Coteaux de la Loire, Jasnières, Montlouis, Sancerre, Vouvray.*
Provence	*Cassis.*
Northern Rhône	*Crozes-Hermitage.*

ROSÉ

Burgundy	*Marsannay.*
Champagne	*Rosé de Riceys.*
Jura	*Arbois.*
Loire	*Cabernet/Rosé d'Anjou.*
Provence	*Côtes de Provence.*
Southern Rhône	*Lirac, Tavel.*

RED

Bordeaux	*Côtes de Bourg, Premières Côtes de Blaye, Fronsac, Graves, Haut-Médoc, Médoc, Pomerol, St Emilion.*
Burgundy	*Beaujolais, Côte de Nuits, Givry, Mercurey, Macon.*
Périgord & Quercy	*Bergerac, Cahors, Pécharmant.*
Languedoc	*Corbières, Faugères, Fitou, Minervois, St Chinian.*
Loire	*Bourgueil, Chinon, Saumur-Champigny.*
Provence	*Bandol, Côtes de P., Palette, Bellet, Coteaux d'Aix-en-P., Coteaux de Baux.*
Northern Rhône	*Cornas, Côte Rôti, Côtes du Rhône, Hermitage, St. Joseph.*
Southern Rhône	*Châteauneuf-du-Pape, Coteaux du Tricastin, Côtes du Rhône Villages, Côtes du Ventoux, Gigondas.*
Roussillon & Pyrenees	*Côtes du Roussillon, Madiran.*

SWEET WHITE

Alsace	*Gewurztraminer (vendange tardive).*
Bordeaux	*Barsac, Cérons, Sauternes.*
Périgord	*Monbazillac.*
Jura	*Vin de Paille.*
Languedoc	*Frontignan, Lunel, Mireval.*
Loire	*Coteaux du Layon.*
Southern Rhône	*Beaumes de Venise, Rasteau.*
Roussillon & Pyrenees	*Banyuls, Jurançon, Maury, Muscat de Rivesaltes.*

SPARKLING WHITE

Alsace	*Crémant d'Alsace.*
Burgundy	*Crémant de Bourgogne.*
Champagne	*(See Section Two).*
Jura & the Alps	*Seyssel, Clairette de Die.*
Languedoc	*Blanquette de Limoux.*
Loire	*Crémant de L., Saumur Mousseux.*
Northern Rhône	*Pétillant de Bugey, St Péray.*

All of these wines go well with white meat – chicken, pork, rabbit, turkey or veal – and with such items of *charcuterie* as *andouilles*, ham, pâtés, *rillons*, *rillettes*, sausages and terrines. They also make an excellent accompaniment for most types of fish (freshwater, salt-water and smoked), and for snails too. Other possibilities include avocado pear, cheese fondue, mousses, pasta dishes, salads, savoury flans (onion tart, *quiche lorraine* etc.) souffles and soups. The best cheeses to eat with these wines are mild and creamy ones. Wines like dry Alsace *Muscat*, *Gewurztraminer*, *Vin Jaune*, *Condrieu* and *Château Grillet* are best as aperitifs or with cocktail eats and spicy or rich food such as smoked fish, *foie gras*, *confit* of goose or duck, and pork.

As above, although these wines are not really suitable for drinking with dishes incorporating a white wine sauce.

Again, if the dish you are eating contains wine it is better to drink a similar wine than one that is going to clash. Otherwise, these red wines can be drunk with almost any type of meat – red, white or in the form of *charcuterie*. These are also the wines for game, whether it has fur (hare, venison, wild boar) or feathers (grouse, partridge, pheasant, pigeon etc.), and for rich stew-like dishes such as *cassoulet*, *civet*, *estouffade*, *potée* and so on. Finally, if you have nuts at the end of your meal, a glass of red wine makes a pleasant change from the more conventional after-dinner drinks, and for strong cheese it is the ideal companion.

Sweet wines tend to be associated with desserts: *crème brulée*, *crêpes*, fruit tarts, *gâteaux*, mousses, pastries and soufflés . . . the list is endless. They also go well with soft fruits like melon, peaches, raspberries and strawberries, but not so well with citrus fruits – oranges, grapefruits etc. Try a sweet wine with *foie gras*, however, or with *Roquefort* cheese. These wines also make good aperitifs.

While dry Champagne can accompany almost any food, like other dry sparkling wines it is better drunk as an aperitif or with rich delicacies such as smoked salmon, caviar and *foie gras*. Sweet Champagne and other sweet sparkling wines are perhaps more suitable for desserts such as those named above.

33

choosing wine(s) to go with your meal you want something that will match the food in strength, richness and style, so that each will compliment the other. The delicate taste of sole will be somewhat nullified if it is accompanied by a powerful red wine such as *Hermitage* or *Cahors*. Equally, the freshness and crispness of a fine dry white such as *Chablis* will be barely appreciated if it is sipped after a mouthful of *bœuf à la bourguignonne*. Apart from such extremes the possibilities are almost endless, and there are few hard and fast rules: in Bordeaux it is not unusual for fish to be accompanied by Claret (red *Bordeaux*), while in Alsace they drink the local dry white wine with red meat and game.

The characteristics of all the main wines of each region are given in Section Two. The chapter on wine which follows is intended to provide you with the essential information on wine in general, including the things to look out for when choosing and tasting wine. It is worth noting that factors such as the weather, the temperature, your mood, the company, the time of day, the time of year, as well as the food itself, all affect the taste of wine: a *Côtes de Provence* rosé leisurely sipped over *bouillabaisse* under a canopy of trailing vines in the lazy summer heat of the Côte d'Azur will taste entirely different over fish pie and peas during the office lunch-hour on a bleak day in January. Heavy colds and heavy spirits (both mental and alcoholic) affect one's perception of wine considerably; so do eggs, artichokes, avocados, vinegary sauces and salad dressings, acidic fruit salads, sorbets, and ice-cream.

Should you find yourself in an expensive restaurant, bewildered by an enormous wine list, you could do worse than follow the recommendations of the wine waiter (*le sommelier*): with his intimate knowledge of the wine-cellar he will (or should) know exactly which wines are ready for drinking.

'Le repas des villes'

This is the name of one of Michel Guérard's *menus dégustations*—a 'sampling' menu of the kind found only in the more expensive restaurants, and usually one practising *nouvelle cuisine*. This is a particularly delicious example, comprising several courses of just two or three mouthfuls each: an extraordinary culinary experience guaranteed to rejuvenate the most jaded gourmand, and one that brings this part of the book to a splendid climax.

Out of interest, we asked M. Guérard to recommend a wine to go with each course, and his selections are listed alongside the translations at the foot of the page.

LE REPAS
DES VILLES

Le foie gras à la mignonnette de poivre en gelée

La raviole de truffe à la crème de mousserons et de morilles

Le demi-homard rôti et fumé dans la cheminée

La rissole d'aile de caille fourrée de cèpes

Le millefeuille à l'impératrice

Foie gras poached in stock, wrapped in a jelly with cracked peppercorn.	A glass of house Sauternes
The ravioli of truffle in a creamy wild mushroom sauce.	Puligny Montrachat 'Les Combettes' 1987 Meursault 'Clos de Barre' 1987 Château Grillet 1988 Château Doisy Daene 1988
Half a lobster grilled and smoked in the fireplace.	
Breast of quail stuffed with ceps and foie gras, wrapped in puff pastry and served with a red wine sauce.	Château Pont Cloquet 1983 Château Beauregard 1979 Château Carbonnieux 1986 Château Haut Badette 1985 Château Dillon 1986
A very light puff pastry filled with crème patissière and served with a puree of raspberries and apricots, and caramelized apples.	To be savoured without any distractions

Useful phrases

S'il vous plaît (see *voo plā*), meaning 'please' is abbreviated to *s.v.p.* throughout.

May I/we see the wine list?
La carte des vins s.v.p.
(lah kart dā vaн s.v.p.)

What wine do you recommend with these dishes?
Qu'est-ce que vous recommendez comme vin pour aller aux plats qu'on a choisis
(kes kө voo rө-ko-mawн-dā kom vaн poor a-lā ō pla kawн ah shwah-zee)

A glass/a bottle of red/white/rosé wine, please
Un verre/une bouteille de vin rouge/blanc/rosé *s.v.p.*
(aн vair/өөn bөө-tā dө vaн roozh/blawн/ro-zā s.v.p.)

I/we would like a light/fruity/full-bodied/sweet/dry wine
On voudrait un vin léger/fruité/charnu/doux/sec
(on voo drā aн van lā-zhā/frwee-tā/shar-nөө, doo, sek)

Something cheaper than that, please
Quelque chose moins cher que ça, s.v.p.
(kel-kө shōz mwaн shair kө sah, s.v.p.)

Would you chill/open the bottle please?
Voudriez-vous rafraîchir/déboucher la bouteille, s.v.p.?
(voo-dree-yā voo-ra-frā-sheer/dā-boo-shā lah bөө-tā, s.v.p.)

The wine tastes good/bad
Le vin a un bon/mauvais goût
(lө vaн ah aн bawн/mō-vā goo)

The wine looks cloudy
Le vin a l'aspect troublé
(lө vaн ah las-pā troo-blā)

Would you taste the wine, please?
Voudriez-vous goûter au vin, s.v.p.?
(voo-dree-yā voo goo-tā ō vaн, s.v.p.)

Could you tell me where I can buy this wine?
Voudriez-vous me dire ou je pourrais acheter ce vin?
(voo-dree-yā voo mө deer oo zhө poo-rā ash-tā sө van)

I want to buy some fine wine of this region
Je veux acheter du vin fin de ce région
(zhө vө ash-tā dөө vaн faн dө sө rā-zhyawн)

Who is the best local producer, in your opinion?
Quel est le meilleur producteur du pays à votre avis?
(kel ā lө mā-yөr pro-dөөk-tөr dөө pā ah vo-trө a-vee)

The best restaurants in France

Michelin 'rosettes' (🏵) and *Gault-Millau* 'toques' (♀) are awarded to a chef not just for culinary skill but also for the rare quality of being able to create new dishes—and as Brillat–Savarin quite correctly said: 'The discovery of a new dish does more for human happiness than the discovery of a new star.' The restaurants in the list that follows have received the greatest number of *rosettes* and points from the two authorities cited. The chef's name is given after the name of the restaurant unless it *is* the name of the restaurant.

Paris

L'Ambroisie—Pacaud (3♀, 3🏵), 9 pl des Vosges, Paris 4. Tel. (Paris) 42.78.51.45.

Lucas-Carton—Senderens (4♀, 3🏵). 9 pl de la Madeleine, Paris 8. Tel. (Paris) 42.65.22.90.

Robuchon (4♀, 3🏵). 32 rue Longchamp, Paris 16. Tel. (Paris) 47.27.12.27.

Taillevent—Vrinat (4♀, 3🏵). 15 rue Lamennais, Paris 8. Tel. (Paris) 45.63.39.94.

Tour d'Argent—Terrail (3♀, 3🏵). 15 Quai Tournelle, Paris 5. Tel. (Paris) 43.54.23.31.

Alsace

L'Auberge de l'Ill—Haeberlin (4♀, 3🏵). Rue de Collonges, Illhaeusern, 68150 H.-Rhin. Tel. 89.71.83.23.

Le Crocodile—Jung (3♀, 3🏵). 10 rue Outre, Strasbourg, 67000 B.-Rhin. Tel. 88.32.13.02.

Burgundy

La Côte St-Jacques—Lorain (4♀, 3🏵). 14 faubourg de Paris, Joigny, 89300 Yonne. Tel. 86.62.09.70.

La Côte d'Or—Loiseau (4♀, 3❀). 2 rue Argentine, Saulieu, 21210 Côte d'Or. Tel. 80.64.07.66.

L'Espérance—Meneau (4♀, 3❀). St-Père-sous-Vézelay, Vézelay, 89450 Yonne. Tel. 86.33.20.45.

Lameloise (3♀, 3❀). 36 pl. d'Armes, Chagny, 71150 Seine/Loire. Tel. 85.87.08.85.

Champagne

Les Crayères—Boyer (4♀, 3❀). 64 bd. Henri Vasnier, Reims, 51100 Marne. Tel. 26.82.80.80.

Gascony

Les Prés d'Eugénie—Guérard (4♀, 3❀). Eugénie-les-Bains, 40320 Landes. Tel. 58.05.06.07.

Jura and the Alpes

Auberge de l'Eridan—Veyrat (4♀, 2❀). 7 av. de Chavoires, Annecy, 74000 H.-Savoie. Tel. 50.66.22.04.

Lyonnais and the Rhône Valley

Alain Chapel (4♀, 2❀). Mionnay, 01390 Ain. Tel. 78.91.82.02.

Georges Blanc (4♀, 3❀). Vonnas, 01540 Ain. Tel. 74.50.00.01.

Paul Bocuse (4♀, 3❀). 50 Quai de la Plage, Collonges-au-Mont-d'Or, 69660 Rhône. Tel. 78.22.01.40.

Pic (4❀, 3♀). 285 av. V. Hugo, Valence, 26000 Drôme. Tel. 75.44.15.32.

Troisgros (4♀, 3❀). Pl. de la Gare, Roanne, 42300 Loire. Tel. 77.71.66.97.

The Massif Central

Michel Bras (4♀, 2❀). Laguiole, 12210 Aveyron. Tel. 65.44.32.24.

The Périgord and Quercy

L'Aubergade—Trama (4♀, 2❀). 52 rue Royal, Puymirol, 47270 Lot/Garonne. Tel. 53.95.31.46.

Provence and Monaco

Jacques Maximin (4♀, 2❀). 2–4 rue S.-Guitry, Nice, 06000 Alpes-Mar. Tel. 93.80.70.10.

Le Moulin de Mougins—Vergé (3♀, 3❀). Notre-Dame-de-Vie, Mougins, 06250 Alpes-Mar. Tel. 93.75.78.24.

Le Louis XV—Ducasse (4♀, 3❀). Hôtel de Paris, pl. du Casino, Monaco. Tel. 93.50.80.80.

THE WINES OF FRANCE

Wine is grown almost everywhere in France. The very best comes from Bordeaux, Burgundy, the Loire and Rhône valleys, Champagne and Alsace. The vast bulk of *vin de table* or *vin ordinaire* (everyday table-wine) is grown in the Languedoc—although that is not to say that all Languedoc wine is 'ordinary' any more than that all Bordeaux wine is top-quality. You will find good, often excellent wines from Savoie, Jura, Provence, Roussillon (the eastern end of the Pyrenees), Bergerac and the south-west, and from Corsica. The shape of the wine bottle varies from region to region—a great aid to speedy identification:

Côtes de Pro-   Anjou   Burgundy   Bordeaux   Alsace   Champagne
vence Rosé   Rosé   'flute'

Hierarchy of French wines

French wine is classified into four categories (indicated on the label); these are as follows, in ascending order of merit:

Vin de table Often sold under a brand name and made from an unrestricted number of different grape-types. It may also be a blend of various wines from all over France as well as from other EEC countries.

Vin de pays Produced from specified varieties of grape in the area indicated on the label.

Vin délimité de qualité supérieure (VDQS) Controlled by stricter rules governing the methods of growing and production.

NB: *Vin de pays* and VDQS wines have to undergo an annual blind-tasting test carried out by an official committee, whose consensus is required each year to grant the wine its classification status.

Vin à appellation d'origine contrôlée (AC or AOC) Subjected to stringent regulations laid down by the INAO (*Institut National des Appellations d'Origine des Vins et Eaux-de-Vie*) and produced in a strictly-defined area under rigorous controls, which determine: the grape-types used, the method of pruning the vines, the quantity planted per hectare, the quantity of wine produced per hectare, the minimum alcohol content and various other aspects of wine production. However, AC win is exempt from any annual tasting test, and although the finest wines come under this category the AC label is no absolute guarantee of quality. A recommended producer is the best source of reliable wine. In Bordeaux, Burgundy and Alsace the best vineyards are further classified into a hierarchy of *crus* and *crus classés* (literally, 'growths' and 'classed growths') which are explained in the paragraphs on wine in Section Two.

The life-span of wines

Of the above four categories, only the last includes wine that improves significantly with age (*vin de garde*). The others are best drunk young, with the exception of the powerful VDQS reds of Provence and the Languedoc, which often benefit from a few years in the bottle.

Generally speaking, the better the wine and the greater the vintage, the longer it will take to mature and the longer its life-expectancy. Dry white wine and rosé is usually drunk young, when it is fresh and fairly acidic; the exceptions to this include some of the great whites of Burgundy and the Loire, and *vin jaune*, which is made only in the Jura and which may keep for over a hundred years. Sweet white wines can also be drunk young, although some may last for fifty years and more. Some of the great sweet whites of *Sauternes* and the *Coteaux du Layon* (Loire Valley) take ten years to mature and may keep for a hundred.

Fine red wine is considered ready for drinking—by non-French drinkers, anyway—when time has softened the tannin and acidity, creating a harmony of all the various elements. In a great red *Bordeaux* or *Burgundy* this process can take up to twenty years, and some of them may keep for sixty years. Loire and Rhône wines tend to mature more quickly, and do not last much beyond twenty years.

Buying and drinking wine in France

Well-matured fine wine is far from being widely available in France. You will find it only in very expensive restaurants and at top-class wine-merchants, where it costs as much as it does in Britain, America and other major wine-importing countries. The lesser ACs and VDQS wines are a far better buy in France, being relatively quick to mature and quite easy on the pocket.

Vin ordinaire and *vin de pays* (often deceptively strong) can be bought extremely cheaply in any grocery (*épicerie*) or general foodstore (*alimentation générale*), while a wider range is available in the big supermarkets (*supermarchés* or *hypermarchés*) that you find on the outskirts of towns. Wine merchants (*marchands des vins*) are now on the increase but they are by no means as common as in Britain or the US, and their selection of wines is relatively limited. In the wine-growing areas you can usually buy from wine cooperatives, which sell local wine by the bottle or in larger containers, or you can take along your own vessel to be filled; you can buy a plastic *bidon* for wine, with its own spigot or tap, from many *co-ops* and *caves*, and at most hardware shops (*quincail-leries*). You will also see notices at the roadside saying *dégustation de vin* or *dégustation et vente* (*directe*) with an arrow pointing to a house or barn. This is a free invitation to taste (and buy) wine direct from the grower; it is good diplomacy to buy one bottle at least, if you do stop; it won't cost very much. For the serious wine enthusiast wanting to stock up the wine-cellar or the cupboard under the stairs with, say, some good Burgundy or claret, the best bet is to go to a recommended producer. A list (by no means exhaustive) of reliable producers—who may be blenders/shippers (*négociants*) or vineyard owners (*propriétaires*)—is given in *Le Guide Hachette des Vins*, published annually. A friendly restaurant owner, or wine-waiter can also point you in the right direction, as can the *Maison du Vin* of the region: addresses are given at the end of each region in Section Two, and the names of some particularly well-known and respected producers are given where relevant.

Serving wine

Most red wine should be drunk at between 60° and 65°F (16°–18°C), i.e. at room-temperature (or *chambré*). And the cork should be removed about an hour beforehand to allow the wine to 'breathe', releasing its full flavour, fragrance and bouquet; in a restaurant the latter is obviously not always possible, unless you order well ahead of time. One exception to this general rule is *Beaujolais Nouveau*, which is popularly served cool at about 54°F (12°C): ideal cellar temperature.

White wine (including champagne) and rosé should be chilled to between 45° and 50°F (7°–10°C), the sweeter ones at the colder end of the range. Warm white wine usually tastes lifeless and insipid.

The ideal wine-tasting glass (which should be of plain glass—never tinted) is as shown on the next page, and it should be slightly less than half-filled, as shown, so that when it is swirled around in the fashion described below, both the wine and its smell remain inside the glass rather than being dissipated about the room.

Tasting wine

The appreciation of wine is largely a matter of personal taste and it can be enjoyed on a number of different levels, from a basic preference for anything dry rather than sweet, or white rather than red, to—in the most elevated wine circles—an inclination towards wine from one particular *château* rather than from its next-door neighbour in the same *commune*. The following notes are intended for wine enthusiasts lying somewhere between these two extremes, but they should be regarded as only very rough guidelines, since the variety of French wine is so huge that it is difficult to generalize. The amateur wine enthusiast is recommended to read *Michael Broadbent's Pocket Guide to Wine Tasting*, the best basic guide to a subject that can only be summarized here.

Appearance

The colour of wine, its depth and clarity, can reveal a great deal about its age and quality. To observe the nuances of colour, the glass should be held by its stem and tipped at an angle away from you against a white background.

Colour and depth: red wine

dark purple (almost opaque) Young, immature wine (especially from Bordeaux and Rhône); the depth of colour often indicates a high tannin content, and the wine will need a long time to reach maturity: hide it away for a few years.

bright, translucent purple Youthful but not necessarily immature wine; typical of young *Beaujolais*, that should be drunk at this stage while it is still fresh.

pale 'watery' red Generally indicates thin wine of inferior quality; sometimes seen in mass-produced *vins de table*; satisfies the thirst but little else.

brick-red Soft, slightly orange-red rather than blue-red is the colour of mature wine, typically *Bordeaux* and *Burgundy*; can be drunk straight away or kept for a while.

mellow red-brown Indicative of a fine *Bordeaux* or *Burgundy* with many years in the bottle: it should be drunk without further delay.

brown Wine that has had its day, or possibly become oxidized (meaning that air has got into it, often through faulty corking); in either case you will not enjoy the taste.

White wine

pale to medium yellow This is the colour range of the majority of dry white wines; white wine darkens with age, but some are darker than others to begin with.

pale tinged with green A characteristic of a number of young dry wines, such as *Muscadet*, *Sancerre* and *Pouilly-fumé*; *Chablis* is more yellow-green; *Graves* and other southern whites rarely bear any trace of green.

gold to deep gold This is the colour range of many sweet wines, including the fortified *vins doux naturels* found in the south (although the latter may also be red or rosé). Very old *Sauternes*, of a great vintage, is usually a deep gold, and some of the top *Burgundies* (dry) take on a soft golden hue after a number of years in the bottle. But in ordinary dry white table-wine, gold—or rather, a flat yellowy-brown colour—usually indicates madirization, meaning basically that it is 'off' through old age and/or oxidation.

brown Whether sweet or dry, wine of this colour is generally over the hill.

Rosé

The colour of rosé wine varies according to the grape-type(s) from which it is made, as well as its region of origin and the method of its production. Generally speaking, it should be a limpid soft salmon-pink colour rather than blue-pink or bright orange. Rosé from the south of France has a natural tendency to be more orange than elsewhere. Almost all rosé is drunk while it is still young and fresh in both colour and taste.

Clarity

Wine that is ready for drinking should be bright and entirely clear: you can assess this simply by holding up your glass to the light.

Red wine that has any age generally throws a certain amount of sediment (dregs), which is quite in order providing that it lies quietly at the bottom of the bottle. If, however, the bottle is shaken about on bumpy roads or through mishandling by a waiter, the disturbed sediment will render the wine cloudy for a while and it should be left to settle or be sent back, according to the circumstances.

In white wine you will occasionally see small white

flakes; these are tartaric acid crystals, which sometimes form if the wine has been exposed to very low temperature. They in no way affect the taste, and do not constitute grounds for complaint.

Bits of cork floating about on the surface of the wine are the result of inept manipulation of the corkscrew and should be fished out without fuss. 'Corked' wine is quite a different matter; recognizable by its cloudiness, stale smell and unpleasant taste, it is wine that has gone 'off', usually because a faulty or damaged cork has allowed oxidation to take place.

The smell (bouquet or 'nose') and taste

A top wine expert can usually pin down the age of a given wine as well as the area, *commune* (parish) and sometimes even the vinyard in which it was made—but not by its taste alone. Having first noted the appearance, the connoisseur then follows his or her nose—to establish the general health, grape-type and state of maturity (as well as other, more elusive qualities)—before bringing the taste-buds into play. To gain the full benefit of the 'nose', swirl the wine round your glass a few times to release the bouquet; then, with your nostrils hovering over the rim, gently breathe in the smell. When you are tasting the wine, take in a good mouthful and let it flow over the whole tongue area so that it reaches all the different taste centres.

General health

The bouquet is one of the most reliable indicators of the soundness of a bottle of wine. Whatever its age or grape-type, wine in good condition should have an enjoyable, clean smell. It may be fresh and flowery, mellow and slightly oaky, sweet and fruity, or barely smell of anything at all—but there should be no trace of mould or mustiness. Oxidized wine has a nasty 'off' odour that is sometimes likened to rotting cabbages. Bacteriological decay can produce a vinegary smell, and the taste will be correspondingly harsh and acetic. But with modern vinification methods and improved hygiene you will rarely come across an unhealthy bottle.

Grape-type and age

To be able to differentiate between the various grape-types and to assess the age of a wine takes years of wine-tasting experience and a brilliant nasal memory. Few people have the necessary time, money or dedication to acquire this skill, but the side-by-side comparison of even a few astutely-chosen wines will speedily expand the wine-tasting abilities of anyone at all interested in the subject. It will also be a help in deciphering the curious jargon of the wine world: descriptions such as supple, complex, hard, thin, stewed, baked, round, concentrated, tannic, acidic, cooked, bite, body etc. will take on fascinating new dimensions! This exercise will be less costly and more fun if you share it with friends, and the better the wine the more instructive it will be; mass-market blended wines rarely produce a bouquet or taste of any note, and anyway they don't improve at all with age.

To discover the effect of 'bottle-age' on wine, try comparing a two-year-old *château*-bottled claret from, say, the Haut-Médoc with one between eight and twelve years of age; in few other red wines does time produce such a marked change—partly because of the high tannin content of the *Cabernet-sauvignon* grape. Hard and drying on the mouth when young, a fine *Médoc* can mellow to an indescribable depth and concentration of flavour when it is fully mature.

Wine vocabulary

appellation contrôlée The top category of wine, under strict government controls.

bouchon A cork.

brut Very dry (of champagne); *brut zéro* or *brut non dosé* is even drier.

cave A wine cellar; wine shops are often called '*caves de vin*'; une *cave co-opérative* is a wine cooperative.

cépage The grape type.

chai An above-ground wine storeroom.

château A large country-house; in wine terms, it means a wine estate—with or without the house.

chambré 'Roomed': brought up to room temperature.

clairet Very light red wine, almost rosé.

claret The British name for red *Bordeaux*.

climat Term used in Burgundy for a vineyard.

clos Literally, an enclosed property—often a walled vineyard or a section of a vineyard (common in Burgundy).

côte(s) or **coteaux** Hillside or slopes where vines are grown.

crémant Semi-sparkling.

cru Literally, 'growth': a term used in the classification of the better vineyards in certain areas (see Bordeaux and Burgundy in Section Two).

cuvée The amount of wine in the vat (*cuve*), or the blend;

in Burgundy, synonymous with *cru: tête de cuvée = grand cru*.

domaine A wine estate.

dosage The amount of sugar added to champagne that determines the final level of sweetness.

doux Sweet.

maître de chai The cellar-master, the man in charge of making the wine and looking after the vineyard.

marchand de vin A wine-merchant.

méthode champenoise Sparkling wine made by the Champagne method.

millésime The year, or vintage, of the wine.

mise en bouteilles (au château) Bottled (at the *château*).

moelleux Mellow (of sweet wines such as *Sauternes*).

mousseux Sparkling.

négociant A wine-shipper; he may also be a blender. *Un négociant-élèveur* buys in young wine and 'brings up' the wine to a state of maturity.

perlant or **perlé** Slightly sparkling.

pétillant Sparkling.

pourriture noble, la 'Noble rot', a mould that grows on ripe grapes under certain climatic conditions and reduces them to a shrivelled concentration of sweetness and flavour which produces the finest sweet white wine in the world.

raisin A grape; a *raisin sec* is a raisin.

seau à glace An ice-bucket.

sec Dry; *demi-sec* means half-dry, but sweet when referring to champagne.

supérieur(e) Denotes a higher alcohol-content, not superior quality (e.g. *Bordeaux Supérieure*).

un tastevin A wine-tasting cup (rarely used nowadays).

un tire-bouchon A corkscrew.

trafiqué 'Cooked' wine.

vendange The grape harvest.

vignoble A vineyard.

vin de garde A wine that should be laid down: it will improve with age.

vin doux naturel (vdn**)** A fortified sweet wine.

vin de pays A country wine.

vin délimité de qualité supérieure (vdqs**)** The second category of wine.

vin ordinaire Everyday, cheap wine (uk: plonk), also called *vin de table* and *vin de consommation courante*.

HOTELS

The *Guide Michelin* (red) is the most informative, comprehensive and easy-to-use guide to hotels of all categories, from the simplest to the most expensive.

During the high season (mid-June to mid-September) and during both the Christmas and Easter holidays, it is essential to book well in advance—up to several months in some hotels—and the same goes for any long-weekend holiday (called a *pont*: 'bridge') such as Ascension or All Saints Day.

For a peaceful night avoid town centres and rooms fronting on main roads. For extra tranquillity choose a *Michelin*-listed hotel which features a rocking-chair symbol.

Not all hotels have restaurants, but if there is one you may be gently urged to take either lunch or dinner there, especially if it is in the country; you are not obliged to do so, but it may prove 'easier' to stay in a hotel without a restaurant if you intend to eat out. Note, too, that a considerable number of what are primarily restaurants also have bedrooms available. *Michelin* denotes these with the symbol *avec ch.*; many are also listed in the *Guide Routiers* and *Logis de France*. Country hotels often do not have a bar, but there is usually a formal sitting-room where you can have drinks before a meal and coffee and digestifs afterwards. Some hotels also serve afternoon tea.

Rooms are not necessarily equipped with a TV or radio, whatever the price, the exception being so-called 'modern' hotels—designated M in *Michelin*, with the TVs presence noted TV. Most rooms will have an internal telephone, however, for ordering breakfast, contacting the desk, or taking outside phone calls.

Most hotels prefer you to take breakfast in your room (though this is not obligatory), and before going to bed it is always wise to ask the hours during which breakfast is served.

Simple hotels economize on soap, so it is advisable to take your own. If you have a room without a shower or bath, you may have to pay a small supplementary charge to bathe.

One potential annoyance in simpler hotels is low-wattage light-bulbs, which tend to be inaccessible and to glare intolerably at the same time, so if you like to read in bed take an inexpensive, low-wattage, clip-on reading lamp (most electrical shops sell them) with a good long lead and a French plug. An English- or American-to-French adaptor plug is also a useful item to include in your luggage, but if you mean to use any high-wattage appliances like a hair-drier or a travel iron in your room, particularly in the simpler country hotels, be prepared for the shock—and embarrassment—of blowing the entire building's circuits. It is best to check before drawing more than about 800 watts. Alternatively, there's likely to be an electrical point somewhere in or near your room that powers the vacuum cleaner: you may have to dry your hair in the corridor, but still . . .

Prices

Except for some in Paris and the fashionable holiday resorts, hotels are generally reasonably priced, particularly in the country, where many are family-run operations (see *Logis et Auberges de France*). Prices, which are displayed in the reception area and on bedroom doors, are usually per double-room (not per person) since French hotels have few single rooms. Family rooms for three to four people are particularly good value. Breakfast is not normally included in the price, and it costs 25–35 francs in an average hotel. For this you can have coffee, tea or hot chocolate, which will be accompanied automatically by rolls, *croissants*, butter and jam (strawberry, apricot and cherry are common; rarely marmalade) and sometimes orange juice. Fruit and boiled eggs are extra. For anything more substantial, the nearest café or brasserie is your best bet. Luxury hotels offer a wider choice of cooked breakfasts—but at a very luxurious price.

Half-board rates (*demi-pension*), which include bed, breakfast and either lunch or dinner, as well as full board rates (*pension*), which include both lunch and dinner, are normally available from any hotel with a restaurant at any season, but you will have to stay for three days or more (see below for details).

The term *service compris* (s.c.) on your bill means 'service included', so there is no need to tip unless you wish to. *Service non compris* means you should add 10%–15% to the bill to cover both maid and restaurant service.

What follows is a rough guide to what you can expect for your money, though standards vary considerably, and the priorities may sometimes seem a little strange: one of the authors once stayed in a small inn where for 80 francs there was a five-course dinner with unlimited wine, a bedroom with an antique mahogany bed of regal dimensions and hand-stitched bed-linen—but no bathroom in the entire building, and only one lavatory! The prices shown below are for a double room, and the higher prices in each category are what you might find in big cities and smart resorts:

simple hotel 150–300 francs: small bedrooms, basically furnished, usually with a basin and perhaps a bidet; poor lighting.

medium hotel 300–450 francs: comfortable though often small bedrooms, probably with a bathroom (and soap!), and lighting you can read by.

good hotel 400–650 francs: spacious bedrooms with bathroom; handsomely furnished, with some attention to decoration.

luxury hotel 600–1500+ francs: these can rank among the best in the world; often palatial bedrooms and bathrooms with meticulous attention to detail; often an excellent restaurant and wine-cellar; highly efficient service, though it can be rather formal and at times intimidating.

Hotel restaurants

Many of France's best restaurants—from the simplest to the most distinguished—will be found in hotels. Outstanding examples at the top end of the market include *L'Espérance* at St Père-sous-Vézelay and *Les Prés d'Eugénie* at Eugénie-les-Bains (see pp. 37–8). Right at the other end of the financial scale, you will come upon tiny, out-of-the-way places like *Le Fayard*, a converted farmhouse at Charavines near Grenoble, where at a rickety table on an uncut lawn covered in wild flowers you could enjoy, for something like 50 francs, the best *friture* you have ever tasted. In between, there are marvellous, reasonably-priced hotel restaurants like *L'Aiguebrun* by the river near Bonnieux, *Le Tournebroche* in the Hotel Frantel in Rouen, or the *Belle Rive*, which stands beside the Aveyron river 2 km from Najac in the Languedoc, and which is a favourite stopping-place for knowledgeable travellers driving to the South of France.

Indeed, one of the great pleasures of journeying through France is having the chance to discover a 'new' hotel restaurant that serves great meals. You needn't be a resident to eat in any French hotel restaurant, but it is wise to book ahead if you can; residents are given preference, and the locals will be just as keen as you are to take the remaining tables.

Useful phrases

S'il vous plaît (see *voo plā*), meaning 'please', is abbreviated to *s.v.p.* throughout.

> I would like (to reserve) a room, please
> *Je voudrais (réserver) une chambre, s.v.p.*
> *(zhә voo-drā rā-zair-vā әәn shawн-brә s.v.p.)*

> for one/two/three people
> *pour une/deux/trois personne(s)*
> *(poor әәn/dә/trwah pair-son)*

> for one night/week
> *pour une nuit/semaine*
> *(poor әәn nwee/sә-men)*

with a double bed/child's bed   with two/three beds
avec un grand lit/lit d'enfants   *à deux/trois lits*
(a-vek aɴ- grawɴ lee/lee dawɴ-fawɴ)   (ah dө/trwah lee)

with w.c./shower/bathtub/bathroom
avec w.c./une douche/une baignoire/une salle de bain
(a-vek vā sā/өөn doosh/өөn bā-nwahr/өөn sal dө baɴ)

The room is too small/dark/hot/cold
La chambre est trop petite/sombre/chaude/froide
(lah shawɴ-brө ā trө pө-teet/soɴ-brө/shōd/frwahd)

Please could I have some lavatory paper?
S.v.p., pourrais-je avoir du papier de toilette?
(s.v.p. poo-rā zhө a-vwahr dөө pap-yā dө twa-let)

I need an iron/hair-drier/pillow . . .
J'ai besoin d'un fer à repasser/sèche-cheveux/oreiller
(zhā bөz-waɴ daɴ fair ah rө-pa-sā/sesh shө-vө/or-rā-yā)

a towel/blanket/light-bulb/needle and thread . . .
une serviette/couverture/ampoule/aiguille et du fil
(өөn sair-vyet/koo-vair-tөөr/am-pool/a-gee ā dөө fee)

The tap/light/lavatory does not work
Le robinet/la lampe/le w.c. ne marche pas
(lө ro-bee-nā/lah lawɴp/lө vā-sā nө marsh pah)

Could you give me a key?
Pouvez-vous me donner une clé?
(poo-vā voo mө don-nā өөn klā)

What time is breakfast/lunch/dinner?
À quelle heure est le petit-déjeuner/déjeuner/dîner?
(ah kel өr în lө ā pө-tee dāzhө-nā/da-zhө-nā/dee-nā)

I would like to order breakfast, please
Je voudrais commander le petit-déjeuner, s.v.p.
(zhө voo-drā ko-mawɴ-dā lө pө-tee dā-zhө-nā, s.v.p.)

I would like black/white coffee
Je voudrais du café noir/au lait
(zhө voo-drā dөө ka-fā nwahr/ō lā)

a hard/soft-boiled egg
un œuf dur/mollet
(aɴ өf dөөr/mo-lā)

toast/cornflakes
du pain grillé/des flocons de maïs
(dөө paɴ gree-yā/da flo/koɴ dө ma-ees)

Could I have the bill, please?
La note, s.v.p.?
(lah not, s.v.p.)

SECTION TWO
The Regions of France

THE MASSIF CENTRAL

This is an extremely rural region consisting of five main areas sharing a similar climate and centring on the rugged mountainous terrain of the Massif Central. Apart from the winter ski resorts around Clermont-Ferrand, there is very little tourism. The countryside is dotted with small agricultural communities where outsiders, let alone foreign travellers, are rarely seen. It is in these tiny villages—in the central restaurant, café or hotel (even more so inside the houses)—that you will find the regional dishes listed below, for the gastronomy is simple and body-filling without the delicacy or finesse found in restaurants recommended by *Michelin* or *Gault-Millau*, or in larger, more sophisticated towns.

The combination of pork, cabbage and potatoes is typical of the Auvergne. Potato and cheese dishes are

popular both in this very mountainous area and in the more clement, rolling landscape of the Bourbonnais. The ham is excellent and *charcuterie* generally is a strong feature all over the region, with many towns specializing in their own pâtés and meat pastries. The mountain pastures are grazed by sheep and multitudes of dairy cattle, for this is cheese country, as witnessed by the long list of cheeses overleaf.

In the Limousin, chestnuts and red cabbage are characteristic accompaniments for pork, beef and game, and everywhere chestnuts are used in soups and stews, or puréed as a vegetable. Mushrooms such as *cèpes*, *morels* and *chanterelles* are found in the wooded hills, and you will see baskets filled with them in the markets (which are very common throughout this region).

In the milder climate north of Clermont-Ferrand, the fertile valleys of the Bourbonnais are cultivated with early

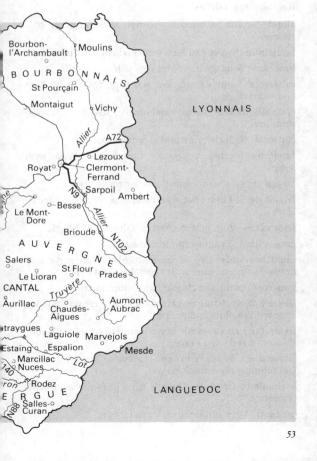

vegetables (*primeurs*) as well as fruit trees. Fruit is also increasingly being grown in the area round Brive, and both the Bourbonnais and Limousin are renowned for their fruit tarts and cherry *clafoutis* (see below), while thick, sweet pancakes filled with fruit or just sprinkled with sugar are popular everywhere.

The mountain streams and lakes are rich in fish —Brioude is known for its salmon and Ussel for jellied eels—but on the whole meat is more commonly eaten. Game, notably hare and partridge, is found in the Bourbonnais and Auvergne, while Marche and Limousin are famous for the quality of their pork and beef, although the delicious hare speciality *lièvre en cabessal* was first created here. Rouergue, on the other hand, seems to excel in offal with various dishes of trotters, tripe and other internal organs to tempt the adventurous diner.

Regional specialities

aligot Similar to *truffade* (below); also the name of a cheese.

bourriolle Sweet and heavy buckwheat flour pancake.

broccana Sausage meat and veal pâté.

cabassols Lamb's head, feet and tripe boiled with ham and vegetables.

clafoutis Baked batter and fruit (usually cherries) pudding.

cousinat Rich chestnut and cream soup.

farcidure Stuffed vegetable dumpling, served with soup.

farçon Fried sausage meat and vegetable cake.

friand de St-Flour Sausage meat wrapped in pastry or leaves.

fricandeau Pork pâté cooked in a thin slice of pork.

gargouillau Pear tart (Bourbonnais).

gigot brayaude Leg of lamb studded with garlic and braised in white wine with vegetables and herbs.

gouerre Potato and cheese flan (Bourbonnais).

lièvre à la duchambais Hare cooked in cream and vinegar with shallots and pepper.

lièvre farci en cabessal Boned, stuffed hare in a blood-thickened red wine sauce.

limousine, à la With red cabbage, chestnuts and (sometimes) *cèpe* mushrooms.

manouls or **trénouls** Sheep's tripe in white wine with tomatoes.

milliard Very similar to *clafoutis* (above).

mourtaïrol Soup-cum-stew of chicken, ham and beef with saffron and vegetables.

œufs auvergnate Poached eggs with cabbage and sausages.

omelette brayaude Omelette with potatoes, ham, cheese and cream.

oyonnade Goose stew (Bourbonnais).

picoussel Meat pâté (Rouergue).

pompe aux grattons Pork and crackling flan.

potée auvergnate or **soupe aux choux** Soup-cum-stew of pork and cabbage with potatoes, onions, turnips, leeks and garlic.

pounti Soufflé of bacon, Swiss chard and perhaps prunes.

sanciau* Thick pancake, sweet or savoury.

tourte à la viande Pork and veal flan.

tripoux Stuffed sheep's feet (St-Flour, Aurillac).

truffade Mashed potatoes mixed with cheese then baked, or fried with bacon and flavoured with garlic.

ventrèche Cured breast of pork.

Cheese: *cow's milk*

Aligot, Tomme d' Supple, fresh cheese (the base of *Cantal* and *Laguiole*), with a slightly sour, nutty taste; irregular shape; made by dairies; best between May and August.

Bleu d'Auvergne Firm blue cheese with a sharp taste; large drum wrapped in foil; commercially made and not seasonal; the farm-made *Bleu de Thiezac* and *Bleu de Causses* are similar; best between June and November.

Cantal, Fourme de or **Fourme de Salers** Supple, with a mild to nutty taste; large drum with a grey rind; commercially made all year; farm-made version best between June and September.

Chambérat Firm and supple with a strong fruity taste; thick disc with a yellowy-brown skin; made on farms; best between June and September.

Creusois or **Guéret** Low-fat, skimmed-milk cheese; firm and mild; thick disc with a hard natural rind; made on farms; best between June and February.

Gaperon Soft, low-fat cheese flavoured with garlic; small flattened ball with a natural rind; made on farms and in small factories; not seasonal.

**Bouguette, crapiau, flagnarde* and *pascade* are all similar types of pancake.

Laguiole, fourme de Firm, with a strong tang; very large drum with a pale grey rind darkening with age; made in creameries; best between June and February.

Murol Supple and mild; flat disc with a pink rind and with a hole in the middle; made in small factories; best between June and September.

St-Nectaire Firm, with a mild tang; flat disc with a grey-purple rind; made on farms and commercially; best between June and September.

Goat's milk

Cabécou d'Entraygues Firm and creamy, with a mild-to-nutty taste; sheep's and cow's milk sometimes mixed in; small flat disc with a pale blue rind; made on farms; best between November and March.

Chevrotin du bourbonnais Supple and creamy, with a mild-to-nutty taste; off-white truncated cone; made on farms; best between June and November.

Rigotte de Pelussin Firm and mildly nutty; small drum with a pale blue rind; made on farms; best between May and November.

Sheep's milk

Tomme de Brach Firm, with a pronounced sheep flavour and smell; drum with a natural rind; made on farms; best between April and September.

Wine

Marcillac, near Rodez, is the only *AC* wine of this region. It made the grade in 1990 with its fruity, full-bodied reds. The whites, of which little is made, are more ordinary, as are the neighbouring (*VDQS*) wines of *Entraygues* and *Estaing*. The other most interesting wine is produced in the north of this area: already well known, the wines of *St Pourçain* continue to gain in reputation. The reds, made from *Gamay* and/or *Pinot Noir* grapes are light and sappy while the whites *(Sauvignon Blanc* and *Chardonnay)* are dry and fruity—not unlike those of the Loire. Good Gamay reds come from *Châteaugay, Boudes, Madargues* and *Chanturgue* in the *Côtes d'Auvergne*, also from this area comes the pale rosé of *Corent.* which is dry and refreshing.

Generally speaking, these are wines to be drunk young.

LANGUEDOC

The traditional food of Languedoc is extremely varied, being influenced by both the rigorous climate of the mountains and the warmth of the Mediterranean. Garlic features strongly everywhere. Olive oil, tomatoes and aubergines are dominant ingredients in the south and east, while to the north and west you will find the more earthy flavours of pork or goose fat, *cèpes*, truffles, chestnuts and various dried beans and lentils.

The most celebrated Languedoc dish is the *cassoulet*. This is a hearty, garlic-steeped concoction of haricot beans, pork and other meats which vary according to local tradition. It is best eaten on a cold day after a long mountain hike! The local lamb and mutton often tastes of the herbs that grow wild on the rugged sheep pastures of the *Garrigues* and *Causses*. Beef, somewhat tough here, is reduced to tenderness in the slowly-cooked stews —*daubes*, *estouffades* and *civets*. Small birds, such as quail and thrushes are popular spit-roasted or cooked in vine leaves or pastry. The *charcuterie* is generally excellent; of particular note are the sausages of Toulouse and ham from the *Montagne Noire*. In the remote mountainous areas offal, especially tripe, is common while further south the massive vineyard area provides a perfect habitat for snails, which are eaten in a number of different ways not encountered elsewhere.

Freshwater fish such as trout and eels can be found but, surprisingly for a region that borders the Mediterranean, there is no great tradition for eating fresh sea-fish other than along the coast itself. Sète is a thriving fishing port bringing in large catches of mackerel, sardines, and even tuna fish among many others, and the cultivation of oysters and mussels in the Thau lagoon is becoming increasingly important. Yet the second most renowned speciality of the region is *brandade de morue*, a dish comprised largely of salt cod and which, from the Middle Ages until fairly recently, formed the staple diet of the country people.

Finally, this is a region for the sweet-toothed, a local characteristic apparently left over from the Arab invasion. Castelnaudary, Narbonne, Carcassonne and Limoux are particularly famed for their pastry, but sweet and sticky delicacies are common everywhere.

Regional specialities

aïgo bouïdo Garlic and herb soup served on bread.

aïllade Garlic flavoured mayonnaise (like *aïoli*).

alicot or **alicuit** Stew of goose or duck's giblets and wings with *cèpes*.

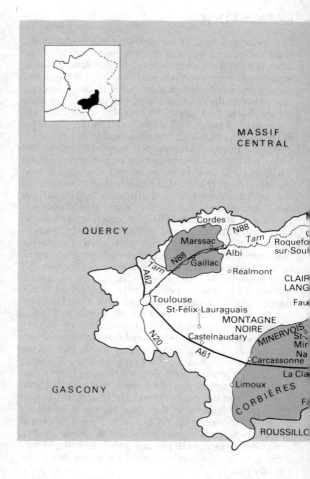

brandade du morue Salt cod pounded to a cream with milk, garlic and olive oil.

caillettes Sausage-meat balls containing liver and spinach.

cargolade Snails stewed in wine.

cassoulet Substantial stew based on white haricot beans, pork and sausage, with herbs and garlic (Castelnaudary version). The Toulouse version includes goose, and in Carcassonne lamb.

civet de langouste Spicy crawfish stew with onions, garlic and white wine.

cousinat Rich chestnut and cream soup (Cevennes).

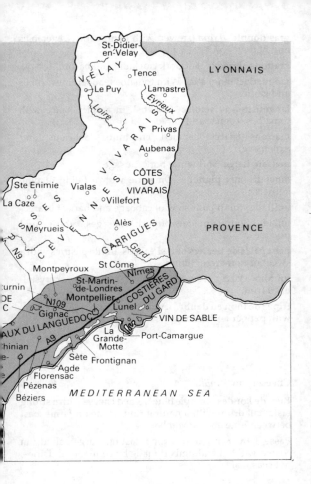

crème d'Homère Egg custard with honey, wine, cinnamon and lemon.

escargots à la languedocienne Snails in a spicy sauce with ham, anchovies, tomatoes and chopped walnuts.

escargots à la narbonnaise Snails in mayonnaise, with ground almonds.

estouffade de haricots blancs White haricot beans stewed with pork, tomatoes and garlic.

féche sec Salted, dried pig's liver served with a radish salad.

foie gras à la toulousaine Goose or duck's liver wrapped in pastry, with garlic.

gras double Tripe (stewed with ham, garlic, vegetables and herbs).

grattons Fried bits of pork crackling and bacon.

languedocienne, à la With tomatoes, aubergines, *cèpes* and garlic.

langouste à la sétoise Crawfish in a spicy sauce with tomatoes, cognac and garlic.

marrons glacés Candied chestnuts (delicious and expensive).

melsat Large, soft white pork sausage.

omelette aux pignons Omelette with a filling of pine kernels.

ouillade Soup-cum-stew of cabbage and haricot beans.

oulade Soup-cum-stew of pork, sausages, cabbage and potatoes.

petit pâtés de Béziers or de Pézenas Little pastries with a sweet or non-sweet filling.

touron Marzipan sweet containing pistachios, or crystallized fruit.

tripes de thon en daube Tuna tripe stewed in white wine with pepper and onions.

Cheese: *cow's milk*

Bleu de Loudes Supple blue-veined cheese with a strong taste; tall drum with a natural rind; made on farms; best between June and November.

Passé l'an Hard and strong tasting; large tall drum coated with oil and umber; made by commercial dairies; not seasonal.

Goat's milk

Pelardon des Cevennes or **d'Anduze** Soft and rich with a nutty taste, small thick disc with a white skin; made on farms; best between June and November.

Picodon de St-Agrève Firm with a nutty taste; small thick disc with a pale blue or yellow rind; made on farms; best between June and November.

Sheep's milk

Roquefort France's most revered blue cheese; firm buttery texture marbled with blue; clean, sharp, sheepy tang; large drum wrapped in foil; cured in the natural limestone caves of Roquefort-sur-Soulzon; good all year except winter.

Wine

Southern Languedoc is the main source of France's *vin de table*. However, in the last decade there has been a widespread movement to upgrade the quality. The most radical activity has occurred in the *vins de pays*: experiments with better grape-types such as *Cabernet-Sauvignon, Syrah, Merlot, Mourvèdre* and, for whites, *Chardonnay* and *Viognier*, along with the *macération carbonique* method of wine-making, have produced some exciting results. Such are the revolutionary *vins des Sables du Golfe de Lion*: on the coastal sand dunes the *Salins du Midi* company (brand name *Listel*) produces some of the best white wine of the area including a sparkling *Brut de Listel*, light fruity reds and, at *Dom. de Jarras*, refreshing rosé, including the excellent *gris de gris*. Striking among the *vins de pays de l'Herault* and *vins de pays des Côtes de Thongue* are *Dom. de l'Arjolle, Dom. la Condamine l'Evêque, Dom. du Bosc* and *Dom. de la Grange Rouge*. At the *Mas du Daumas Gassac* glacial soil produces an intensely concentrated red (80% *Cabernet*) and white (*Chardonnay* and *Viognier*) of similar promise.

In the 1980s several wines were given *AC* status: in the *Coteaux de Languedoc* reds of note include *La Clape* (good white too), *St Saturnin, Montpeyroux, St Georges d'Orques, Cabrières* (also known for rosé), *Faugères* and, in particular *St Chinian* with top producers being the *co-op de Berlou* and *Château Coujan*. The white *Picpoul de Pinet* is dry and nutty when well made. *Minervois* produces some good robust red wine of which *Château de Bourgazaud* and *Dom. de Ste. Eulalie* are worthy examples. The wines of *Corbières* continue to improve: the best sources (of mainly red wine) include *Castelmaure, Cascastel, Paziols, Dom. de Villemajou* and *Dom. de Fontsainte*. The powerful reds of *Fitou* are well known. In the west, the *Côtes de Malapère* and *Cabardes* are *VDQS* wines trying hard for the *AC* rating, while at the eastern extreme, the *Costières de Nîmes* has now made the grade.

White AC wines include the dry *Clairette de Languedoc* and *Clairette de Bellegarde*, the former having the greater character. *Blanquette de Limoux* is a delicious sparkling white, fruity yet dry and very good value.

The *Muscats* of *Frontignan* (probably the best), *Lunel, Mireval* and *St-Jean-de-Minervois* are *vins doux naturels* (VDNs), fortified sweet wines heady with the scent of the *Muscat* grape. Well chilled, they make a good aperitif.

Gaillac, near Albi, produces some fairly ordinary reds and rosés but the whites and sparkling *Gaillac Perlé*, made from the local *Mauzan* and *L'en de L'El* grapes (some *Sauvignon* too) are well worth trying.

Most Languedoc wines should be drunk young but the better reds, such as those named above, would improve with a little age. A year to avoid might be 1987.

THE PYRENEES, ROUSSILLON AND GASCONY

The cooking of the Pyrenean provinces varies little from west to east despite great differences in both agriculture and climate. Béarn and the Pays Basque, buffeted by the cold Atlantic Ocean, cook largely with goose-fat from geese raised on the maize-rich land between the Adour and the Oloron rivers. In Bigorre and the country of Foix they make more use of butter from the Pyrenean cows that graze in high mountain pastures watered by tumbling fish-filled streams. The Roussillon, basking beside the warm waters of the Mediterranean, is abundant in fruit, spring vegetables, grape-vines—and olive trees, whose oil dominates the cooking.

Parallel with these contrasting elements are the mountains and neighbouring Spain, which are common to all three areas. And these are the overwhelming influences in the distinctive and highly-spiced *cuisine* of this fiery and fiercely independent people. Garlic, peppers, onions, tomatoes, and various herbs and spices occur in many meat, fish and egg dishes. Strong-tasting mountain sausages and Bayonne ham are popular, and often form

part of the body-warming meaty stews and soups of the mountains (*garbure* and *estouffat*).

The Catalan influence is very strong in Roussillon, with an emphasis on garlic and bitter Seville oranges in many meat dishes and a love of sweet pastries. From the mountains come some very good sheep's-milk cheeses (mainly in the west), and lamb from the Ossau valley is renowned for its tenderness. Bayonne (birthplace of the Bayonet) is famous for its delicious salt-cured ham which is eaten raw (in paper-thin slices), or cooked in various vegetable and meat dishes. Less well-known is that, until about 300 years ago, the only chocolate in France was made in Bayonne.

North of the Pyrenees lies the old province of Gascony, a region of high gastronomic repute where the strong, spicy flavours of the mountains are considerably tempered by the more elegant influences of Bordeaux and the Périgord.

Inland from its immense sandy beaches, the poor soil of the Landes yields little. However, there is a string of lagoons that are rich in fish, and huge pine forests sheltering countless small birds which are, sad to say, hunted ruthlessly during the autumn season by enthusiastic

marksmen. In restaurants, such birds are served stuffed and spit-roasted, wrapped in delicate pastry or in a rich *salmis* (see below). The Armagnac area is best known for its fine brandy, which is also used in many of its superb meat and game dishes, in particular the famous *estouffat de Nöel*. You will also come across *foie gras* and *confits* which, though more closely associated with the Périgord, are just as good here.

Regional specialities

alose de l'Adour Shad stuffed with sorrel and baked with ham.

becfigue or **becfin** A figpecker, a tiny bird usually served spit-roasted.

bonite Fish similar to tuna.

bouillinade Fish stew with onions, peppers, garlic and potatoes.

braou bouffat Hearty country soup of rice and cabbage.

cargolade Local name for snails (Roussillon).

chipirones Squid (Pays Basque) often stewed in its own ink.

chorizo Very spicy sausage.

chou farci Stuffed cabbage.

collioure sauce Mayonnaise flavoured with anchovies and garlic.

confit Duck or goose cooked and preserved in its own fat.

coudenat Large pork sausage eaten hot in slices.

cousinette Soup of sorrel, spinach, chicory, mallow and Swiss chard.

cruchades Maize-flour fritters or pancakes.

daube (à la Béarnaise) Beef stewed in wine (with ham, onions and tomatoes).

elzekaria Haricot bean and cabbage soup, with garlic.

estouffat (de Nöel) Meat stewed in wine with herbs, vegetables and pork (beef stewed in Armagnac and wine with shallots).

foie aux raisins Goose or duck liver cooked in white wine with grapes.

galabart Large black pudding.

garbure Hearty vegetable soup (cabbage, peas, haricot beans and garlic) enriched with pork, sausage or *confit* (see above).

gâteau Basquaise Pastry filled with custard or fruit (cherries or plums).

isard, civet d' Mountain antelope (rare) stewed in red wine.

jambon de Bayonne Delicately-cured ham often eaten raw in thin slices.

loukinka A small, highly-spiced garlic sausage.

millassou Sweet maize-flour flan.

mouton en pistache or **à la catalane** Mutton braised in white wine with 50 cloves of garlic, ham and vegetables; *aux pistaches* means with pistachio nuts.

ortolans à la landaise Buntings (type of) stuffed and spit-roasted.

ouillade Thick soup of cabbage and haricot beans with garlic.

ouliat Onion and garlic soup (may include leeks, tomatoes and cheese).

pastis landaise Pastry filled with prunes.

perdreau à la catalane Partridge stew with peppers and bitter oranges.

pétéran Tripe, sheep's trotters and ham stewed in wine.

pipérade Omelette or scrambled eggs with peppers, ham, tomatoes and garlic.

poitrine de mouton farcie à l'ariégeoise Breast of mutton stuffed with ham and garlic.

pommes basquaise Baked potatoes stuffed with peppers, ham, tomatoes and garlic.

poule en compote Chicken stew with shallots.

poule au pot d'Henri IV Chicken stuffed with ham and liver and cooked in wine.

salda Soup of bacon, sausage, cabbage and haricot beans.

salmis de palombes Roast pigeon finished in a red wine sauce with onions, ham and mushrooms.

saucisse à la catalane Sausage fried with garlic, orange peel and herbs.

saupiquet Piquant wine-and-cream sauce (with hare and venison).

soupe du berger Same as *ouliat* (see above).

toulia Local name for *ouliat* (see above).

tourin (tourain) Onion-and-milk soup, sometimes with cheese.

touron Sweet made of ground almonds, pistachio nuts and crystallized fruit.

tripotcha Spicy black pudding.

ttoro Fish soup with onions, garlic and tomatoes.

Cheese: *sheep's milk (fromage de brebis)*

The following are all fairly similar in appearance and type. They are farm-made in large discs (about 14 inches in diameter), with rinds varying from pale yellow to orange. The taste ranges from mild to nutty, becoming stronger with age. Best from May to October: *Amou* (Gascony), *Ardi-Gasna* (Pays Basque), *Esbareich/Oloron* (Bigorre), *Iraty* (Pays Basque) and *Laruns* (Béarn).

Cow's milk

Bethmale, Cierp de Luchon or **Oustet** Firm, with a pronounced taste; large disc; made on farms; not seasonal.

Les Orrys Firm but supple, with a fairly tangy taste; large disc; made in mountain cottages; best between June and February.

Wine

Madiran, grown just south of *Armagnac* country, is a powerful red wine of great depth and longevity. Drunk too young and the *Tannat* grape, which provides its character, gives it a harsh taste but after five years, or better, ten, it mellows to a silky-smooth, rich wine which has been compared, often favourably, with *Cahors*. Top producers include *Château de Peyros, Dom. Barrejat* and *Dom. Laplace*. Avoid the years 1987 and 1989.

Similar to *Madiran*, though less weighty, is the red of

Irouléguy. The rosé is less notable. The red and rosé *Vins de Béarn* are generally fruity and light.

Jurançon and *Jurançon sec* are the most noteworthy whites of the region. The former, famous in the time of Henri IV, is a luscious sweet wine, richly scented. *Jurançon sec* is dry but with a depth of flavour and spiciness that makes it a delicious aperitif. Both can age to about ten years. *Pacherenc du Vic Bilh* is a similar though less striking wine. It may be dry or slightly sweet.

The above are all *AC* wines; among the *VDQS* wines worth trying are *Tursan* and *Côtes de St-Mont*, described as minor 'Madirans', and watch for the robust reds and full, fragrant whites of the up-and-coming *Vin de Pays des Côtes de Gascogne*.

In the *Côtes du Roussillon* and superior *Côtes du Roussillon Villages* (both *AC*), changes in grape-type, the use of *macération carbonique* and the ageing of wine in oak barrels, have all had a favourable influence on the production of red wine. Recommended are *Château de Jau* and the villages of *Caramany* and *Latour de France* which gained their own *ACs* in 1977. The small *AC* of *Collioure* makes a strong red wine, Spanish in style. It may be drunk young but after five or more years develops considerable depth and richness. Some sharp whites (*vins verts*) and light rosés are made as well as the fortified sweet wines (*vins doux naturels*) of *Maury*, *Rivesaltes* and *Banyuls* and the *Muscat de Rivesaultes*. A *little* like port they are enjoyed locally as an aperitif or dessert wine. *Banyuls*, the best, may age to around fifteen years.

In the Pays Basques a rather sharp cider is made called *Pittara*; also a herb-flavoured liqueur called *Izarra*.

Armagnac

Though less famous than *Cognac*, *Armagnac* is the oldest brandy of France and preferred by many for its softer and slightly earthy quality. It is produced by continuous distillation (unlike Cognac), which enables it to retain greater flavour and fragrance. After twenty years maturing in an oak cask it should be fiery but velvety smooth, and have the 'unmistakable aroma of plums and violets' according to Georges Samalens of Laujazan, one of the best producers. However, more often it is drunk when still young and lacking in elegance. The very best Armagnac comes from *Bas-Armagnac* and, apart from *Samalens*, the better labels to look out for include *Marquis de Montesquiou*, *Domaine de Gayrosse* and *Domaine de Boingnères*. *Haut-Armagnac* and *Ténarèze* produce Armagnac of lesser quality which is usually blended.

The local aperitif is called *Floc*, a delicious mixture of Armagnac and fresh grape juice.

For information on Armagnac contact: Maison de l'Armagnac, Place de la Liberté, 32800 Eauze.

THE PÉRIGORD AND QUERCY

This is one of the most beautiful and interesting parts of France. Man was first drawn here over two million years ago, when he took advantage of the shelter afforded by the extraordinary grottoes and caverns in the limestone hills around the Dordogne valley. Today, the tourist is attracted by those same caves, with their incredible wall-paintings (at Les Eyzies, Domme and elsewhere), by the unspoilt, rural countryside dotted with clusters of charming red-tiled farmhouses, the fairytale castles teetering on the cliffs above the meandering Dordogne, the generous hospitality of the people and, not least, by the superb gastronomy.

In this warm, unhurried southern atmosphere a great

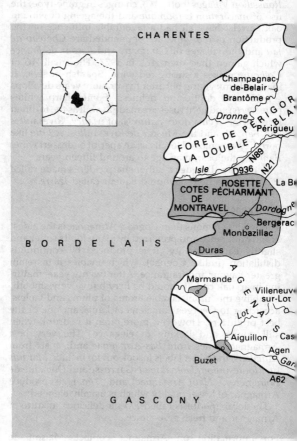

deal of time is taken over the preparation and consumption of meals. As a general rule, each dish is small and delicate, and even the most humble restaurant may offer you five courses or more. But if you are starving at lunchtime, look for a very simple café-cum-restaurant (not in the guide books!) where you can join the local farmworkers stocking up on a thick soup of vegetables and pork, sausages or mutton (*sobronade* or *cassoulet*).

The gastronomy is more or less uniform over this whole region, with neighbouring invasions on the fringes. Dominated by the truffle (known locally as the 'black diamond') and by *foie gras* (see below), it is unusually sophisticated for such a rustic area. The truffle is a jet-black fungus with an earthy, woody taste, and it is used in soups, sauces, stuffings, pâtés and meat preparations.

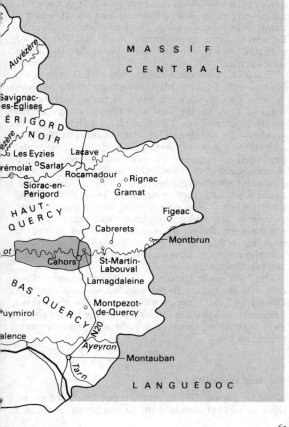

Truffles are delicious and expensive, and you can buy them fresh only between November and March, when they are 'hunted' using pigs or hounds specially trained to recognize their telltale pungent scent around the roots of certain oak trees. *Cèpe*, another local fungus, similar to a field mushroom though much fleshier, is a tasty and far cheaper alternative; *omelette aux cèpes* is excellent.

Foie gras, the other gastronomic wonder of the region, forms part of many other dishes as well as being served on its own as a starter (very rich). The idea of force-feeding may seem repugnant, but the geese wandering over the vineyards and meadows look happy enough. The rest of the bird is made into a *confit* (see below) and every local household will have one prepared as an instant, delicious meal for the unexpected guest. Goose-fat, rather than olive oil or butter, is used for cooking in general, and it gives the local dishes their own particular character.

The region is particularly known for the quantity and quality of its walnuts. These are eaten whole, or made into a liqueur (*brou de noix*) or pressed for their oil, which is delicious in salad dressing. The fertile area between the Lot and Garonne rivers (known as the Agenais) is filled with fruit trees, most notably plum trees—Agen is famous for its prunes.

The small town of Sarlat, the old capital of Périgord Noir (so called for the black appearance of the hillsides densely packed with oak trees) is particularly rich in regional fare. In the narrow winding streets of the medieval quarter you will find shops selling a host of goodies—tins of *foie gras*, *confits*, bottles of truffles, jars of fruit (plums, raspberries, greengages and chestnuts) preserved in liqueurs, sweets made of walnuts and chestnuts and all the local fruit *eaux-de-vie*.

Markets are often the best places to find local specialities and, since it is such an agricultural area, most villages have markets at least once a week. The *charcuteries* and *pâtisseries* are particularly good, and numerous! For some reason, there are also many small but flourishing potteries selling a variety of garden urns, kitchen paraphernalia and tableware—inedible but very pretty, and relatively inexpensive.

The lush green countryside of the Dordogne valley contrasts strongly with the arid limestone plateaux of Quercy and the rocky, scrub-covered hills of northern Périgord but as you drive along empty lanes, through tiny sleeping villages, there is everywhere a feeling of space, peace and time.

Regional specialities

alicot or **alicuit** Giblets and wings (usually of goose, duck or turkey) stewed with haricot beans, garlic and mushrooms in wine.

ballottine de lièvre à la périgourdine Boned hare stuffed with rabbit, veal or pork, *foie gras* and truffles, and flavoured with brandy.

boudin blanc quercynoise Fat, soft white pudding made with minced chicken and veal or pork.

bougras or **soupe à l'eau de boudin** Vegetable soup (celery, leeks, potatoes, cabbage, onions, carrots and turnips) using the stock from black pudding.

cajasse sarladaise Rum-flavoured cake or pastry.

carpe à la Neuvic Carp stuffed with truffles and *foie gras*.

cassoulet périgourdin Stew of haricot beans, mutton, garlic sausage and stuffed goose-neck.

cèpes à la périgourdine *Cèpes* (a fleshy sort of mushroom) cooked with bacon, parsley, garlic and *verjus* (juice from unripe grapes).

chou farci Whole cabbage stuffed with minced pork, veal and mushrooms, and cooked in white wine for five hours.

confit: de canard, de dinde, d'oie or **de porc** Pieces of duck, turkey, goose or pork salted then cooked, and preserved in their own fat in earthenware jars.

cou d'oie farci Goose-neck stuffed with *foie gras*, minced pork and truffles; served cold in slices.

daube Beef stewed in red wine with *cèpes*, onions and bacon.

dodines de volaille Boned, marinated pieces of chicken which are then stuffed and braised.

foie gras Enlarged liver of goose or duck that has been force-fed on maize; cooked and served hot or cold in slices, or made into a *pâté* with truffles added (*truffé*); fresh only from November to February, otherwise tinned.

fricassée de volaille aux écrevisses Chicken and crayfish stewed in a cream and white wine sauce.

gougnette A large sweet fritter.

jacque Apple pancake.

lièvre à la royale Marinated hare boned and stuffed with veal and bacon, cooked in wine and brandy and served in a rich sauce garnished with truffles.

magret or **maigret de canard** Boned breast of duck, grilled or fried.

merveille Sweet fritter flavoured with brandy.

millas Maize flour flat cake served either savoury with stew, or sprinkled with sugar as a pudding.

milliassou Sweet maize-flour pastry.

mique sarladaise Dumpling made with maize flour and pork fat, usually served with stews.

œufs à l'agenaise Eggs baked with fried chopped onion, aubergine, garlic and parsley.

œufs en cocotte périgourdine Eggs baked with *sauce périgueux*.

omelette aux truffes or **aux cèpes** Omelette filled with sliced truffles or cèpes.

périgourdine, à la Accompanied by, with a sauce of, or stuffed with truffles and, usually, *foie gras*.

pintade rotie, flambée et bardée de truffes de Gourdon Guinea fowl stuffed with truffles and served in a flaming brandy sauce.

pommes de terre à la sarladaise Potatoes and truffles layered in a casserole and baked (sometimes includes *foie gras*)

poulet rouilleuse Chicken in a rich, blood-thickened white wine and garlic sauce.

roussette Sweet maize flour fritter.

sauce périgueux *Demi-glace* (brown) sauce flavoured with madeira and truffles.

sobronade Thick soup of pork, ham, white beans, turnips, onions, garlic and herbs.

tourin or **tourain périgourdin** Onion soup with tomatoes, egg yolks, and occasionally grated cheese (*gratinée*).

tourte de truffes à la périgourdine A lidded tart filled with slices of truffles and *foie gras* sprinkled with brandy.

tourtière Chicken and salsify pie.

tripe à la cadurcienne Tripe cooked with saffron.

truffe en croûte or **en pâte** Truffle with bacon and *foie gras* wrapped in crispy pastry.

truffe sous les cendres Truffle sprinkled with brandy, wrapped in a thin slice of pork and cooked in hot ashes.

Cheese: *cow's milk*

Bleu de Quercy Firm and blue-veined, with a strong taste and smell; large drum wrapped in foil; made by commercial dairies; best between October and February; *Bleu de causses* is similar.

Goat's milk

Cabécou de Rocamadour or **Livernon** Soft, with a fairly nutty taste; small, thin disc with a faint blue rind; made on farms on the Gramat plateau; best between June and

November; also made with sheep's milk; there are many different *cabécous* (the local word for a little goat's cheese), which vary from mild to very strong in taste.

Picadou *Rocamadour* that has been wrapped in leaves and aged in crocks; soft, and very strong.

Sheep's milk

Roquefort Considered by many to be the finest blue cheese; very salty and tangy; aged in caves in Roquefort (see entry in the Dictionary which follows).

Wine

The red wines around Bergerac are made largely from the same grape-types as their grand neighbours in Bordeaux. They have a light-weight claret taste that develops little with age: enjoyable for lunch and good value. *AC Côtes de Bergerac* is superior to plain *AC Bergerac*. Top producers include *Chât. Panisseau* and *Chât. La Jaubertie*. The best reds are considered to come from *Pécharmant*, although the wines of *Buzet* are of a similar style and quality (note the *Cuvée Napoléon*). *AC Côtes de Duras* and the recent *AC Côtes du Marmandais* make light, everyday reds and whites. *Côtes du Tarn, Coteaux de Quercy, Côtes du Bruhlois* and *Côtes du Agenais* are country wines of particular note.

The best dry whites are *Bergerac Sec*. The semi-sweet whites of *Saussignac, Rosette* and *Côtes de Montravel* are declining and more dry is being made. But the star is *Monbazillac,* a rich and potent (13° minimum) sweet white wine known as the 'poor man's *Sauternes*': delicious chilled as an aperitif or to accompany *foie gras* or fruit tarts. It may be drunk young but after ten or more years gains in depth and complexity. *Château de Monbazillac* is the main producer and interesting to visit. Best years: 1971, '75 '76, '78, '79, '80, '81, '82, '83, '85, '86, '88, '89, '90.

For red-wine enthusiasts the most interesting wine of the region is undoubtedly that of *Cahors*, the old capital of Quercy. Made largely (70%) of the *Malbec* grape (or *Auxerrois*) which provides its deep 'black' colour, it is a full, robust wine of considerable longevity. Some, however, is made in a lighter style (and colour) and has a less distinctive taste. The best includes *Clos de Gamot, Château de Cayrou, Prince Probus* and *Château de Haute-Serre*. These heavier-style wines are superb with red meat and game. Growers recommend that *Vin de Cahors* should be drunk cool. Best years: 1979, '81, '82, '83, '85, '86, '88, '89, '90.

For information on Bergerac wines contact: Maison du Vin—Comité Interprofessionnel des vins de la région de Bergerac, 2 place du Docteur Cayla, 24100 Bergerac.

THE BORDELAIS AND CHARENTES

The two areas making up this region are better known to English-speakers as Bordeaux and Cognac, and these names seem far more appropriate, for the vine dominates the countryside and economy as does its fruit the table. You can see from the list below that almost every regional speciality uses grapes, grape juice or wine, and *à la bordelaise* typically means 'with a wine sauce' although it *can* indicate other accompaniments. The city of Bordeaux is very definitely the heart of the region; a great gastronomic centre, it is here that the regional *cuisine* has developed to complement the finesse and variety of the surrounding wines. Both Charentes and the Bordelais grow superb vegetables and fruit, and there are other very stylish raw ingredients close at hand such as truffles and *foie gras* from Périgord and *cèpes*, game and *foie gras* from the Landes in Gascony, and many specialities from both areas can be found in this region. Along the coast are major centres for oysters (Arcachon, Marennes), mussels (La Rochelle) and shrimps (la Cotinière) whilst the Gironde estuary is rich in eel, lamprey and shad, which are very popular locally.

Gastronomic sophistication dwindles as you move away from Bordeaux and big coastal resorts such as Arcachon and La Rochelle. Charentes, in particular, is a very rural area, largely by-passed by tourists and little known for its culinary performance; the great gourmet Curnonsky described its *cuisine* as 'simple, honest and countryfied'. However, the area boasts fine butter, delicious Charentais melons and, even more than the Bordelais, it makes use of the wealth of shell-fish along the coast.

Neither the Bordelais nor Charentes produces cheese of any note. There is a long tradition around Bordeaux of eating Dutch Edam (*croûte rouge d'Hollande*) with red wine, a delicious combination. In both areas small goats' cheeses are popular: *cabécous*, as they are known, from Périgord, and *chabichous* from Poitou.

Regional specialities

agneau de prés-salés Tender lamb raised on the salt marshes.

alose à l'oseille Baked shad with sorrel sauce.

anguilles aux pruneaux Eel stewed in red wine with prunes.

anguilles au verjus Eels steeped in the juice of unripe grapes, then grilled.

bordelaise, à la With a red wine sauce; with garlic or shallots and parsley; with artichoke bottoms, new potatoes and onions; with *cèpe* mushrooms.

cagouilles à la vigneronne Snails (local name) cooked in white wine with garlic, or shallots, and parsley.

cèpes à la bordelaise *Cèpes* (fleshy type of mushroom) sautéed in oil with garlic, parsley and (sometimes) grape juice.

chaudrée rochelaise Fish soup-cum-stew of tiny sea fish and white wine.

crèpinettes truffées Small truffled pork sausages, often eaten with oysters.

entrecôte à la bordelaise or **marchand de vin** Entrecôte steak in a wine-and-shallot sauce with (sometimes) sliced beef-marrow.

entrecôte maître de chai Entrecôte grilled over vine twigs (*sarments*).

farée Stuffed cabbage (Charentes).

foie gras aux raisins Goose or duck's liver cooked with grapes.

gigorit Pig's head in a red wine and blood sauce (Charentes).

lamproie à la bordelaise Sliced lamprey in a red wine and blood sauce with leeks.

mouclade Mussels in a creamy wine sauce with herbs (Charentes).

pain de brochet d'Angoulême Fish terrine or 'loaf' made of pike.

pibales Baby eels, usually fried.

soupe des vendanges A hearty country soup of meat and vegetables, traditionally served at the grape harvest.

Cognac

The most famous brandy in the world, Cognac is distilled from white wine and gains its earthy finesse and amber colour only after being aged in oak casks for a number of years. All Cognac is blended from different years and areas (marked A to F in order of quality on the map over) except for *Fine* or *Grande Champagne* (no relation!) which is blended from *Grande* and *Petite Champagne* alone.

Three stars on the label denotes a minimum age of $2\frac{1}{2}$ years, 'VO' and 'VSOP' (Very Superior Old Pale) a minimum of $4\frac{1}{2}$ years, whilst 'Extra', 'XO', 'Napoléon' and 'Grande Réserve' may be fifty or more years old.

Pineau des Charentes is a mixture of Cognac and fresh grapejuice, and quite delicious as an aperitif.

Bordeaux

The Bordeaux wine-growing region, which covers almost the whole of the Gironde department, was first planted with vines by the Romans; the vineyard of one Ausonius, a Roman consul, remains to this very day (see *Château Ausone* below). Under the auspices of Henry II (Plantagenet) who married Eleanor of Aquitaine in 1152, the wine trade was considerably expanded to meet the needs

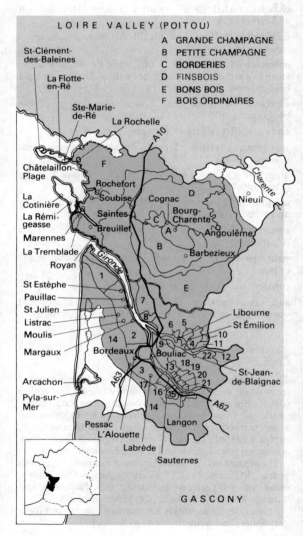

LOIRE VALLEY (POITOU)

A GRANDE CHAMPAGNE
B PETITE CHAMPAGNE
C BORDERIES
D FINSBOIS
E BONS BOIS
F BOIS ORDINAIRES

St-Clément-des-Baleines
La Flotte-en-Ré
Ste-Marie-de-Ré
La Rochelle
Châtelaillon-Plage
Rochefort
La Cotinière
Soubise
Saintes
La Rémigeasse
Breuillet
Marennes
La Tremblade
Royan
Cognac
Bourg-Charente
Nieuil
Angoulême
Barbezieux
Gironde

St Estèphe
Pauillac
St Julien
Listrac
Moulis
Margaux
Bordeaux
Libourne
St Émilion
Bouliac
St-Jean-de-Blaignac
Arcachon
Pyla-sur-Mer
Pessac
L'Alouette
Labrède
Langon
Sauternes

GASCONY

of its new English admirers who dubbed the then clear, light red wines of this region 'claret', derived from the French *clairet* meaning pale or clear red. The name has stuck, but today it applies to the whole enormous variety of Bordeaux reds, dark and pale alike.

The five top wine areas are *Médoc*, *St Emilion* and *Pomerol* (all red), *Graves* (white and—more notably —red), and *Sauternes/Barsac* (all sweet white).

Red wine

Top appellations
Médoc and Graves

1 Médoc
2 Haut-Médoc
  St-Estèphe
  Pauillac (Lafite,
  Latour,
  Mouton-Rothschild)
  St-Julien
  Listrac
  Moulis
  Margaux (Margaux)
3 Graves (Haut-Brion)
  Pessac-Léognan

St Emilion and Pomerol

4 St Emilion (Cheval
  Blanc, Ausone)
  St-Georges-St-Emilion
  Lussac-St-Emilion
  Puisseguin-St-Emilion
5 Pomerol (Pétrus)
  Lalande-de-Pomerol

Lesser appellations

6 Fronsac
  Canon Fronsac
7 Premières Côtes de
  Blaye
8 Côtes de Bourg
9 Graves de Vayres
10 Bordeaux Côtes de
  Francs
11 Bordeaux Côtes de
  Castillon
12 Ste-Foy-Bordeaux

Regional appellations

13 Premières Côtes de
  Bordeaux
14 Bordeaux and

Bordeaux Supérieur
14 Bordeaux Clairet
14 Bordeaux Rosé

Sweet and medium-sweet white wines

Top appellations

15 Sauternes (d'Yquem)
16 Barsac (Coutet,
  Climens)

Lesser appellations

17 Cérons
18 Cadillac
19 Loupiac
20 St-Croix-du-Mont
21 Côtes de Bordeaux-
  St-Macaire
12 Ste-Foy-Bordeaux
3 Graves Supérieures

Regional appellations

13 Premières Côtes de
  Bordeaux
14 Bordeaux Supérieur

Dry white wines

Top appellation

3 Graves

Lesser appellations

7 Côtes de Blaye
8 Côtes de Bourg
9 Graves de Vayres
22 Entre-Deux-Mers

Regional appellations

14 Bordeaux and
  Bordeaux sec

Red Bordeaux derives from three main grape types: the classic *Cabernet-Sauvignon, Sauvignon Franc* and *Merlot*. Significantly, St Emilion and Pomerol use a high ratio of *Merlot*, while in the Médoc *Cabernet-Sauvignon* is the key variety. The white wine is made mainly from *Sauvignon Blanc* and *Semillon* grapes. In the dry whites of *Graves, Sauvignon* predominates (from about 60% to 100%), while *Sauternes, Barsac* and other sweet whites are made from 65% to 100% *Semillon* whose 'nobel rot' gives the wine its luscious richness. A little *Muscadelle* is often added too.

The châteaux in these areas have been categorized into a hierarchy of classed growths (*crus classés*). They are too numerous to list here except for the handful of those at the top of the *premiers crus* or *premiers grands crus* which are bracketed in the lists overleaf. (See Hugh Johnson's *World Atlas of Wine* for a fuller explanation.) These *crus classés* wines are very expensive but there are an enormous number of *crus bourgeois* wines which share the characteristics of the classics at more affordable prices (a selection of addresses is given below). Some of the big châteaux make a second wine similar in style to their *grand vin* but again cheaper: Château Latour's *Les Forts de Latour* is an example.

The map and lists on these pages give a broad idea of what is the world's largest fine wine area.

Notes on the main wines

Médoc The flagships of Bordeaux; typically tannic when young; full and elegant with a fine Cabernet nose after eight to ten years.

Graves The best dry whites in Bordeaux—full and rich yet very dry; some outstanding reds—soft and rounded with an earthy flavour.

St Emilion Noted for their roundness and fruity bouquet.

Pomerol Warm and gentle, with great concentration of taste; probably the most instantly appealing of all the clarets; both *St Emilion* and *Pomerol* mature more quickly than *Médoc* and *Graves*.

Fronsac and Canon Fronsac Big fruity wines—worth trying.

Sauternes and Barsac Deep golden whites famous for their honeyed and luscious richness; delicious with desserts, *foie gras* or *Roquefort* cheese!

Cérons and *St-Croix-du-Mont* Lacking in the richness of *Sauternes*, but excellent and much cheaper alternatives.

Premières Côtes de Blaye and *Côtes de Bourg* Good robust reds; indifferent dry whites.

Entre-Deux-Mers Crisp, light and dry whites—a good buy.

Regional appellations Variable though generally above average everyday light wines; *Bordeaux Supérieur* has more alcohol.

Best years

Red: 1966, 1970, 1975, 1978, 1979, 1981, 1982, 1983, 1985, 1986, 1988, 1989, 1990.

Sweet white: 1967, 1971, 1975, 1979, 1980, 1981, 1983, 1985, 1986, 1988, 1989, 1990.

Poor years

Red: 1968, 1969, 1972, 1974.

Sweet white: 1968, 1972, 1973, 1974, 1977, 1987.

Addresses

General information on Bordeaux wine: Conseil Interprofessionnel du Vin de Bordeaux, 1 Cours du XXX Juillet, Bordeaux 33000.

Information on *Crus Bourgeois*: Le Syndicat des Crus Bourgeois de Médoc, 24 Cours de Verdun, Bordeaux 33000.

Bordeaux wines are sold by: Vinothèque de Bordeaux, 8 Cours du XXX Juillet, Bordeaux 33000.

Information on Cognac: Maison du Cognac, 3 allée de la Corderie, 16100 Cognac.

THE LOIRE VALLEY

There is no culinary style in the Loire Valley that you can put your finger on, for along with the Île de France it is the gastronomic (as well as cultural) heart of France and its regional dishes have been largely adopted into the general repertoire of international *cuisine française*. Highly-skilled chefs employ superb local ingredients to produce fine, sophisticated food in keeping with the elegance of the chateaux in whose kitchens a number of the dishes were probably first created.

The flat, tranquil and tree-lined countryside of the valley itself, often referred to as 'the garden of France', is filled with fruit trees, soft fruits and an enormous variety of vegetables. Many places have their own particular speciality, such as the famous prunes of Tours which are commonly added to local fish or meat stews. As might be expected, there is a wide range of delicious fruit tarts; of special note are the cherry *clafoutis* of Berry and Poitou

and *tarte tatin* which was first created in Lamotte Beuvron.

The Loire itself, along with its tributaries, is the other main source of food, and freshwater fish can be found on menus everywhere. Eels are very popular in stews, and *beurre blanc* is the traditional accompaniment for pike and shad, as well as for eels.

This is an area rich in *charcuterie*, which is distinguished by the inclusion of game in the many different pies, sausages, potted meats, pâtés and terrines, together with the more usual pork meat. This is no doubt due to the abundance of game, both winged and footed, in the watery forests of Sologne and the marshland north of Niort in Poitou.

North of the valley in Maine and the Beauce the cooking alters little although the lush green Loire landscape gives way to plateaux and flat plains largely cultivated with cereal crops or grazed by cows and sheep. The southern parts of Poitou and Berry are very rural and untouristed.

With the exception of the coastal plains, where early vegetables (*primeurs*) thrive in the damp maritime climate, the land is largely given over to pasturing cattle, sheep, pigs and especially goats, whose milk provides the whole region with delicious *chabichous* (small goats'-milk cheeses). In remote corners you may come across such rustic 'delicacies' as *fressure vendéen* or *gigorit*, but only in farmhouses or the simplest of eating-places outside the ken of *Gault Millau* and *Michelin*. The coast of Poitou is a mecca for the lover of seafood and particularly of shell-fish, notably mussels, lobsters and the oysters of the Bay of Aiguillon. The Sables d'Olonne is an important fishing port, and there are many fish markets up and down the coast which are well worth visiting.

Regional specialities

alose, carpe or **tanche à l'oseille** Shad, carp or tench stuffed with sorrel.

andouille Large pork and tripe sausage served cold in slices.

andouillette Smaller version of *andouille*, served hot.

beurre blanc Butter whipped up with vinegar or white wine and shallots.

boudin blanc White sausage of minced chicken, rabbit or pork.

bouilliture d'anguilles Eels stewed in wine with prunes and onions.

cerneaux aux verjus Green walnuts steeped in unripe grape juice.

chaudrée Sea-fish stew with white wine, onions and garlic.

chouée Boiled cabbage with butter and/or cream.

citrouillat Pumpkin pie (Berry).

clafoutis Baked batter and fruit (often cherries) dessert.

cotignac or **pâté de coings** Sweets made of quince paste (Orléans).

far(ci) poitevin Cabbage stuffed with bacon, pork, onions and herbs.

fressure vendéen Pig's liver, heart, lungs and spleen cooked in blood and served cold.

friture de la Loire Small fish deep-fried and served with lemon.

gâteau de Pithiviers Puff pastry with a creamy almond filling.

gigorit Pig's head stewed in blood and red wine (Poitou).

gouéron A type of cheesecake made with goat's cheese.

matefaim Type of heavy pancake (Berry).

matelote Freshwater fish stew with wine, onions and mushrooms.

pain d'épices or **nonnettes** Spiced honey and ginger cakes.

pâté de Chartres (partridge in a pastry case); **de foie gras** (duck or goose liver); **de Paques** (pork, chicken or rabbit with hard-boiled eggs); **de Pithiviers** (lark in a pastry case); **vendéen** (rabbit and pork).

porc (noisette de) aux pruneaux Pork (tenderloin) with prunes in a wine and cream sauce.

poulet en barbouille Chicken in a blood-thickened wine sauce.

quenelles de brochet Small pike mousses in a cream sauce.

rillettes Potted meat paste (pork, rabbit, duck or goose).

rillons Similar to *rillettes* but the meat is left in pieces rather than being pounded into a paste.

sandre Freshwater fish known as a pickerel or pike-perch.

tarte tatin Upside-down apple tart.

tartouffe or **truche** Local name for potato (Berry).

tourteau fromagé Type of goat's-milk cheesecake.

truffiat Potato cake.

Cheese: *cow's milk*

Bondaroy au foin Also called *Pithiviers au foin*, this is a supple and tangy cheese cured in hay; flat disc with a grey rind; made by farms and small dairies; best between June and November.

Caillebotte Fresh and soft with a mild, creamy taste; home- and farm-made; best in spring and summer.

Crémet Fresh, mild and creamy; eaten with fruit, sugar and cream; speciality of Anjou; not seasonal.

Olivet bleu Supple and rich with a fruity taste; flat disc with a bluish rind, often wrapped in plane leaves; made by dairies; best between August and November; *Vendôme bleu* is similar.

Olivet cendré Firm and supple with a pronounced taste; flat disc cured and coated in ashes; made by farms and dairies; best between June and November; *Pannes cendré* is similar.

Goat's milk

Chabichou fermier Firm with a sharp, tangy taste; a

truncated cone with a bluish rind; made by farms; best between May and February.

Couhé-Vérac Firm with a nutty taste; square-shaped covered with chestnut or plane leaves; made on farms; best between May and February.

Crottin de Chavignol Aged, dry cheese, very sharp tasting with a rancid smell; roughly shaped flattened ball with a red-brown or grey rind (like *crottin*, which means horse-dung!); made on farms, and best in winter.

Gien Firm and nutty tasting; drum or truncated cone coated in ashes or plane leaves; made on farms; best between May and February.

Mothe-St-Héray Supple and strong-tasting; flat disc with a white downy rind; boxed; made by the dairy of la Mothe-St-Héray; best between May and November.

Ste-Maure Firm with a very goaty tang; long log with a white rind; commercially made; best between May and November.

Valençay or **levroux** Firm with a mild to nutty taste; a truncated pyramid with a blue rind; made on farms; best between May and February.

Wine

Rosés and whites—both dry and semi-sweet—sparkling rosés and whites to rival those of *Champagne*, luscious sweet whites which can compare with *Sauternes*, as well as some very fine reds make up the immense diversity of *Loire* wines.

In Anjou-Saumur and Touraine the *Chenin Blanc* is the dominant grape for white wine, and *Cabernet Franc* for red and rosé. *Rosé d'Anjou* and the superior, more fragrant *Cabernet d'Anjou Rosé* are generally fairly dry. Cheaper rosé is sold under the general appellation, *Rosé de Loire*. The *Coteaux du Layon* produces luscious and long-lived sweet white wine redolent of peaches, hazelnuts and apricots. The *Quart de Chaumes* and *Bonnezeaux* are outstanding vineyards with their own AC. The *Coteaux de l'Aubance* produces similar, though less fruity wine, and both areas make rosé and a little light red. In the *Coteaux de la Loire* some of the best dry white wine comes from *Savennières*, and of particular note are the powerful and fragrant whites of the *Coulée de Serrant* and *Roche-au-Moines Communes*—superb with salmon, though delicious by themselves. Sparkling white and rosé is made round Saumur, known as *Saumur Mousseux*—a delicious and far cheaper alternative to *Champagne* —while *Saumur-Champigny* is among the better reds of the Loire.

The best reds of Touraine are *Chinon, Bourgueil* and *St-*

Nicholas-de-Bourgueil, with their bouquet of raspberries and taste reminiscent of redcurrants. The white wine of *Vouvray* ranks among the finest of Loire wines; it may be dry, semi-sweet, sparkling or, at its very best, luscious sweet wine (described as *moelleux*) with rich flowery, honeyed fruit and a life-span longer than the comparable wines of *Sauternes*. Worth visiting in Vouvray are the natural limestone cellars where you can taste both the wine and the local specialities in the restaurants now housed there. *Montlouis*, across the river, is a similar wine of slightly less quality but very good value. Both wines are excellent with the local specialities, *rillons*, *rillettes* and *boudin blanc*, as well as with fish. Under the general *appellation* of *Touraine* you will find reds, whites and rosés, with the best wine coming from the villages of *Azay-le-Rideau*, *Mesland* and *Amboise* (their name is added to 'Touraine' on the label). North of Tours, alongside the respectable reds, whites and rosés of the *Coteaux du Loir*, is the tiny *appellation* of *Jasnières* whose white wine, in a good year, can rival that of *Vouvray*. Both Touraine and Anjou produce *Crémant de Loire*, a dry, softly sparkling wine of high repute. In the eastern part of the Loire the *Sauvignon Blanc* grape produces white wine of an entirely different nature. The most famous are *Sancerre* and *Pouilly Fumé*, which are almost indistinguishable from each other: simple, fresh and short-lived wines with a dry, smoky fruitiness and the distinctive Sauvignon nose that are instantly appealing. *Chavignol* produces some of the best *Sancerre* and this village—once renowned for its walnut, hazelnut and almond oil—is now famous for its strong-smelling goat's cheese called *Crottin de Chavignol*. Of the lesser-known *Sancerre*-style whites, *Quincy* is deemed to have the edge over *Reuilly* and *Ménétou-Salon*.

Among the best of the VDQS wines are the light reds and *Sauvignon* whites of *Cheverny* and the *Coteaux du Giennois* and *du Vendômois*, as well as the *Gamay* (Beaujolais grape-type) reds and rosés of *Châteaumeillant*. A number of fruit liqueurs are made in the Loire, including *Cointreau* and *Guignolet* (cherry brandy), both made in Angers, and *eau-de-vie de coings*, the famous quince liqueur of Orleans.

Best years—red: 1976, 1981, 1982, 1983, 1985, 1986, 1988 and 1990.
Best years—white: 1971, 1976, 1978, 1979, 1982, 1985, 1986, 1988, 1989 and 1990.

For general information on Loire wines contact:
Comité Interprofessionnel des Vins d'Anjou et de Saumur, Hotel Godeline, 73 rue Plantagenet, 49023 Angers. Comité Interprofessionnel des Vins de Touraine, 19 Square Prosper Mérimée, 37000 Tours.

BRITTANY

Unlike most regions of France, Brittany does not have its own distinctive style of cooking, a fact which might seem odd for such a highly individualistic people as the Bretons. But there are two likely reasons for this unFrench attitude to food: until recent improvements in farming techniques were introduced, the Bretons could only just about scrape a living off the unyielding land, and such poverty provided little scope for culinary exploration and development. Furthermore, Brittany did not become part of France until the sixteenth century, and even then the Bretons refused to associate with the French; right into this century they have had more in common with the Welsh (both in language and customs), whose Celtic ancestors colonized the province in the fifth century.

Progress has since altered all that. New motorways have opened up the countryside, giving easy access to the beautiful rugged coast and unspoilt undulating landscape. A flourishing tourist industry has risen up, along

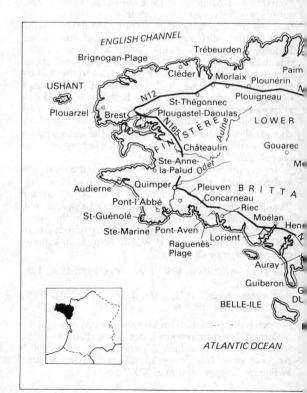

with an encouraging number of good restaurants (see map). The chefs display their culinary art in skilful but simple preparations of the local produce. Naturally, seafood dominates the menus and there are no heavy traditional sauces to smother the delicate flavour of fish fresh from the sea. With the mild Breton climate, fresh vegetables of superb quality are available most of the year round and need only light boiling. Such simplicity is in the style of the latest and most sophisticated of culinary trends, *nouvelle cuisine*, but simplicity is its only common link with the latterday diet of the Breton farmer and fisherman.

Pancakes (*crêpes* and *galettes*) are the only true Breton speciality, and filled with sweet or non-sweet stuffings they can provide a complete meal at little cost. There are *crêperies* in almost every town where you can watch your pancake being cooked. The other dish, ubiquitous along the whole coast of France, is fish stew; it is called *cotriade* here, and traditionally consisted of any fish left over from the day's catch, always including conger eel.

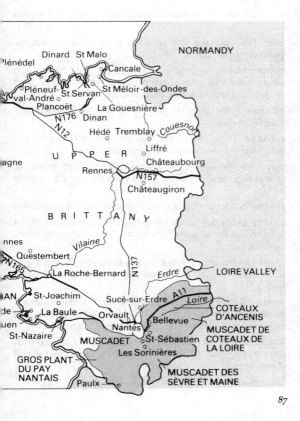

The tender young lambs raised on salt-meadows (*prés-salés*) are particularly good, as are poultry and *charcuterie* (pork products). The Bretons are very partial to their butter, and they also like to drink buttermilk (*lait baratté*) or thinned yoghurt (*lait ribot*) with pancakes—but, surprisingly for a dairy-farming region, they produce few cheeses.

The original name for Brittany, *Armor* (country of the sea) is responsible for a long-standing gastronomic debate on the origins of the famous lobster dish *homard à l'armoricaine* or *américaine*. From the taste it would seem to have come from Provence, but nevertheless you will frequently find it on the Breton menu.

Regional specialities

alose à la crème Shad served in a creamy sauce.

andouille Smoked pork and tripe sausage usually served cold.

andouillette Similar to *andouille*, but smaller and served hot.

bardatte Cabbage stuffed with hare or rabbit accompanied by chestnuts.

beurre blanc A creamy sauce of chopped shallots in white wine and vinegar whipped up with butter; served with pike (*brochet*) and shad (*alose*).

civelles Baby eels, generally deep-fried (particularly round Nantes).

cotriade Fish stew of various fish, shellfish and conger eel, with onions, potatoes, herbs and cream.

crêpe (dentelle) Large pancake (very thin) made of wheat-flour and generally eaten with a sweet filling: fruit or jam.

far breton Sweet batter pudding with raisins or prunes.

galette de blé noir or **de sarrasin** Thick pancake made of buckwheat flour, usually with a filling of cheese, meat, eggs or fish.

gigot (d'agneau) de pré-salé à la bretonne Roast leg of lamb from the salt-meadows served with white haricot beans.

homard à l'armoricaine or **à l'américaine** Lobster sautéed in olive oil, flambéed in cognac and served in a cream and wine sauce with onions, garlic, tomatoes and herbs.

kig ha fars Meat (beef, pork or oxtail) slowly cooked with vegetables, and served with cabbage and buckwheat dumplings.

kouign amann Puff-pastry cake layered with sugar.

lait baratté Buttermilk; *lait ribot* is a thinned yoghurt drink.

palourdes (moules) farcies Clams (mussels) stuffed with chopped shallots, garlic, herbs and butter, then baked.

pot au feu d'homard Lobster stew with shrimps, scallops, mussels and oysters.

Cheese: *(all cow's milk)*

Campénéac, Trappiste de Mild, supple cheese; yellow interior with tiny holes; large flat disc with a greyish yellow rind; made by the nuns of Campénéac Convent; not seasonal.

Crémet nantais Very soft, mild cream cheese; usually served with fruit or jam, or just sprinkled with sugar; not seasonal.

Fromage du Curé or **Nantais** Supple, with a pronounced tangy taste; square-shaped with a yellowish rind; made in small factories; not seasonal.

La Meilleraye, Abbaye de Supple and fairly tangy; large square slab with an ochre-yellow rind; made at the Abbey of La Meilleraye; best between May and February.

Mingaux Very similar to *Crémet nantais* above.

Wine and cider

Cider is the drink traditionally associated with Brittany, but though delicious with pancakes it is not generally of the same quality as the Normandy brew, except for that made at Beg-Meil and Fouesnant, which is worth looking out for.

Although now administratively part of the Loire, the wine-growing region around Nantes is regarded by the Bretons as their territory, and *Muscadet* as their wine: justly so perhaps, for this crisp, dry white wine is particularly delicious with seafood (though also excellent with the freshwater fish of the Loire!). Made from the single grape-type, *Muscadet de Bourgogne*, it is a fresh wine which should be drunk as young as possible, and of the three 'appellations' *Muscadet de Sevre-et-Maine* is the best. *Sur lie* on the label indicates the wine has been bottled on its lees, thereby giving greater freshness of flavour. *Gros Plant* is a dry white *VDQS* wine of a somewhat coarser quality but the *Coteaux d'Ancenis* (also *VDQS*) produces a light and cheerful red not unlike *Beaujolais* and a light, refreshing white, both of which are worth trying.

For general information on wine contact: Comité Interprofessionnel des Vins de Nantes, Maison des Vins—Bellevue, 44690 La Haye Fouassière.

NORMANDY

After William the Conqueror, Normandy is most well known for its dairy produce and its apples, and both of these feature prominently in most of the regional dishes. The Normans are notoriously big eaters and they like their food to be coated thickly with creamy sauces flavoured with apples, cider or *Calvados* (preferably all three!). *Nouvelle cuisine* seems to have given the area a wide berth, and the classic regional fare, which is of a heavy rustic quality, is still very much alive—and very fattening!

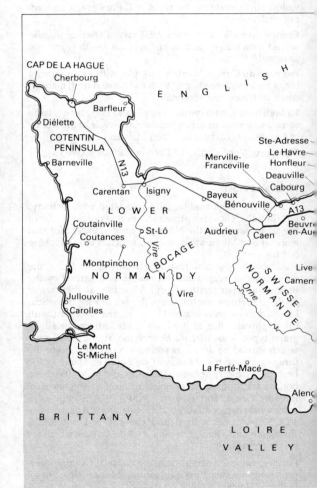

Pork products are rated highly here; the *andouilles* (see below) of Vire and the *andouillettes* of Caen are amongst the best in France. Tripe too is popular, with *tripes à la mode de Caen* being one of the most famous dishes of the province. The Duclair and Rouen breeds of duck are renowned, and chicken is also extremely good. The sheep raised on the salt-meadows (*prés-salés*) of the Cotentin Peninsula produce superb lamb and mutton. However, it is the produce of the brown and white Normandy cow that is of outstanding quality. Today, most of the milk is sent directly to factories for processing, and the results

lack some of the taste and richness of the old-fashioned farm-made products. Nevertheless, cheeses such as *Camembert* and *Pont l'Évêque* still rank among the best in the world, and the famous butter of Isigny has managed to retain its delicious nutty taste.

The relatively flat and treeless landscape of upper Normandy is given over to large-scale arable farming with wheat, sugarbeet and flax being the main crops. Lower Normandy is completely different; the Cotentin Peninsula is thought by some to resemble the wild beauty of Cornwall, while further south, orchards and little villages decorate the countryside, and in the *bocage* green meadows surrounded by a network of high hedges provide lush pasture for the dairy cattle. In May the most beautiful part is the Auge Valley where contented cows chew the cud beneath endless dazzling canopies of apple blossom destined to provide the nation's top cider and *Calvados*.

The sea plays a prominent role in the lives and the cooking of the Normandy people; its salt-tang, carried on the wind, can be detected miles inland, and so can the presence of its fruits, which provide a refreshing change from the rather rich repertoire of cream, apples and pork. The coast abounds in an enormous variety of fish and shellfish: you can be sure that those on the menus of the coastal restaurants will have been bought that day from one of the many fish-markets, such as those at Fécamp, Honfleur or Dieppe, where freshly-caught fish are auctioned daily.

Regional specialities

andouilles de Vire Smoked and cooked pork and tripe sausage, generally served cold in slices as a starter.

andouillettes Similar to *andouilles*, but smaller and served hot.

barbue à l'oseille Brill served in a sorrel sauce.

boudin blanc Fat white sausage made of chicken, white meat and/or game.

bourdelot Whole apple cooked in a pastry case.

caïeu A giant type of mussel which grows near Isigny.

caneton à la rouennaise Lightly-roasted duck stuffed with its own liver and served in a blood-thickened sauce.

colin à la granvillaise Hake, marinated then fried, and served with shrimps.

demoiselles Baby lobsters, fished mainly round Cherbourg.

douillon Whole pear cooked in a pastry case.

ficelle normande Pancake stuffed with ham, cheese or mushrooms in a creamy sauce.

filet mignon de porc normande Pork tenderloin cooked with apples and onions in cider, and served with caramelized apple rings.

fouace A plain sweet cake.

graisse normande A mixture of pork and beef fat, with vegetables and herbs, used for cooking.

jambon au cidre Ham baked in cider.

marmite dieppoise Fish and shellfish stewed in white wine with leeks and cream.

mirlitons Tartlets with an almond-and-cream filling.

moules à la marinière Mussels cooked in white wine with shallots and parsley.

moules à la normande Mussels in a white wine and cream sauce.

omelette à la Mère Poulard Plain, fluffy omelette cooked over an open log fire.

omelette normande Omelette filled with mushrooms and shrimps, or with apples, cream and *Calvados*.

pieds de mouton à la rouennaise Stuffed sheep's trotters, either fried or grilled.

plateau de fruits de mer Cold seafood platter of oysters, mussels, scallops, prawns, winkles, cockles etc.

poulet (or veau) Vallée d'Auge Chicken (or veal) cooked in cider and *Calvados* with cream and apples.

sablé Sort of crumbly shortbread.

salade cauchoise or **normande** Diced potatoes, celery and ham in a cream dressing.

sauce normande Wine or cider and cream sauce, served with fish, meat, eggs or vegetables such as leeks and cauliflowers.

sole normande Original version: Dover sole poached in cider and cream with shrimps; Parisian version: Dover sole poached in wine, served in a cream sauce with oysters, crayfish and truffles.

soufflé normande Soufflé flavoured with *Calvados* and apples.

sucre de pommes Apple sugar sticks.

tarte aux pommes Apple tart, usually served hot.

tord-goule or **tergoule** Rice pudding with cinnamon.

tripes à la mode de Caen Tripe cooked very slowly with trotters, onions, carrots and herbs in cider and *Calvados*.

tripes de la Ferté-Macé Tripe cooked in small 'packets' on skewers.

Cheese: *(all cow's milk)*

Bondard Soft double-cream cheese with a pronounced fruity taste; log with a reddish-grey downy rind; made on farms; best in October/November.

La Bouille Firm and fruity double-cream; drum with a downy white rind; made by small dairies; best between June and February.

Bricque-bec, Trappiste de Supple and mild; large flat disc with a greyish-yellow rind; made by monks; not seasonal.

Brillat-Savarin Soft and mild triple-cream; flat disc with a white downy rind; made by a small factory; not seasonal.

Camembert Supple to soft and creamy; mild becoming fruitier with age; flat disc with a downy white rind; commercially made and non-seasonal; *Camembert fermier* (farm-made) is now hard to find; mellow fruity taste; best between June and November.

Carré de Bray Fairly soft and salty with a mushroom smell; small square with a white downy rind; made by dairies; best between May and August.

Cœur de Bray Soft and supple with a fruity taste; heart-shaped, with a downy white rind; made mainly in factories; best in summer.

Excelsior Firm, delicate-tasting double-cream; flat disc with a downy white rind (boxed); made by small dairies; not seasonal.

Gournay Supple, mild and slightly salty; small disc with a downy white rind; made by dairies; best between May and February; *Gournay frais* (or *Malakoff*) is a fresh cheese, salty and slightly sour; not seasonal.

Livarot Supple with a strong, spicy taste; thick disc banded with sedge; made mainly on farms; best between May and February.

Monsieur Fromage Firm with a fruity taste and strong smell; drum with a downy white rind with red speckles; made by small dairies; best between May and February.

Neufchâtel, Bondon de Smooth and salty; variable shape with a downy white rind; made by small factories and farms; not seasonal.

Pavé d'Auge or **de Moyaux** Supple with a spicy, tangy taste; square with an ochre-yellow rind; made by farms or small dairies; best between June and February.

Pont l'Évêque Soft and supple with a pronounced tangy taste; square with a golden rind; made mainly on farms; best between June and February.

Drinks

The cider apple takes the place of the grape in Normandy, for no wine is grown here. Good cider (*bon bère*) is made from pure apple juice which is fermented in the bottle, producing a naturally sparkling drink (*cidre bouché*) that is either dry (*brut/sec*) or sweet (*doux*) and can be extremely potent! Today's factory-made cider is somewhat characterless, but the traditional methods are being revived on a small scale, notably at the Duche de Longueville near Dieppe, where a delicious old-fashioned brew is made using single varieties of apple: look out for the brand name '*le Duc*'. Perry, the pear equivalent of cider, is also popular.

Calvados is the 'brandy' distilled from cider. Coarse and fiery when young, after fifteen years it should be smooth and dry with the scent of ripe apples mingled with the oakiness of the casks in which it is aged. The best comes from the Auge Valley and is the only *Calvados* to have its own *appellation contrôlée*. There is a local tradition of knocking back a glass of '*Calva*' in the middle of a meal; this is known as *le trou normand* (*trou* means 'hole'), and it is meant to create a space for the next course.

Bénédictine was first 'invented' at Fécamp in 1510 by a monk who made this now-famous sweet liqueur from the aromatic herbs growing on the cliffs.

THE NORTH AND CHAMPAGNE

The north of France is predominantly flat, monotonous and treeless—a landscape not unlike the English fenland. Huge hedgeless fields of beet, grain and hops are dissected by sluggish rivers and dotted with lonely-looking farmhouses; most of the population is concentrated in the

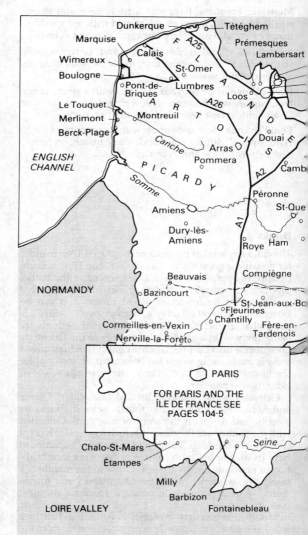

FOR PARIS AND THE
ÎLE DE FRANCE SEE
PAGES 104-5

industrial areas around Lille. Champagne is similar, although the monotony is broken in the north by the thickly-wooded hills of Ardennes, in the south-east by large forests and lakes, and around Reims by the vine-covered slopes that produce the most famous bubbly wine in the world.

Gastronomically, the link between these two regions is

a tenuous one which stems largely from Flanders. Champagne has no distinctive *cuisine* of its own. It simply eats the food of its neighbours: Lorraine (*potée*), Burgundy (*gougère, quenelles*), the *haute cuisine* of Île de France and—in common with Artois and Picardy—the rather heavy, simple fare of Flemish inspiration. Flanders (now in the *Nord* department) did not become part of France until 1668, and the names of several local dishes such as *kokeboterom* and *waterzooi* are decidedly unFrench, as is the combination of dried fruit with meat (*lapin valenciennes* and *veau flamande*); nor are you likely to find beef cooked in beer (*carbonnade*) elsewhere in France.

Charcuterie is particularly popular throughout the north and Champagne. The *andouilles* and *andouillettes* of Troyes, Arras and Cambrai have a formidable reputation, while pâtés and terrines wrapped in pastry feature strongly around Amiens and Reims. The forests of Ardennes are full of game and during the hunting season in winter, venison and wild boar appear on local menus—roasted, casseroled or in game pies and pâtés. Hearty vegetables such as potatoes, leeks, onions, pumpkins and cabbage perform major roles in the numerous soups and stews, and in the ubiquitous *flamiche* (literally, Flemish).

The influence of the sea does not penetrate very far inland in Artois and Picardy, but in Flanders and around Boulogne (which is France's largest fishing port) mackerel and herring are part of daily life, and a host of different methods have been devised for curing them—herrings especially. In Champagne you will come across freshwater fish such as trout, salmon and pike.

Both regions make fine fruit tarts (apple, plum, cherry or blackcurrant) and in the north pancakes, waffles and sweet *brioche* buns are popular. Several good cheeses are produced here too; those of the north are mainly very strong and fruity, with a powerful smell to match, whilst in Champagne they are generally mild and creamy.

Regional specialities

agneau de prés salés Tender lamb raised on the salt-meadows (north).

andouille Large pork, chitterling and tripe sausage, served cold.

andouillette Smaller version of *andouille*, eaten hot.

anglois Plum tart.

anguille au vert Eel in a green herb-and-wine sauce.

biscuit de Reims Small oblong macaroon.

cachuse or **caqhuse** Pork braised with onions (north).

carbonnade flamande Beef braised in beer with onions and spices.

caudière or **caudrée** Sea-fish stew with onions and mussels (north).

chou rouge à la flamande Red cabbage stewed with vinegar, sugar and apples.

coq à la bière Chicken cooked in beer and *genièvre* (juniper *eau-de-vie*) with mushrooms (north).

courquignoise Soup/stew of sea-fish cooked in white wine with mussels, leeks, onions and herbs (north).

craquelots Small herrings lightly smoked over hazel and walnut leaves (north); also called *bouffis*.

ficelle picarde Ham and mushroom pancake with *béchamel* sauce.

flamiche or **flamique** Leek or pumpkin and cream tart.

galopin or **galopiau** Small, thick bread pancake sprinkled with sugar.

gaufre Waffle sprinkled with sugar.

gougère Cheese choux pastry.

goyère A tart filled with strong cheese (*Maroilles*) and cream.

hareng saur Salted and smoked herring, sometimes called a *gendarme*—literally, a policeman.

hénon Cockle (Picardy), otherwise called *coque*.

hochepot Stew of beef, pork, mutton and oxtail with vegetables.

jambon en croûte Cooked ham in a pastry case.

jets de houblons à la crème Hop shoots in a cream sauce (north).

kokeboterom Small raisin bun.

langue de Valenciennes Lucullus Smoked tongue with *foie gras*.

lapin (de garenne) valenciennes (Wild) rabbit, stewed with prunes and raisins.

marcassin ardennaise Young wild boar roasted with bacon and celeriac in a red wine sauce with juniper berries.

pain d'épices Spiced honey gingerbread.

pâté: d'anguille (eel), **de bécasse** (woodcock), **de canard** (duck) and **de grives** (thrush), sometimes *en croûte*: in a pastry case.

pieds de porc à la Ste Menehould Pig's trotters cooked slowly for several hours until the bones are soft enough to eat.

potée champenoise Country stew of ham, bacon and sausage with cabbage.

potje flesh or **vleesch** Rabbit, veal and chicken terrine.

quenelles de brochet Poached pike mousses in a creamy sauce.

rabote Whole apple cooked in a pastry case; also called *talibur*.

salade de pissenlits au lard Salad of dandelion leaves with diced bacon and fried bread or new potatoes.

sauterelles Shrimps (Picardy), otherwise called *crevettes grises*.

soupe: à la biere (beer, cream and onion), **au potiron** (pumpkin) and **maraîchère** or **des hortillons** (vegetables: leeks, onions, carrots etc.).

talibur See *rabote*.

veau flamande Veal braised with dried apricots, prunes and raisins.

waterzooi Chicken or freshwater fish stewed with vegetables in a creamy sauce.

Cheese: the north

All of the cheeses listed here are made from cow's milk.

Boulette d'Avesnes Powerful taste and smell; made from *Maroilles* (see below) mashed up with herbs and pepper, and hand-shaped into a rough cone; made in farms and factories; best between June and February.

Dauphin Supple and spicy, with a penetrating smell; crescent- or fish-shaped, with a brown rind; best between June and February.

Fromage fort de Bethune Well-aged *Maroilles* mashed with herbs and stored in crocks; home-made; best between October and May.

Maroilles Supple, very tangy and strong-smelling; a square slab with a red-brown rind; originally made by the monks in the monastery of Maroilles about 1000 years ago, now made in farms and factories; best between June and February.

Mont des Cats, Abbaye de Supple and mild; a large flat disc with a golden rind and a pale yellow interior; made by monks; best between June and November.

Puant de Lille Softish, with a very spicy taste and a powerful smell (*puant* means 'stinking'!); thick square slab with a pinky-grey rind; made by farms and small dairies, and also known as *Gris de Lille*; best between October and May.

Rollot Supple, with a tangy taste; small drum or heart with a yellow rind; made by small dairies; best between June and November.

Cheese: Champagne

Barberey Soft, skimmed-milk cheese; mild and musty-smelling; flat disc coated in ashes and boxed; made by small dairies; best between July and November.

Caprice des Dieux Soft, mild double-cream cheese; oval, with a white downy rind; boxed; commercially made and not seasonal.

Carré de l'Est Supple and bland, with a mushroomy smell; square, with a downy white rind, and boxed; commercially made; not seasonal.

Cendré des Riceys or **de Champagne** Soft, skimmed-milk cheese; flat disc coated with ashes; nutty taste; made by farms and small dairies; best between July and November.

Chaource Supple, with a delicate, fruity taste; thick disc with a downy white rind; made by small dairies; best between July and November.

Chaumont Supple, with a spicy taste and a strong smell; a small truncated cone with a white downy rind; made by farms and small dairies; best between July and November.

Ervy-le-Châtel Firm and fairly mild, with a mushroomy smell; truncated cone with a downy white rind; made by farms and small dairies; best between May and October.

Igny, Trappiste de Supple and mild; large flat disc with a yellow rind; made by monks in the monastery of Igny; best between May and October.

Langres Supple and tangy, with a strong smell; truncated cone with a light red-brown rind; made by small dairies; best between May and October.

Champagne

Champagne is known by the brand-name (*marque*) of the maker and not by the vineyard, for its quality results from the careful blending (*cuvée*) of wines produced from the grapes of different vineyards and different years, except for vintage champagne, which is made from a single and exceptionally good year. Although sparkling white wine is made by the *méthode champenoise* elsewhere, none can equal the rich, round elegance and the mature bouquet of an old-style champagne such as *Krug* or

Bollinger, or the light, grapy sleekness and the clean, flowery *bouquet* of the modern style—*Taittinger*, for instance.

The *méthode champenoise* was discovered in the seventeenth century by Dom Pérignon, a monk at the abbey in Hautvilliers. Briefly: once the wine has been fermented and blended, a second fermentation is induced in the bottle by adding the *Liqueur de Tirage*, a mixture of cane sugar and yeasts that provides the 'sparkle'. Then, after a maturation period of one to five years, the cork is removed and so is any sediment; before recorking, the *Liqueur d'Expedition* or 'dosage' is added, which determines the final level of sweetness, which is labelled as follows:

Brut zéro	No sugar at all
Brut	Very dry
Extra sec	Dry
Sec	Slightly sweet
Demi-sec	Sweet
Doux	Very sweet

Champagne is generally drunk very dry as an aperitif, slightly fuller with main courses, and fairly sweet with desserts. In each case it should be served cooled, but not ice-cold.

Two-thirds of the total production is made by the champagne houses based mainly in Reims, Épernay and Ay. You can visit their cellars, which in some cases run for several miles through the chalk rock thirty metres beneath Reims and Épernay, and which provided shelter for the townspeople during the terrible bombing raids of the last world war. The remaining third, rarely seen outside France, is made by the growers themselves; it is of less consistent quality, and usually considerably cheaper.

Champagne is made from three grape types, and the very best comes from the grapes grown in the following three areas: the *Côtes de Blancs*, planted mainly with the white *Chardonnay* grape which gives freshness and finesse to the blend; *Montagne de Reims*, planted with the *Pinot Noir* for strength, backbone and the round, fruity bouquet that so distinguishes champagne; and the *Vallée of the Marne* (unhappily more famous for the battle fought there), where both the *Pinot Noir* and *Meunier* grapes grow, the latter having a softening effect on the blend.

The top *marques* include Bollinger, Deutz & Gelder-mann, Charles Heidsieck, Piper-Heidsieck, Heidsieck Monopole, Joseph Perrier, Krug, Lanson, Laurent-Perrier Louis Roederer, Marne & Champagne, Mercier, Möet & Chandon, Mumm, Perrier-Jouet, Pol Roger, Pommery & Greno, Taittinger and Veuve Clicquot-Ponsardin. Many of them make a De Luxe champagne as well: Moët & Chandon's *Dom Pérignon* and Roderer's *Cristal* are the two most famous.

Blanc de Blancs is champagne made from the white grapes only—very light and delicate. Pink champagne (*rosé*) has a little red wine blended in. *Crémant* has less fizz than the standard: *Crémant de Cramant* is a good example.

Coteaux champenois is the term given to the still wines of the region, which include an excellent red from *Bouzy* which is delicious with *Boursault* cheese; other good local reds are *Vertus, Damery* and *Cimières*, and there is the fine *Rosé de Riceys. Ratafia de champagne*, an aperitif, is a delicious mixture of brandy and unfermented grape juice.

Champagne vintages: 1969, 1970, 1971, 1973, 1975, 1976, 1978, 1979, 1982, 1983, 1985.

Beer and Genièvre

No wine is grown in the northern region of France, but the endless fields of hops and barley provide a quarter of the country's beer. Before the First World War there were 2600 breweries, but today only 37 remain; most of them are around Lille and Armentieres in Flanders, but beer is also produced in Chalons-sur-Marne and in Sedan, Ardennes. There are various types of beer ranging from light, fizzy lager to soft, dark-brown ale. The local spirit, *Genièvre*, is basically gin flavoured with juniper berries. Traditionally, a meal would be washed down with beer and finished off with a glass of Genièvre or a *bistouille*, which is coffee laced with a liqueur.

Paris and the Île de France

Paris is the undisputed gastronomic centre of France and possibly of the western world. The very word 'restaurant' was invented here in 1765. The vast repertoire of rich creamy soups and sauces, elaborate garnishes and exotic gâteaux which constitute *haute cuisine* are largely the inventions of Parisian chefs of the last four centuries. Classic sauces such as *béchamel, béarnaise, hollandaise* etc. are now household names and have long since lost any special association with Paris, but the creative imagination of the city's chefs has never been more active than now, and Paris today is an exciting melting-pot of gastronomic ideas new and old. You will find *nouvelle cuisine* at its most adventurous and classic and regional dishes at their best, as well as superb examples of cooking from all over the world, and if you want to cater for yourself there is also an enormous number of *charcuteries* and *pâtisseries* where you can buy takeaways fit for the most discerning gourmet.

The international expense-account and tourist end of the restaurant world centres around the Champs Elysées

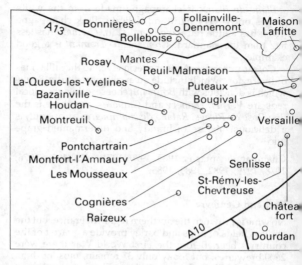

and the Rue St Honoré in the 8th *Arondissement* (district), as well as around the Eiffel Tower in the 7th. The more authentic French restaurants, bistros, cafés and nightclubs frequented by fashionable Paris are to be found in the Latin Quarter on the left bank and in the Les Halles area on the right bank of the Seine. Les Halles used to be the food market of Paris, and there have always been restaurants in the area ready at all hours to fortify late-night revellers and early morning traders with onion soup and such delicacies as pigs' trotters. The tradition of late-night restaurants continues, but in place of agricultural produce the halls now house everything from cinemas and a concert hall to chic clothes boutiques and fashionable eating-places.

Ethnic food can be found everywhere, but specifically in the following areas: the Temple quarter for Chinese, Belleville for Jewish and Arabian, the Marais for Jewish, Barbès-Rochechouart for African and the southern part of the 13th *arondissement* for Vietnamese.

The Île de France takes its gastronomic cue from Paris. Traditionally it supplied most of the raw ingredients for the capital's culinary needs, but this function has been taken over by the massive food market of Rungis, near Orly (1500 acres of food halls, with produce from every region in France and most other countries in the world), and today the beautiful lush landscape with its ancient forests and elegant châteaux provides a weekend escape for the city dweller. There are numerous restaurants which cater mainly for the expensive, sophisticated tastes of the affluent Parisian. At lunchtime on Sundays they are jam-packed: be warned!

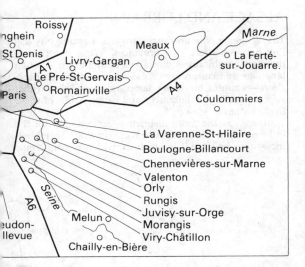

What were once the specialities of Paris and the Île de France are now an integral part of classic French food and far too numerous to list. The region grows no wine, but there are some fine local cow's-milk cheeses and one very special one:

Brie Declared by many to be the 'king of cheeses' and dating back to the 8th Century and beyond, *Brie* is produced in the area to the east of Paris and comes in flat discs of various sizes. The main types are *Brie de Coulommiers, Brie de Meaux fermier* and *Brie de Melun affiné*, as well as a factory-made *Brie laitier*. The perfect *Brie* should be supple to the touch, soft without being actually runny inside, and with an indescribably rich yet delicate fruity flavour. Factory-made *Brie* is made all year round, those made by farms are best between June and February.

Explorateur A firm triple-cream cheese with a mild flavour; drum-shaped, with a downy white rind; commercially made and available all year.

Feuille de Dreux Soft, partly skimmed-milk cheese with a very fruity taste; flat disc with a bluish-grey rind covered in chestnut leaves; made by small factories; best between June and February.

Fontainebleau A fresh, light cheese mixed with whipped cream; eaten as a pudding with fruit or just sprinkled with sugar; commercially or home-made, and available all year.

Lucullus or **Boursault** Rich, soft cheese with a mild, slightly nutty flavour; drum with a pinkish downy rind; made commercially; best between October and February.

ALSACE AND LORRAINE

The Vosges mountain range provides a strong physical link between these two provinces. While it separates them geographically and acts as a barrier to the Alsatian language and culture, it also serves as a common back-cloth—beautiful, but with a damp and rugged climate that affects equally the daily lives and eating habits of those living within its view.

Alsace has the more distinctive gastronomy, for the influence of neighbouring Germany (to which both provinces once belonged) is much in evidence: *choucroute*

(sauerkraut), rich sausages, *brioche* cakes, dumplings, noodles, and spices such as carraway seeds are all very popular—and many traditional dishes have decidedly unFrench titles. However, the region is noted for the skill of its chefs and in their hands the rather heavy nature of German food is carefully balanced by a delicacy and finesse that is the hallmark of French cooking. The food of Lorraine differs mainly in that once away to the west of the Vosges, the *cuisines* of Champagne and the Île de France outweigh the culinary influence of Germany. Nevertheless, the fine though hearty quality of the gastronomy has much in common with that of Alsace.

Tarts, sweet or otherwise, are popular throughout this area, with *quiche lorraine* being the most famous. Less well known is the delicious *flammekueche* or *tarte flambée* of Alsace, which is a traditional Sunday dish (eaten with the fingers by those in the know!). Pork is favoured above all other meats, and the *charcuterie* is excellent. There are pâtés and terrines of all types imaginable, but most notable is *pâté de foie gras* for which Strasbourg and Nancy are the main centres. The local *foie gras* (enlarged goose or duck liver) is far paler than its counterpart in Périgord, perhaps because the birds are purportedly force-fed on noodles instead of corn.

There is a wide variety of game, including wild boar, to be found in the thickly-wooded hills, as well as an abundance of mushrooms such as morels and the elusive truffle. Mountain lakes and rivers provide superb pike and trout, while the Rhine is noted for its salmon.

Apart from the fine asparagus for which Metz is famed, the range of vegetables is somewhat restricted: cabbages (red and white), potatoes, turnips and other root vegetables are the most common, and form part of many traditional dishes such as *potée lorraine* and *choucroute garnie*. Nuts are plentiful and in Lorraine particularly, poultry and game are often stuffed with chestnuts.

Fruit of all kinds is abundant and plays an important role in cooking, particularly in Alsace where the alluvial plain between the Vosges and the Rhine is filled with fruit trees. Alsatian fruit tarts are exceptionally good, and fruit—often dried—is also used in many meat dishes, which is unusual in France. Bar-le-Duc is famous for its redcurrant jelly, whilst fruit liqueurs and *eaux-de-vie* are made everywhere (see under wine below).

Regional specialities

backenoffe or **baeckaoffa** Marinated pork, mutton and beef stewed in wine with potatoes and onions.

berawecka or **birewecka** Rich fruit cake with dried pears, prunes, figs or dates.

boudin noir (à langue) Blood pudding (made with tongue).

carpe à la juive Braised carp served cold in aspic.

choucroute (garnie) *Sauerkraut*—pickled cabbage with juniper berries (cooked in wine with pork, sausages and perhaps goose, then served with potatoes).

cochon de lait à la gelée Suckling pig served cold in aspic.

coq au Riesling Chicken in a white wine and cream sauce with onions and mushrooms.

flammekueche Flat open tart filled with a mixture of bacon, onions, cream cheese and cream.

kaffekrantz Raisin cake eaten with coffee.

kassler Rolled and smoked pork fillet.

knackwurst Small sausage like a frankfurter.

knepfle Small dumpling, sometimes fried.

kugelhopf Ring-shaped *brioche* cake with almonds and raisins.

lewerknopfles Liver dumplings.

madeleines Little shell-shaped cakes, with orange or lemon essence.

marcassin Young wild boar (October to March).

matelote Stew of freshwater fish, particularly pike and eel.

oie à l'alsacienne Roast goose stuffed with sausage and served with sauerkraut.

porc (côtes de) à la vosgienne Pork chops cooked with onions, wine, vinegar and plums.

potée lorraine Hearty stew of pork, bacon, sausage, cabbage and various other vegetables.

quiche lorraine Open tart containing egg custard and bacon.

ramequin Cheese tartlet.

salade de cervelas Sliced white sausage served cold in vinaigrette sauce.

sauce au raifort Horseradish sauce.

saucisse de Strasbourg Smoked pork and beef sausage.

schifela Smoked pork shoulder served with pickled turnips.

soupe aux grenouilles Frogs' legs soup with white wine and cream.

spaetzle Type of noodle dumpling.

tarte à l'alsacienne Open fruit tart or custard tart.

tarte flambée See *flammekueche* above.

tarte au m'gin or **mougin** Open tart filled with a mixture of eggs, cream and a fresh cream cheese called *Fremgeye*.

totelots Hot noodle salad with hard-boiled eggs.

tourte à la lorraine Tart filled with pork and veal in cream.

truite au bleu Fresh trout poached in vinegar.

waffelpasteta Truffled *foie gras* wrapped in pastry.

zewelwai Onion and cream tart, sometimes with spring onions.

Cheese

All of these cheeses are made from cow's milk.

Gérardmer or **Lorraine** Firm, with a mild, slightly acidic taste; large disc (boxed) with a pale pink rind; made commercially; best between June and November.

Géromé Supple and spicy with a strong smell; thick disc with a reddish-coloured rind; made commercially; not seasonal.

Munster The most famous cheese of the region; soft and supple, with a strong tangy taste and a powerful smell; thick disc with a smooth red rind; commercially-made version available all year; farm-made variety best between June and November.

Saint-Rémy Supple and strong smelling with a spicy taste; square, with a light reddish rind; made by local factories; best between May and February.

Wine

The wines of Alsace were grouped under a single *Appellation Contrôlée* in 1963, and until recently they have been differentiated solely by the name of the grape from which they are made—*Riesling, Gewurztraminer, Muscat, Tokay d'Alsace, Sylvaner, Pinot Blanc*—rather than by an area, *commune*, vineyard or *château*, as elsewhere in France. Increasingly, however, the names of the better vineyards may also appear on the label. Almost all Alsace wine is white with the exception of *Pinot Noir*, a dry, fruity rosé or light red wine.

Riesling, generally considered to be the king, is dry, yet fruity and powerful—excellent with fish, *choucroute* and white meat. *Tokay d'Alsace* (or *Pinot Gris*) is full-bodied and heady with a delicious lingering aftertaste—a fine match for *foie gras* and roast meat. *Gewurztraminer* is a bold, spicy wine with an overwhelming fruity bouquet and immediate appeal; in great years such as 1976 it may be vinified to become slightly sweet, with an alcohol content of 14° and this is indicated on the label by the term *Vendange Tardive* or, sweeter still, *Sélection des Grains Nobles*. It goes well with highly-seasoned food, smoked salmon, pungent cheeses (such as *Munster*), as well as with *tarte à l'alsacienne*. *Muscat* here is completely dry (unlike the luscious sweet *Muscats* of the Midi), yet its fruitiness and full *Muscat* flavour are quite overpowering and best savoured alone as an aperitif. *Sylvaner*, the most widely planted and less 'noble' grape, is fresh and dry, yet fruity (sometimes sparkling) and an appropriate accompaniment to *hors d'œuvres* and fish.

There are other less important grapes such as the *Chasselas* and *Pinot Blanc* (or *Klevner*), which is also used for making sparkling *Crémant d'Alsace*. *Zwicker*, a no more than average table wine, is a blend of these and other, lesser grapes, while *Edelzwicker* is blended from the more noble varieties.

Most of the best wine is grown in the area south of Sélestat, an exception being Barr, where excellent *Riesling* is made. The N59 takes you past the impressive castle of Koenigsbourg to the *Route des Vins*, which meanders among picturesque wine villages such as Kayserberg and Riquewihr. Important producers like Hugel, Dopff, Dopff-Irion and Preiss Zimmer are based in Riquewihr, and you can buy their wine in the retail shops below their offices. The cooperative of nearby Kientzheim is another source of excellent *Riesling*. Some of the top vineyards entitled to the recent *Grand Cru appellation* are also in this area; look out in particular for *Kaefferkopf, Schlossberg, Sporen* and *Schoenenburg*. A red seal—*Le Sigille de la Confrerie St-Etienne*—signifies wine of exceptionally good quality, while *Alsace Grand Vin* or *Réserve* indicates that the wine has more than 11° alcohol. Most Alsace wine should be drunk very young but *Riesling, Gewurztraminer* and *Tokay d'Alsace* will improve after a few years in the bottle. Best years: 1971, 1976, 1978, 1981, 1982, 1983, 1985, 1986, 1988, 1989, 1990. Poor year: 1977.

Between the vineyards are orchards, providing fruit for macerating to make sweet fruit liqueurs, or for distilling into dry colourless *eaux-de-vie* (or *alcools blancs*): *Fraise* (strawberry), *Framboise* (raspberry), *Mirabelle* (yellow plum), *Quetsch* (purple plum), *Reine-claude* (greengage), *Kirsch* (cherry), *Mûre* (blackberry), *Myrtille* (bilberry) and *Houx* (holly).

Lorraine produces some wine, which is of unremarkable quality; the best known are *Vin de Moselle* and *Côtes de Toul*, and both areas make dry white, light red or, most commonly, a refreshing pale rosé called *Vin Gris* which should be drunk well chilled.

Alsace and Lorraine also produce very good beer, which is mainly of a light lager type: Strasbourg, Champigneulles, Metz and Schiltigheim are big brewing centres. And finally, there is the famous mineral water of Vittel.

For general information on Alsace wine contact: Maison du Vin, Comité Interprofessionnel des vins d'Alsace, 12 ave de la Foire aux vins, 68012 Colmar.

CHAMPAGNE

ALSACE

Fougerolles

Luxeuil

Port-sur-Saône

Belfort

Saône

Vauchoux

Ognon

Baume-les-Dames

Étuz

Roches-les-Blamont

Goumois

Besançon

Bonnevaux-le-Prieuré

Morteau

Doubs

Loue

Mouchard

Arbois

Pupillin

Château-Challon

Étoile

Courlans

Lons-le-Saunier

Crissier

Lausanne

Les Rousses

St Amour

Gex

Ain

Fernay-Voltaire

Geneva

St-Julien

Lake Geneva (Lac Léman)

Evian

Thonon

Sciez

Crepy

Avoriaz

Bogève

Frangy

Seyssel

Bonneville

Annecy

Talloires

Chamonix

BUGEY

Rhône

Virieu-le-Grand

Megève

Montagnieu

Belley

Aix-les-Bains

Le Bourget

Beaufort

Albertville

RHÔNE VALLEY & LYONNAIS

Faverges-de-la-Tour

Chambéry

Montmélion

Tignes

Courchevel

Val d'Isère

Apremont

St Marcellin

A48

A41

Grenoble

L'Alpe-d'Huez

Les-Deux-Alpes

Briançon

Château-Queyras

La Chapelle-en-Vercors

Pelvoux

Drôme

Die

DAUPHINÉ

Gap

Serres

PROVENCE

A36

Isère

112

JURA AND THE ALPS
[FRANCHE-COMTÉ, SAVOIE AND DAUPHINÉ]

A predominantly harsh climate and rugged terrain unite these mountainous regions gastronomically as much as geographically. The traditional dishes are plain, hearty and designed to keep out the cold. Cheese, potatoes and various types of cured meat are prominent ingredients. Their ability to keep indefinitely was once of vital importance during the months when snow cut off all communication with the outside world. Today, mountain culinary customs are still strong, although in the larger towns and popular skiing resorts the food is largely international.

In the Alps, cheese and potatoes are combined to make the famous *gratins*, *dauphinois* and *savoyard*. *Gratins* (meaning dishes with a browned topping, often of cheese or breadcrumbs) are made of other vegetables too—leeks, celeriac, pumpkins, Swiss chard and cardoons—as well as of minced meat, macaroni, *cèpes* and, grandest of all, crayfish tails (*queues d'écrevisses*). Cheese *fondue*, more commonly associated with Switzerland, is popular in both the Alps and Jura. Long experience in curing meat is reflected in the superb *charcuterie*, notably the smoked mountain hams, and sausages such as *Jésu de Morteau*. *Brési*, thinly-sliced cured beef is a delicious speciality of Franche-Comté.

The thickly forested foothills abound in a wide range of game, both furred and feathered, and here too can be found a large variety of wild mushrooms, providing the perfect accompaniment. Bonneville and Besançon specialize in various types of game pâté. Fish are also plentiful, especially trout from cascading mountain rivers such as the Ognon and Doubs, and the highly-prized *omble de chevalier*, *féra* and *lavaret* (all members of the salmon family), which are virtually exclusive to Lakes Annecy and Geneva (Léman), though a few are caught in the lakes of Jura as well. Freshwater crayfish are the speciality of Nantua—*à la Nantua* means 'with crayfish'—for Lake Nantua was once filled with these sought-after crustaceans.

The Isère Valley is famous for nuts; hazelnuts, chestnuts and particularly the walnuts around Grenoble. The city has various walnut specialities and walnut oil is often used in salads. In the fertile lowlands of Franche-Comté there is more variety in the cooking and a wider range of vegetables and fruit—cherries, especially. Likewise, the western edge of the Alps has easy access to the rich larders of Burgundy, Bresse and the Rhône Valley while the arid hills of the extreme south, where milk-fed lamb (*agneau de lait*) is a speciality, begin to look towards Provence for culinary inspiration.

Regional specialities

biscuit de Savoie Light sponge-cake with almonds.

brési Dried, smoked beef served in thin slices.

brochette jurassienne Skewered pieces of cheese wrapped in ham and fried.

croustades jurassiennes Bacon- and cheese-filled toasts or pastries.

défarde Stew of tripe and lambs' feet (Alps).

diots au vin blanc Pork sausages poached in white wine (Alps).

escalope de veau belle comtoise Veal escalopes breadcrumbed and baked with slices of cheese and ham (Jura).

Farçon or **farcement** Potatoes mixed with eggs, sugar and dried fruit, and baked as a dessert.

fechun Cabbage stuffed with bacon and vegetables (Jura).

fondue Cheese melted in white wine with kirsch (and eggs in Jura), into which pieces of bread are then dipped.

gâteau grenoblois Rich walnut cake.

gratin dauphinois Thinly-sliced potatoes baked in milk with nutmeg and (sometimes) cheese.

gratin de queues d'écrevisses Freshwater crayfish tails cooked in a creamy sauce containing white wine and Cognac, then browned in the oven.

gratin savoyard Thinly-sliced potatoes with cheese baked in stock.

jésu(s) de Morteau Large smoked sausage.

langues fourrées Stuffed tongues (Besançon).

mont blanc Meringue with chestnut purée and whipped cream.

omelette savoyarde Omelette filled with fried potatoes and cheese.

pauchouse Stew of freshwater fish (pike, carp, trout etc.) in wine.

pets de nonne 'Soufflé' fritters made with a sort of *choux* pastry; literally, 'nuns' farts'!

pommes dauphiné Deep-fried potato and choux pastry croquettes.

poulet au vin jaune Chicken with morels in a creamy sauce made with this potent local wine (Jura).

quenelles de brochet Nantua Poached pike mousses in *sauce Nantua*.

ravioles Pastries made with goats' cheese.

sauce Nantua Creamy sauce with truffles and freshwater crayfish tails.

soupe aux cerises Hot cherry soup.

soupe aux grenouilles Creamy frogs' legs soup.

soupe montagnarde or **savoyarde** Thick vegetable soup with grated cheese.

Cheeses of Jura: *cow's milk*

Bleu de Gex Firm and blue-veined, with a sharpish taste; a thick disc with a natural rind; made by small dairies; best between June and November.

Bleu de Septmoncel Very similar to *Bleu de Gex* in all aspects.

Cancoillotte Pale yellow, runny, very fruity; made from *Metton* (a skimmed-milk cheese) melted with butter, garlic and eggs; eaten warm on toast; sold in cartons; not seasonal.

Comté, gruyère de Similar to *Swiss Gruyère*—firm and yellow, with small holes and a sharp taste; large flattened drum (77 lbs); made commercially; best between August and February.

Emmental français Similar to *Swiss Emmental*—very supple; yellow with large holes; fruity taste; vast drum (176–220 lbs); made commercially; available all year.

Mamirolle Supple and fairly strong; oblong with a reddish rind; made at the Mamirolle dairy school; not seasonal.

Morbier Firm but supple, with a black streak through the middle; fairly fruity taste; thick disc with a grey rind; made by cooperatives (*fruitières*); best in spring.

Vacherin Mont d'Or Firm and supple; mild-tasting; flat disc with a pale pink rind; made by farms; best between November and February.

Goat's milk

Chevret Soft with a nutty taste; square, rectangle or flat disc with a pale blue rind dotted with pink; made on farms; best between June and November.

Cheeses of Savoie: *cow's milk*

Beaufort, gruyère de Firm (almost no holes) with a salty, fruity tang; large flattened drum (88–132 lbs) with a natural rind; made in mountain chalets; best in winter, spring and summer.

Beaumont Supple and mild-tasting. Flat disc with a yellow rind. Made commercially; best between June and November.

Bleu de Sainte-Foy Brittle and blue-veined with a rather sharp taste; large drum with a natural rind; made on mountain farms; best between June and November.

Bleu de Sassenage Supple and blue-veined; slightly sharp taste; thick disc with a natural rind; made by dairies; best in summer.

Bleu de Tignes Blue-veined and similar to *Bleu de Sainte-Foy*.

Chambarand, Trappiste de Supple, mild and creamy; small, flattened drum with a yellow-pink rind; made by monks; best between June and February.

Fondu au Marc or **au raisin** Processed and fairly mild; flat disc covered in grape pips. Made commercially; not seasonal.

Reblochon Supple, creamy and mild; flat disc with a pale pink skin; made by farms and cooperatives; best between June and November.

St Marcellin, Tomme de Supple and mild; small drum with a blue-grey rind; made commercially; not seasonal.

Tamié, Trappiste de Similar to *Beaumont*; made by monks.

Tomme de Savoie Supple with a nutty taste; thick disc covered by a grey rind with red and yellow spots; made by farms and factories; best between May and February.

Vacherin d'Abondance Supple to runny; mild; flat disc with a pink rind (boxed); made on farms; best between November and February.

Goat's milk

Chevrotin des Aravis Firm; mild goaty taste; drum with a grey rind; made in mountain chalets; best between June and November.

Persillé des Aravis Firm and blue-veined with a sharp taste; log-shaped, with a grey-brown rind; made on farms; best between June and November.

Tomme de Vercors Firm with a nutty taste; small drum with a pale blue rind; made on farms; best between May and February.

Note: there are many more types of *Tomme*: the ones included here are typical examples.

Wine

The regional appellation *Côtes du Jura* includes red, rosé and white wines (some sparkling), as well as the unique *vin jaune* (yellow wine) and *vin de paille* (straw wine).

AC Arbois covers the whole range, but its dry rosé and *vin jaune* are the most noteworthy. Henri Maire is by far the biggest producer, but Christian Rolet and Émile Rousseau compare well for quality. *Château-Chalon* produces some of the finest *vin jaune*; this is a golden wine with a nutty bouquet—dry yet potent, with immense longevity. Made from the *Savignin* grape it undergoes a fermentation process similar to that of sherry, remaining in the cask for 6–10 years before it is bottled. *AC Étoile* is best known for its dry, often sparkling, white wine as well as for *vin de paille*. The latter is made by drying the grapes (on straw, traditionally) before pressing them; this produces a small amount of very sweet juice which makes a very full, fragrant and powerful wine (15° minimum) which, like *vin jaune*, is expensive.

Apart from the excellent *Kirsch* of Mouthiers and Fougerolles, the speciality of Jura is *Hypocras*, which is red wine mixed with sugar and spices.

Most Savoie wine is white, sparkling or still, and generally light and dry—a fine accompaniment for the heavy cheese dishes and creamy *gratins* of the region. The villages of *Apremont*, *Ayse*, *Abymes* and *Chignin* produce some of the best wine in the *Vin de Savoie* appellation, while under *AC Roussette de Savoie* look out for *Frangy* and *Marestel*. *AC Crépy* is a light, dry wine from the *Chasselas* grape, and *AC Seyssel* is noted for its delicate sparkling wine from the *Altesse* grape. Some of the best reds come from *Montmelian* and *St-Jean-de-la-Porte*, and a light fruity *Gamay* (*Beaujolais* type) is made at *Chautagne*.

West of the Savoie wine region lie the *VDQS* wines of *Bugey*: *Montagnieu*, *Manicle* and *Virieu-le Grand* are dry whites worth looking out for. There is also some sparkling *Pétillant de Bugey*, as well as light reds and fruity rosés.

Clairette de Die, out on a limb in southern Dauphiné, is a full and fragrant sparkling white wine made from the *Clairette* and *Muscat* grapes. It is made dry and semi-sweet, and both are best drunk alone as aperitifs.

A number of liqueurs are made in the Alps, of which the most famous is *Chartreuse* (said to hold life-prolonging properties!); there is also the excellent dry vermouth of *Chambéry*.

PROVENCE

The spectacular terracotta landscape of Provence shimmers in brilliant sunshine. On the steep, parched hillsides sheep and goats graze among wild thyme, rosemary and lavender which, with pines, evergreen oaks and olive trees, thrive miraculously on the stony ground. Below, in sharp contrast, lie the lush river valleys—in particular, the wide alluvial plain of the River Rhône, whose abundance of fruit and vegetables have earned it the title 'the market garden of France'.

The dominating influence on Provençal cooking was determined 2500 years ago when the Greeks brought over

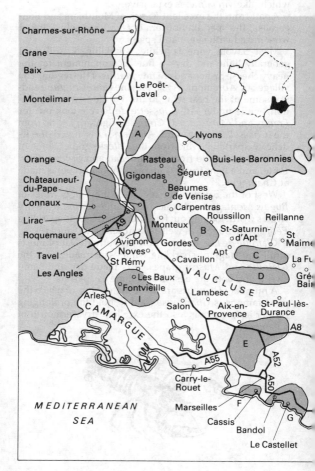

the olive tree. Olive oil is used unreservedly in cooking—vegetables as well as fish and meat—and in salads. The olives themselves, along with fat sweet tomatoes, pungent garlic, sweet and hot peppers, raw onions, artichokes and herbs, are typical ingredients of many dishes.

For lovers of fish and shellfish, Provence is a haven; Marseilles is the home of *bouillabaisse*, but fish—in soups, stews or simply fried—fill menus all along the coast, and far inland as well. Red mullet *(rouget)*, tuna *(thon)*, monkfish *(lotte)*, sea bass *(loup)*, scorpion fish *(rascasse)* and sardines are very popular, and salt anchovies *(anchois)* appear in various dishes. The fish

DAUPHINÉ

A COTEAUX DU TRICASTIN
B CÔTES DU VENTOUX
C COTEAUX DE PIERREVERT
D CÔTES DU LUBERON
E PALETTE; COTEAUX
   D'AIX-EN-PROVENCE
F CASSIS
G BANDOL
H BELLET
I COTEAUX DE BAUX

ITALY

HAUTE
PROVENCE

Digne

âteau-
noux

Moustiers-
Ste-Marie

es-

VAR

Tourtour

Cotignac

CÔTES DE

PROVENCE

Solliès Toucas

Hyères

Toulon

St-Martin-du-Var

Cagnes-sur-Mer

Vence

St-Paul-de-Vence

La-Colle-sur-Loup

St-Vallier-
de-Thiey   Grasse

Mouans-Sartoux
Mougins

La Motte

Fréjus

Grimaud

St Tropez

La Galère

La Napoule

Gassin

Cavalière

Le Lavandou

Bormes-les-Mimosas

ALPES-
MARITIMES

St-Pancrace

Peillon

Roquebrune-
Cap-Martin

Monte-Carlo

Nice   Èze

Beaulieu

St-Jean-
Cap-Ferrat

Villefranche-
sur-Mer

Antibes

Cap-d'Antibes

Juan-les-Pins

Cannes

Golfe-Juan

markets of Marseilles, Toulon, Cannes and Nice are particularly worth seeing. Locally grown beef or mutton is generally tough, but in slowly- cooked stews such as *estouffade* and *daube*, or *civets* of venison and hare, the meat is reduced almost to melting point.

There are few dishes devoid of garlic. *Aïoli* (garlic mayonnaise) is used in vegetable and egg dishes, salads and *bourride* (the virtually indistinguishable alternative to *bouillabaisse*), while *rouille* (see below) is also added to fish soups. Vegetables are another important part of the Provençal meal, either baked or fried in oil as in *tian* and *ratatouille*, or eaten raw in salads and *hors d'œuvres*, and they make a dazzling display of colour in the markets that proliferate in the Rhône Valley and all along the coast.

The cooking of the Nice area is a blend of Provençal and Italian. Here you will find pasta such as *canelloni* and *ravioli* as well as *gnocchi*, a type of potato and flour dumpling. *Pissaladière* is very closely related to *pizza*, as is *pistou* to the Italian *pesto*, and the soup it accompanies is almost identical to *minestrone*. The best time to visit the area is in early summer when the flowers (and not the tourists) are in full bloom, and the flower market in Nice is at its most spectacular. Earlier still, in March, the inimitable scent of mimosa hits you as you approach this most colourful and vibrant corner of France.

Regional specialities

aïgo bouïdo Garlic-and-herb soup, poured over bread.

aïgo sou Fish soup-cum-stew with potatoes and garlic.

aïoli Garlic mayonnaise.

anchoïade Anchovy paste, usually eaten on toast or with raw vegetables.

artichaut à la barigoule Artichoke stuffed with mushrooms, pork and sausage-meat.

bouillabaisse Fish soup-cum-stew with conger eel, scorpion fish, gurnet and others, plus saffron, fennel, garlic and bitter orange peel; served with *aïoli* or *rouïlle*.

bourride Similar to *bouillabaisse*.

brandade de morue Salt cod creamed with oil, milk and garlic.

calissons Boat-shaped marzipan sweets.

capoun fassum Cabbage stuffed with rice and sausage-meat; also called *sou fassum*.

catigou Eel stewed in wine and oil with garlic and tomatoes.

clovisse Type of small clam (local name).

esquinado (à l'huile) Local name for a spider crab (puréed and served cold in its shell).

limaces Small snails (local name).

loup au fenouil Sea bass with fennel, flambéed in Pernod or brandy.

mesclun Salad of lettuce, lamb's lettuce, chicory, endive, dandelion leaves, fennel and herbs.

niçoise, à la As *à la provençale* plus (usually) olives, capers, anchovies and tarragon.

pan bagna Bread roll soaked in olive oil and filled with tomatoes, anchovies, onions, boiled eggs, olives etc.

pieds et paquets Sheep's or calf's trotters and stuffed tripe packages' in a wine and tomato sauce.

pissaladière Open tart with tomatoes, onions, anchovies and olives.

pistou Sauce of basil, garlic and cheese, pounded in oil.

poutargue Paste of mullet roe mashed up in oil.

poutina et nonnat Tiny fish served fried (as a *friture*) or in an omelette.

provençale, à la With tomatoes, garlic, olive oil, onions, herbs and (sometimes) eggplant or aubergine.

raïto or **rayte** Sauce of red wine, tomatoes, garlic and ground walnuts, served with fish.

ratatouille Mixture of courgettes, onions, tomatoes and aubergine (eggplant) cooked in oil.

rayte See *raïto*.

rouille Hot chili-and-garlic mayonnaise.

salade niçoise Salad of tomatoes, beans, anchovies, olives, peppers and boiled eggs.

Château de la Bégude

CÔTES DE PROVENCE
APPELLATION CÔTES DE PROVENCE CONTRÔLÉE

MIS EN BOUTEILLE AU CHATEAU

J. LEFEBVRE, propriétaire-vigneron 13790 ROUSSET

socca Chick-pea flour pancake.

sou fassum See *capoun fassum*.

soupe au pistou Soup of vegetables and pasta (like minestrone), served with *pistou*.

soup au poissons Smooth soup of puréed white fish with *rouille*.

soupe d'épautre Soup-cum-stew of meat, vegetables and garlic.

stocaficada Dried salt cod stewed in oil with vegetables and olives.

tapenade A paste of olives pounded with anchovies, capers and tuna; served on toast.

tian Layered mixed vegetables baked in a *gratin* dish.

Cheese

Banon Supple, with a mild to slightly nutty taste; made from goat's, sheep's or cow's milk; small disc wrapped in chestnut leaves; dairy-made cow's milk version available all year; farm-made sheep's or goat's milk best in late spring and summer.

Brousse de la Vesubie White, creamy, fresh cheese made from goat's or sheep's milk; soft and very mild; often served with fruit; commercially made all year, but farm-made version best in spring and early summer.

Picodon de Valréas Supple, semi-fresh, goat's-milk cheese with a delicate nutty taste; a small disc, made on farms; best between May and September.

Poivre d'âne *Banon* cheese containing savory; made by farms and dairies; sold in boxes filled with sprigs of savory.

Tomme arlesienne or **Tomme de Camargue** Soft, fresh sheep's-milk cheese; creamy, with a hint of thyme and bayleaf; square-shaped; made by a dairy; Best in winter and spring.

Wine: *Southern Côtes du Rhône*

The vast bulk of wine with the basic appellation *Côtes du Rhône* is red: very drinkable, and good value. Some dry white and rosé is also made. One step up are the more substantial *Côtes du Rhône-Villages*; of the sixteen villages in this appellation the white of *Laudun* and the reds of *Vinsobres*, *Chusclan*, *Cairanne* and *Vacqueyras* stand out. At the heart of the region are the full-bodied, richly-scented reds of *Châteauneuf-du-Pape*; most are ready for drinking after four years, although the heavier styles of, for example, *Domaine de Beaucastel* and *Château Fortia* take longer to mature. *Domaine de Mont-Redon* is our wine-adviser's recommendation. Neighbouring *Gigondas* makes a similar wine—*Domaine les Paillières* is excellent. *Côteaux du Tricastin* and *Côtes du Ventoux* are noted for red and rosé and the quality continues to improve. *Beaumes de Venise* is a *vin doux naturel*, a fortified sweet wine with a wonderful flowery bouquet— pure nectar of the *Muscat* grape and delicious with strawberries. *Rasteau* is similar but inferior. *Tavel* rosé, once rated the best in France, is fruity and supple, it should be drunk young (when pink rather than orange). Maby and Bernard are main producers. *Lirac* also makes a good rosé but the reds are now of greater interest. The Auberge de Tavel has a good selection of both *Tavel* and *Lirac*.

Best years: 1978, 1980, 1983, 1985, 1986, 1988, 1989, 1990. Poor years: 1975, 1987.

Provence

The *Côtes de Provence* are best known for dry, strong, fruity rosé, delicious with fish and good value on its home ground. However, in recent years, experiments with non-Provençal grape-types have led to great improvements in the reds. *Domaine Ott*, with *Château de Selle* and *Clos Mireille* (good white), is the biggest producer. Look out for Château Ste-Rosaline and the superb Château de la Bégude (see p. 121). The reds of *Bandol*, powered by the *Mourvèdre* grape, are smooth and full. *Domaines Tempier* and *Pibarnon*, and *Château Vannières* are among the best as are the rosés of *Doms. Tempier* and *de Terrebrune*. *Château Simone* in tiny *AC Palette* is justly famed for its elegant red. Its whites and rosés are full and long-lived. *Cassis* (no connection with the liqueur) produces a dry white wine, fragrant and refreshing. *Bellet*, near Nice, makes small amounts of all colours, the dry, full white is most notable. The reds of the *Côtes du Luberon* are increasingly good, in particular *Chât. Val-Joanis* and *Chat. la Canorgue*. In the *Coteaux d'Aix-en-Provence* the supremacy of *Chât. Vignelaure* is being put to the test by *Chât. Fonscolombe* and *Chât. de Beaulieu*. *Domaine de Trévallon* in nearby *Coteaux de Baux-de-Provence* looks set to outstrip them all. Of the *VDQS* wines the *Coteaux du Pierrevert* are for everyday drinking, the rosés can be good. Experiments with *Cabernet-Sauvignon* and *Syrah* have produced some great results in the *Coteaux Varois*.

Most Provence wine should be drunk young, but *Bandol* and other good reds, such as those named above, improve with age. Avoid 1984. For further information on *Côtes de Provence* wines contact: Comité Interprofessionnel des Vins des Côtes de Provence—RN7, 83460 Les Arcs sur Argens.

THE LYONNAIS, BRESSE AND
THE NORTHERN RHÔNE VALLEY

The Lyonnais is a largely industrialized district famous for the manufacture of silk and enthusiasm for food. The outlying areas of Bresse, la Dombes, Beaujolais, Forez and the Rhône valley have traditionally provided the superb raw ingredients upon which its culinary achievements are based. You may come across such delectable inventions as *quenelles de brochet* or *poularde en demi-deuil* in any part of this region, but the focal point of lyonnais gastronomy is the city itself.

Lyon has a long and distinguished culinary history dominated, unusually, by women (fondly called *les mères*). The emphasis on good eating continues still, and there are more restaurants blessed with *Michelin* stars and *Gault-Millau toques* than in any other area of its size in France. The style of cooking varies from rich and elaborate concoctions involving the liberal use of cream

MASSIF CENTRAL

LANGL

and truffles, to simpler, more solid dishes of potatoes, onions, tripe and almost every part of the pig. Lyon is particularly known for its *charcuterie* (pork cookery) with *pâtisserie* and chocolate also high on the list of goodies. It is not a city for the calory-conscious although some chefs are now redirecting their skills to *nouvelle cuisine* in deference to the more modest modern appetite.

At the extremities of the region, the city's culinary influence becomes somewhat diluted. The kitchens of the Bresse produce more lightweight fare, omitting the body-building dishes of pork and tripe and concentrating more on chicken—their own tender white breed fed on maize and buckwheat and bathed in milk after slaughter! The startling lake-strewn landscape of la Dombes is a haven for birds and fish—pigeon, woodcock, crayfish and pike all appear on the menu, as do snails and frogs' legs.

In the Beaujolais area the splendid charollais cow provides superb beef often prepared *à la bourguignonne* and accompanied by the local red fruity wine.

The high wooded hills of Forez abound with game, which during autumn and winter arrives on the table roasted or made into delicious pâtés and terrines. In the fertile plains to the east you will come across salmon and trout fresh from the Loire, while to the west can be found the mountain food of the Massif Central.

The Rhône valley, covered with vines, fruit trees and Roman ruins, represents a bridge between northern and Mediterranean France, and a dividing line between earthy Languedoc and the sparsely-populated plains of the Bas Dauphiné. As might be expected, it is a gastronomic and cultural crossroads, with specialities coming from any one of the neighbouring regions. However, as you head south past Valence the mood changes, and with the heat of the sun, the olives and herbs of Provence begin to flavour the air and the food.

Regional specialities

Bœuf à la mode Piece of beef braised in red wine, served hot with onions and carrots or cold in aspic.

boudin aux pommes de reinette Blood pudding cooked with apples.

bugne Sweet fritter (often flavoured with acacia flowers).

cardons à la moelle Cardoons (similar to celery in looks, Jerusalem artichoke in taste) baked with a bone-marrow and cheese sauce.

cervelas aux truffes et aux pistaches (en brioche) Smooth, smoked pork sausage containing truffles and pistachio nuts (cooked in brioche pastry).

chapon de Bresse gros sel Bresse capon baked in rock salt with sliced truffles.

cocons Liqueur-flavoured marzipan sweets shaped like a silkworm's cocoon.

gras-double à la lyonnaise Ox-tripe fried with onion, vinegar and parsley.

gratinée lyonnaise Beef consommé with port and eggs (sometimes onions) topped with toasted bread and cheese.

grenouilles à la bressane Frog's legs in butter, cream and herb sauce.

jambon au foin Smoked ham simmered in water with fresh hay, or more often now with herbs—rosemary, thyme and sage.

lièvre (civet de) de Diane de Châteaumorand Hare stewed in red wine with onions and mushrooms (Bresse).

omelette à la lyonnaise Omelette filled with onions and parsley.

pommes lyonnaise Sliced potatoes fried with onions.

pogne Large brioche cake which is filled with fruit or jam (Valence).

poularde, poulet, volaille or **chapon de Bresse** A breed of chicken from the Bresse: reputedly the best in France:

  célestine With tomatoes, mushrooms in a wine and cream sauce.

  demi-deuil (à la mère Fillioux) Cooked with sliced truffles beneath the skin; stuffed with sausage and served with a cream sauce, often accompanied by lambs' sweetbreads.

  aux écrevisses With crayfish in a white wine and cream sauce.

  en vessie Stuffed and poached in a pig's bladder.

  au vinaigre With shallots and tomatoes, in a white wine, vinegar and cream sauce.

Quenelles de brochet Small pike mousses poached and usually served in a cream sauce.

rosette A large pork sausage rather like salami.

sabodet A sausage made from pig's head. Served hot in thick slices.

saladier lyonnaise Calf's head, sheep and pig's trotters, and ox muzzle, served in a dressing of oil and vinegar with chopped shallots.

tablier de sapeur Ox tripe coated in egg and bread-crumbs, fried and served with tartare or *béarnaise* sauce.

tendresses Rum-flavoured nougat sweets in a meringue case.

Cheese: *cow's milk*

Bleu de Bresse A creamy, blue-veined cheese with a mild taste; a drum wrapped in silver foil; commercially made; not seasonal.

Cervelle de Canut or **Claqueret** A fresh cheese, home-made round Lyon, with herbs, white wine and vinegar (originally made by the silk-workers (*canuts*) of Lyon); not seasonal.

Fourme de Monbrison Firm, with a pronounced, slightly bitter taste; large drum with a grey rind speckled with red and yellow; made by small dairies in Forez; best between June and November.

Mont d'Or Soft, with a mild, delicate taste; thin disc with a blue rind; made near Lyon; not seasonal.

Rigotte de Condrieu Supple and mild, with a slightly milky taste; small drum with a thin reddish rind; made by small dairies; not seasonal.

Goat's milk

Bressan or **Petit Bressan** Firm, fruity with a slightly goaty smell; small truncated cone with a whitish rind; made on farms; best between June and November.

Brique du Forez or **Cabrion du Forez** or **Chevreton d'Ambert** Firm with a nutty taste; slim brick with a white and blue rind; made only on farms in Forez and the Auvergne; best between June and November.

Wine

Lyon lies roughly midway between the wines of *Beaujolais* and the *Côtes du Rhône*. Both flow liberally in the bars and restaurants of the region and both are predominantly red, but here the similarity ends.

Beaujolais

The granite hills of Beaujolais are ideal for the *Gamay*—the grape variety which gives the wine its delicious red fruity taste. The southern end of the region produces the great mass of wine (15 million gallons a year) with the simple *AC Beaujolais* or slightly stronger *AC Beaujolais Supérieur* classifications. Most of this is best drunk young— *Beaujolais Nouveau* just a few weeks after the grape harvest. It is a light and extremely gulpable wine, delicious with the local beef.

The wine of the northern end is more serious (and more expensive). Among the thirty-five villages given the higher appellation of *Beaujolais Villages* there are nine with their own individual appellations (see map). Given a little time, these wines (*Morgon, Moulin-à-Vent* and *Chénas* in particular) develop a greater depth and richness, yet still retain the fruity grapiness characteristic of all *Beaujolais*. (*Grumé* indicates wine that ages well.)

The *Gamay* reds of *AC Coteaux du Lyonnais*, as well as those of the *Côtes du Forez* and the *Côtes Roannaises* (both *VDQS*), are great value minor '*Beaujolais*'.

Best years: 1985, 1987, 1989, 1990.
Poor years: None to speak of since 1984.

Rhône valley

The Rhône valley is divided into two very different wine-growing areas by 50 miles of vineless no-man's-land. Both are called *Côtes du Rhône* but only the northern section is dealt with here; the southern section comes within Provence.

Under the simple *AC Côtes du Rhône* you will find a variety of inexpensive red wines, some deep-coloured and full-bodied, others lighter and fruitier. The whites are dry, often grapy, and can be very heady. Some palatable dry rosés are also made. There are eight superior (and much pricier) wines with their own appellations. The *Syrah* is the dominant grape-type used for the reds and the *Marsanne* and *Rousanne* for the whites.

Starting in the north near Ampuis, the *Côte Rôtie* is said by many to produce the finest of all the Rhône red wines. It has a sappy, rich taste which improves vastly with age: a rare and expensive wine, of which one of the top producers is Marcel Guigal at Ampuis; Paul Jaboulet is another name worth looking out for.

Further south around Condrieu, two even rarer (and pricier) wines are grown: the whites of *Condrieu* and *Château Grillet*, the latter consisting of only four acres. Both are made uniquely with the *Viognier* grape, which gives the wine an extraordinarily alcoholic fruity richness with the scent of Muscat (almonds, to some). Both wines should be drunk young, on their own or with a highly-seasoned dish such as snails. Guigal and Delas Frères are among the best producers.

Hermitage, near Tain, makes the 'biggest' wine of the region. Deep and full-bodied (often described as 'manly'), it is a wine that should be well aged and one that goes particularly well with red meat and game. There is also a full and heady white *Hermitage* which is good with richer fish such as salmon and turbot. *Crozes-Hermitage* nearby produces a lighter (and cheaper) red that matures more quickly, and a palatable white wine which is delicious with most *hors d'œuvres*. Paul Jaboulet and M. Chapoutier produce excellent examples of all these.

St Joseph, to the west, is a highly-scented red wine with a pronounced earthy flavour (best drunk youngish). Small quantities of a potent white wine are also made here. The cooperative of St Désirat at Champagne is a commendable producer.

Cornas produces a rich and elegant red wine which keeps for a long time and is ideal with game. Top producers are Delas Frères and Auguste Clape of Cornas.

St Péray, at the southern end of this region, produces a heady white, most of which is made into a sparkling wine—good as an aperitif. Look out for M. Milliand and J. F. Chaboud.

Best years (red and white): 1971, 1976, 1978, 1979, 1980, 1982, 1983, 1985, 1986, 1988, 1989, 1990.
Poor years: 1975, 1987.

For general information on Beaujolais and Rhône wines contact:
Maison du Vin de Beaujolais, 69220 St Jean d'Ardières.

Maison du Tourisme et du Vin, 41 cours Jean Jaurès, 84000 Avignon.

BURGUNDY (BOURGOGNE)

The departments of Yonne, Nièvre, the Côte d'Or and Saône-et-Loire that make up modern Burgundy, share a chunk of France upon which the best of almost everything edible grows, grazes, swims or flies. It is the land of the big but discerning eater whose culinary traditions date back to the Middle Ages and remain virtually unchanged to this day. Burgundian food is in the best *bourgeois* style of fine, unfussy cooking. The dominant ingredients are

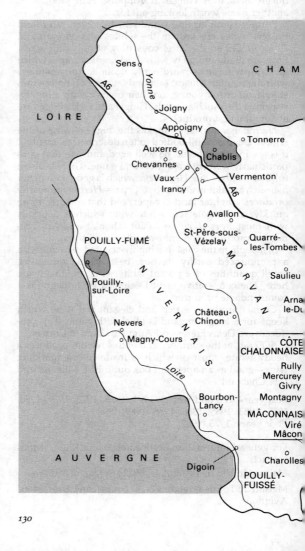

beef, pork and chicken, onions and mushrooms of various types, snails and their pungent companion garlic, and cream (though the latter is kept under control).

The Côte d'Or, incorporating two of the most distinguished wine-growing areas in France, is considered to be the heart of Burgundy. Some of the finest regional cooking can be found here and all down the Saône valley, through the other wine regions of Chalonnais and Mâconnais. Dijon's gastronomic history can be traced back to the massive medieval banquets held by heroes like Philip the

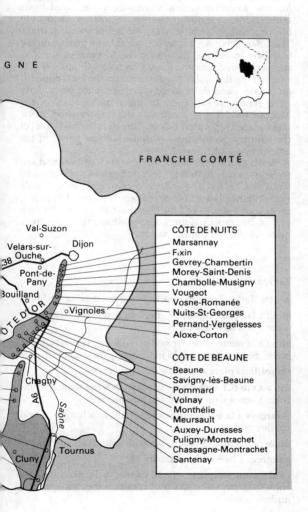

GNE

FRANCHE COMTÉ

Val-Suzon
Velars-sur-
Ouche
38
Pont-de-
Pany
Bouilland
Dijon
Vignoles
CÔTE D'OR
Chagny
A6
Saône
Cluny
Tournus

CÔTE DE NUITS

Marsannay
Fixin
Gevrey-Chambertin
Morey-Saint-Denis
Chambolle-Musigny
Vougeot
Vosne-Romanée
Nuits-St-Georges
Pernand-Vergelesses
Aloxe-Corton

CÔTE DE BEAUNE

Beaune
Savigny-lès-Beaune
Pommard
Volnay
Monthélie
Meursault
Auxey-Duresses
Puligny-Montrachet
Chassagne-Montrachet
Santenay

Bold and John the Fearless at the Palais des Ducs de Bourgogne (now the Musée des Beaux Arts, but you can still see the kitchen with its six enormous fireplaces). Today the city is best-known for its mustard. *Pain d'épices*, a kind of honey gingerbread, is another speciality, and the blackcurrants growing just beyond its suburbs are made into *Crème de Cassis*, a blackcurrant liqueur often mixed with white wine to make the aperitif *Kir*—named after Canon Kir, a mayor of Dijon who was particularly fond of this combination.

The beautiful wooded hills of the Morvan are renowned for fine game (including *marcassin*, young wild boar) which is available during the hunting season (October to March), and its gushing rivers are full of excellent trout. The Charollais cow, a splendid white beast producing the best beef in France, thrives on the Morvan pastures as well as in Nivernais and among its native Charollais hills north of the Beaujolais mountains, and the local pigs, fed on potatoes and dairy by-products, produce particularly good ham and sausages. In the remoter parts of the Morvan and Nivernais you may still find the solid, rustic dishes listed separately below. These are the body-fuel of the country people and are unlikely to be found in the other more sophisticated areas.

North of the Morvan, the dominance of beef and red wine gives way to delicate fish dishes and the fine white wine of Chablis. The influence of neighbouring Île de France, birthplace of *haute cuisine*, is reflected in richer, more lavish sauces and the liberal use of cream, although one of the most ubiquitous specialities, the *gougère* is quite simple and unpretentious.

Regional specialities

andouillette Tripe and pork or veal sausage, served hot.

bœuf à la bourguignonne Beef stewed in red wine, with onions and mushrooms

bœuf à la mode Beef stewed in red wine, vegetables and herbs. Served hot, or cold in its own jelly (*en gelée*).

charol(l)ais pièce de Charollais beef (steak).

coq au vin (Chambertin) Chicken in a red wine (Chambertin) sauce with onions and mushrooms.

escargots à la bourguignonne Snails in a hot garlic and parsley butter.

fouée Cream and bacon flan with walnut oil.

gougère Cheese *choux*-pastry ring.

jambon en saupiquet (à la crème, à la morvandelle) Ham in a piquante sauce of cream, wine, vinegar and juniper berries.

jambon persillé Cold pressed ham layered with parsley, in jelly.

lièvre (râble de) à la Piron Saddle of hare marinated in *marc* and roasted with grapes and shallots, with a peppery cream sauce (Dijon).

marcassin farci au saucisson Young wild boar stuffed with sausage.

matelote Freshwater fish (eel, pike or trout) stewed in red wine.

meurettes Red-wine sauces served with meat, eggs or fish.

mousserons à la crème St George's mushrooms in a cream sauce.

nonnettes See *pain d'épices.*

œufs pochés en meurette Poached eggs in a red wine sauce.

pain d'épices Spiced honey gingerbread (baked in different shapes—a Dijon speciality).

pauchouse or **pochouse** Freshwater fish (eel, carp, trout or pike) stewed in white wine (Dijon area).

pognon Flat- or girdle-cake.

poulet en matelote Chicken cooked in red wine with sliced eels, onions and bacon (Nivernais).

queue de bœuf des vignerons Oxtail stewed with white grapes.

rigodon A brioche flan, either with bacon, or sweet, with nuts and fruit.

tartouillat Apple tart.

Country food (Morvan and Nivernais)

fressure or **ferchuse** Pig's fry (heart, liver and lungs), usually stewed in red wine with onions and herbs.

jau (poulet) au sang Chicken in a rich, blood-thickened sauce.

omelette au sang Omelette with a thickened blood filling.

potée bourguignonne Thick soup or stew of vegetables and pork, and sometimes chicken, beef and garlic-sausage.

rapée morvandelle Grated potato baked with cream, eggs and cheese.

sansiot Calf's head (often accompanied by onions and mushrooms).

133

Cheese: *cow's milk*

Aisy-cendré Firm and very fruity; flat disc or truncated cone covered in wood ashes (in which it has been stored); best between October and May.

Cîteaux Supple, tangy and fairly fruity; flat disc with a yellowy-grey rind; made in the monastery of Cîteaux; best between June and November.

Époisses Soft and supple with a tangy, slightly acid taste; drum with an orange-red rind; best between June and March.

Les Laumes Rare supple cheese with a strong, spicy and slightly smoky taste; made on farms in thick squares which are washed in coffee, giving the rind a dark-brown colour; best between October and February.

Pierre-Qui-Vire Supple, tangy and strong-smelling; flat disc with a reddish rind, sold on a straw base; made in the monastery of the same name; sometimes eaten fresh; best between June and November.

Saint-Florentin Tangy and supple; flat disc with a smooth reddish-brown rind; mostly made commercially now; best between June and November.

Soumaintrain Very similar to St-Florentin in appearance and taste though also eaten fresh when white and creamy; best between May and November.

Goat's milk

Charollais Firm with a nutty taste; small log with a bluish rind; made on farms round Charolles; sometimes eaten fresh when still milky-tasting; best between June and November.

Chevreton de Mâcon Firm and nutty tasting, though also eaten fresh when creamy; small truncated cone with a light-blue rind; made by farms and factories; best between June and October.

Claquebitou A fresh cheese tasting of herbs and garlic; only available between June and October.

Montrachet Mild and creamy; log wrapped in vine or chestnut leaves; made by small dairies; best between May and October.

Wine

Burgundy is famous the world over for its wine, and since demand well outstrips a relatively small supply prices are high. But in spite of strict controls, quality does not necessarily reflect price. The most reliable sources of top-quality wines are top-quality restaurants and recommended wine producers such as those listed in Hugh

Johnson's *Wine Companion*. You can also buy wine direct from the grower; *vente directe* (direct sale) is increasingly common in Burgundy—but although it is cheaper, it is a much less reliable method.

With the exceptions of *Chablis* and *Pouilly Fuissé*, the *Grands* and *Premiers Crus* (top and second growth wines) are all grown on the Côte d'Or. The N74 (known as the *Route des Grands Crus*) runs past the villages (see the map) which contain vineyards producing some of the most expensive wine in the world. However, lesser vineyards within these same village parishes use the same grape varieties (*Pinot Noir* for reds and *Chardonnay* for whites) to produce excellent wine at more enjoyable prices. But care should be taken not to confuse a general village appellation such as *AC Gevrey-Chambertin* with say *AC Chapelle-Chambertin* or *AC Chambertin Clos de Bèze*, which are *Grand Crus* appellations applying to individual vineyards; see Hugh Johnson's *World Atlas of Wine* for a full explanation of the incredibly complicated system of classifying wine in Burgundy.

The *Côte de Nuits* is the main classic red Burgundy area producing firm, powerful wines with a deep rich colour and, after a few years in the bottle, a fine *Pinot* aroma. It is the perfect wine for game and beef. *Marsannay*, the exception, produces the best rosé in burgundy—pale pink, fine and mouth-watering. The *Côte de Beaune* is renowned for both red and white wine. The reds have plenty of body, a delicate flavour and reach maturity more quickly than their northern neighbours. The whites are dry, crisp and pale in colour, with an exquisite bouquet.

Further south, the *Côte Chalonnaise* produces wines well worth trying. *Mercurey* and *Givry* make mainly red wines, which can rival those of the *Côte de Beaune* in body, bouquet and finesse. The whites of *Montagny* and *Rully* are dry, light and fruity and a certain amount is made into the sparkling *Crémant de Bourgogne*, which is delicious as an aperitif. *Bouzeron*, near Chagny, produces one of the best *Bourgogne Aligoté* wines (named after the grape variety from which it is made), which is the white wine traditionally mixed with *Crème de Cassis* (blackcurrant liqueur) to make *Kir* or *vin blanc Cassis*, but it is also good on its own.

The *Mâconnais* produces eminently drinkable light red wines but is better known for its dry whites. *St Véran* is a name to look out for, and the village of *Viré* also makes a fine white, but the most famous of all is *Pouilly-Fuissé* —one of the best wines in France to accompany seafood. The neighbouring vineyards of *Pouilly-Loché* and *Pouilly-Vinzelles* make wine of comparable character and at lower cost.

The small town of *Chablis*, near Auxerre, is famous for its limpid greeny-golden white wine—dry, fine, powerful, superb with fish and pricy; the best (*Grands* and

Premiers Crus) need at least three years to mature. *AC Petit Chablis* is not in the same league, but can be good value. The nearby villages of *Irancy* and *Coulanges la Vineuse* produce good reds, and the *Clos de la Chainette* a fine rosé.

The area round Pouilly-sur-Loire produces two white wines. The lesser, made from the *Chasselas* grape, is called *Pouilly-sur-Loire*. The more well-known *Pouilly-Fumé* (no relation to *Pouilly-Fuissé*) is made from the *Sauvignon* grape, which gives it a dry, slightly smoky flavour with immediate appeal, very similar to that of *Sancerre* just across the river (see under Loire Valley), and delicious with shellfish.

There are many other wines which, if labelled *AC Bourgogne* are all made from the same grape-type as the grand wines. *AC Bourgogne Ordinaire* can taste very like *Beaujolais*, being made from the same grape-type, the *Gamay*. *AC Bourgogne Passe-tout-grains* is red wine made from a mixture of both *Pinot Noir* and *Gamay* grapes.

Finally, there is the *Marc de Bourgogne*, an *eau-de-vie* distilled from the residue of the grapes after they have been pressed for making wine. *Marcs* are made in many parts of France but the fine flavour and smooth potency of the Burgundian variety have earned it a high reputation.

Best years—red: 1969, 1971, 1972, 1976, 1978, 1982, 1983, 1985, 1988, 1989, 1990.
Best years—white: 1971, 1973, 1977, 1978, 1979, 1981, 1982, 1983, 1985, 1986, 1988, 1989, 1990.
Poor year both: 1984.

For general information on the wines of Burgundy contact:

Bureau Interprofessionnel des Vins de Bourgogne, 12 boulevard Bretonnière, 21200 Beaune.

SECTION THREE
A Dictionary of French Menu Terms

PRONUNCIATION GUIDE

The phonetic symbols which appear in brackets after each dictionary entry are intended as a rough guide to the French pronunciation for those with no knowledge of the language. Pronounce each syllable as you would say it in English and the word will come out sounding more or less as it should in French. The result won't always be perfect, but it will be close enough to get the meaning across and to avoid major disasters.

Some syllables are connected by hyphens, while others are separated by spaces. Try to run the connected syllables together as smoothly as possible, but for clarity's sake keep the words themselves separate. Remember that French is an *unstressed* language, and give equal weight to each syllable: don't say *GA-tō* for cake, but *ga-tō*.

Most of the phonetic symbols are ordinary letters from the English alphabet, a bar over a vowel indicating that the sound is long rather than short. The five symbols at the foot of the page represent sounds with no direct equivalent in English, so we have added a few hints on how these should be pronounced.

a as in c*a*fé	*ī* as in w*i*ne
ā as in t*a*ste	*j* as in *j*uicy
aw as in *aw*ning	*k* as in coo*k*ing
a as in écl*ai*r	*n* as in di*n*e
e as in Fr*e*nch	*ɴ* as in ta*ng*
ee as in ch*ee*se	*o* as in b*o*ttle
g as in *g*arlic	*ō* as in h*o*tel
i as in dr*i*nk	*oo* as in f*oo*d

ah represents the slightly broadened French *a* in words like *fromage*, and *à la*. The sound is less broad than the English 'a' in 'bar' but not as sharp as the English 'a' in 'café'. The American 'a' in 'bar' is just about right. So is the English 'a' sound in 'cup' or 'yah'. English readers might also try saying 'bar' while smiling broadly.

ə represents the sound somewhere between *e* and *o* in words like *de*, *le*, *yeux* and *bœuf*. To produce this sound, which falls half-way between the vowel-sounds of 'pull' and 'fur', English readers should round the lips and say 'urgent', while Americans should round the lips and say 'pull'.

əə is a longer version of the above which occurs in words like *du*, *rue* and *suprême*. Say 'ee' while sharply rounding the lips, and you'll be close.

əy is the *ə* sound followed by 'ee' in words like *chevreuil*. The two sounds need to be run together as a single syllable, rather like the 'oy' in 'boy'.

r in French is growled from the back of the throat. An English 'r' will be understood, but it's worth trying to do the authentic growl. Practice by saying 'grrr' with the mouth wide open.

zh represents the soft *j* sound in *courgette* and *beige*.

à *(ah)* To, at, in, on, by, with, from . . . this multi-purpose word (its alternative forms are *au* and *aux*) appears on menus in such forms as:

  à point (just right)
  à l'os (on the bone)
  à la carte (from the menu)
  au pot (in a pot)
  aux abatis (with giblets)

When followed by the name of a town, region, country, a nationality or a particular person, it means 'in the style of' and is really a contraction of *à la mode de.* Otherwise it means 'served with', 'cooked with' or 'accompanied by' whatever sauce, stock, garnish etc. follows it.

abatis *(a-ba-tee)* Giblets of poultry or game fowl.

abats *(a-ba)* Offal: the edible internal organs of animals.

ablette *(a-blet)* Bleak: a small, white-fleshed freshwater fish, usually fried.

abricot *(a-bree-kō)* Apricot.

acajou *(a-ka-zhoo)* Cashew nut.

actinie *(ak-tee-nee)* Member of the sea anemone family.

Adèle, consommé *(kawн-so-mā a-del)* Clear soup garnished with carrots, peas and chicken *quenelles* (tiny poached mousses).

adour, alose de l' *(a-loz də la-door)* Shad baked with ham and a sorrel stuffing.

aeglé *(ā-glā)* Hybrid tangerine/grapefruit called ugli fruit.

africaine, à l' *(ah laf-ree-ken)* In the North African style: with aubergine (eggplant), mushrooms, potatoes and tomatoes.

agenaise, œufs à l' *(əf ah la-zhen-ez)* Method of cooking eggs by frying them in goose fat, with eggplant (aubergine) and onions.

agneau *(an-yō)* Lamb; for mutton see *mouton.* The principal cuts of lamb are:
  baron *(ba-rawн)* Saddle and both hind legs.
  carré *(ka-rā)* Rack, best end of neck, crown, rib chops or cutlets.
  côtelette *(kōt-let)* Cutlet or lamb chop.
  épaule *(ā-pōl)* Shoulder.
  gigot *(zhee-gō)* Leg.
  medaillon *(mā-dī-yawн)* See *noisette.*
  mignonette *(meen-yawн-net)* See *noisette.*
  noisette *(nwah-zet)* Small, round, boned cutlet; also called *medaillon* and *mignonnette.*
  poitrine *(pwah-treen)* Breast.
  selle *(sel)* Saddle.

agnelet *(an-yə-lā)* Baby milk-fed lamb.

agnelle *(an-yel)* Ewe lamb.

aiglefin *(ā-glə-faн)* Haddock.

aïgo bouïdo *(ī-ee-go boo-ee-doh)* Provençal garlic soup, served on slices of bread; a traditional Christmas Eve and wedding dish. Also called *bouïdo* and *bullido.*

aïgo sa(o)u *(ā-gō sā-oh)* Provençal fish soup not unlike *bouillabaise.*

aigre *(ā-grə)* Bitter, sour.

aigre-doux *(ā-grə doo)* Sweet-and-sour; for *soupe aigre-douce* see mehlsuppe.

aigrefin *(ā-grə-faн)* Haddock: see *aiglefin.*

aigrette *(ā-gret)* Cheese fritter.

aigroissade *(ā-grwah-sahd)* Vegetables, including chick-peas, served with *aïoli* sauce.

aiguille *(ā-gwee)* Garfish: spectacular to look at, but dull-tasting.

aiguillette *(ā-gwee-yet)* A long, thin slice of meat, poultry or fish; also a name for a piece of top of beef rump *(pièce de bœuf)*, and for a garfish: see *aiguille*.

ail *(ī)* Garlic.

aile *(el)* Wing.

aïllada *(ī-yah-dah)* Oil-and-garlic sauce for snails.

aïllade *(ī-yahd)* Garlic sauce; also, dishes based on garlic or with a strong garlic taste.

aillé *(ī-yā)* With garlic.

aïoli *(i-yo-lee)* Garlic mayonnaise; also, various main dishes with garlic mayonnaise; also spelled *ailloli*.

air, en l' *(awʀ lair)*
pommes *(pom . . .)* Fried slices of apple.
pommes de terre *(pom də tair . . .)* Fried potato puffs.

airelle *(ā-rel)* Bilberry, huckleberry or wortleberry.
airelle rouge *(. . . roozh)* Cranberry.

à l' and **à la** *(ahl, ah lah)* See *à*.

Albert *(al-bair)*
sauce *(sōs . . .)* Creamed horseradish sauce.
sole *(sole . . .)* Sautéed sole with vermouth.

Albertine, sauce *(sōs al-bair-teen)* Sauce for poached fish made with mushrooms, truffles and white wine.

albigeoise, à l' *(ah lal-bee-zhwazh)* In the style of Albi, in SW France: with ham, stuffed tomatoes and potato croquettes.

albignac, salade d' *(sa-lahd dal-been-yak)* Salad of celeriac, chicken, crayfish, hard-boiled eggs and truffles.

albuféra, à la d' *(ah lah dal-bəə-fai-rah)*
caneton *(kan-tawʀ . . .)* Roast duckling with ham, garnished with a rich *sauce madère*.
sauce *(sōs . . .)* A white sauce with pimento butter.

alcazar, gâteau *(gat-oh al-ka-zahr)* Almond and apricot cake.

alcool *(al-kol)* Alcohol; spirits.

alénois(e) *(a-lān-wah(z))* With watercress.
soupe *(soop . . .)* Watercress soup.

alésienne, tripes à l' *(treep ah la-lā-zyen)* Tripe cooked with carrots, celery and tomatoes.

alexandra *(a-leks-awʀ-drah)*
pêche *(pesh . . .)* Cold, poached peach served with ice-cream and puréed strawberries.
poulet *(poo-lā . . .)* Sautéed chicken with an onion-and-cream sauce.

algérienne, à l' *(ah lal-zhā-ryen)* In the Algerian style: with a garnish of small tomatoes cooked in oil, with sweet potatoes cooked in butter or served as croquettes.

alicot or **alicuit** *(a-lee-kō, a-lee-kwee)* Duck or goose wings accompanied by giblets stewed with mushrooms and chestnuts.

aligot *(a-lee-gō)* Potatoes mashed with *aligot* cheese and garlic, then fried.

alimentation *(a-lee-mawʀ-ta-syawʀ)* Food shop or grocery store (also called an *épicerie*); food in general.

all grenat *(al grə-na)* Sauce for snails or fish: see *bouillade*.

alleluia *(a-lā-looyah)* Little cake, popular in S France.

allemande, à l' *(ah lal-mawnd)* In the German style: with noodles and mashed potatoes; also, a cream or sour cream sauce for game.
bifteck *(bif-teck . . .)* Slang term for a hamburger.
salade *(sa-lahd . . .)* Salad made of apple, herring, onion and potato.

sauce *(sōs . . .)* Rich white *velouté* sauce.

allongé *(a-lawн-zhā)* Stretched, extended, diluted.
  café allongé de l'eau *(ka-fā . . . də lō)* A weak black coffee.

allumette *(a-lөө-met)* 'Matchstick': puff-pastry cut into fine strips, or shoe-string potatoes.

alma, poire *(pwar al-ma)* Pear poached in port wine.

alose *(a-loz)* Shad: 'the king of herrings', delicious but bony.

alouette *(al-wet)* Lark or skylark, often prepared as a pâté or terrine.

alouette de mer *(al-wet də-mair)* Sandpiper or snipe.

aloyau *(al-wah-yō)* Sirloin or tenderloin of beef; also, a large joint consisting of the sirloin and rump together.

alphée *(al-fā)* Shellfish roughly half-way between a crawfish and a prawn.

alsacienne, à l' *(al lal-za-syen)* In the style of Alsace in NE France: this covers many preparations, which usually include sauerkraut, sausages, potatoes and sometimes *foie gras*; the term also applies to chicken or fish cooked in Riesling.
  escargots *(es-kar-gō . . .)* Snails stuffed with herbs and spiced butter, and cooked in Alsace wine.
  tarte *(tart . . .)* Open fruit and custard tart, or a jam-filled tart made with lattice-work almond pastry.

amande *(a-mawнd)* Almond.

amandine *(a-mawн-deen)* With almonds.

américaine, à l' *(ah la-mā-ree-ken)*
  bifteck *(bif-tek . . .)* Slang term for *steak tartare*.
  faisan *(fā-sawн . . .)* Sautéed pheasant, grilled

with bacon and served with tomatoes, mushrooms and watercress.

homard *(ō-mar . . .)* Classic method of cooking lobster, in which it is sautéed in oil, flambéed in cognac and served in a cream-and-wine sauce with onions, garlic, tomatoes and herbs; also called *homard à l'armoricaine*.

salade *(sa-lahd . . .)* Salad of celery, cucumber, tomatoes and hard-boiled egg.

amiral, à l' *(ah la-mee-rahl)* A garnish for large fish, consisting of various shellfish with truffles.
  œufs *(өf . . .)* Scrambled eggs mixed with pieces of lobster.
  sauce *(sōs . . .)* Anchovy-and-herb sauce.

amuse-gueule *(a-mөөz gөl)* Appetizer or cocktail snack.

amygdalin *(a-meeg-da-laн)* Made of almonds.

ananas *(a-na-nas)* Pineapple.

anchoïade *(awн-shō-yahd)* Paste made of anchovies and garlic, usually eaten on toast.

anchois *(awн-shwah)* Anchovy.

anchois de Norvège *(awн-shwah də nor-vaizh)* Sprat: see *esprot*.

ancienne, à l' *(ah lawn-syen)* 'In the old style': a traditional way of cooking beef by first braising and then slowly simmering it; the name is also applied to traditional blanquettes and fricassées of lamb, veal or chicken.
  consommé—see *croûte-au-pot.*
  sauce *(sōs . . .)* Wine-and-cream sauce with mushrooms, onions and shallots.

andalouse, à l' *(ah lawн-dah-looz)* In the Andalusian style: with tomatoes, or indeed anything vaguely Spanish; also, a garnish of pimentos (sweet peppers), rice, aubergine (eggplant) and sometimes sausage.

œufs *(ef . . .)* Fried eggs with grilled tomatoes.
poulet *(poo-lā . . .)* Chicken stuffed with rice and ham, plus paprika seasoning.

andouille *(awʀ-dwee)* Large sausage made from chitterlings, tripe etc.; usually eaten cold.

andouillette *(awʀ-dwee-yet)* Small chitterling sausage, usually fried or grilled and eaten hot.

anémone de mer *(a-nā-mon de mair)* Sea anemone: a general name for various edible sea polyps, including the starfish.

aneth *(ah-net)* Dill, often used as a seasoning for such fish as salmon.

aneth doux *(a-net doo)* Fennel: see *fenouil*.

anges à cheval *(awnzh ah she-val)* 'Angels on horseback': grilled oysters wrapped in bacon.

angélique *(awʀ-zhā-leek)* Angelica, used in cakes, pastry creams and various liqueurs, among them Bénédictine.

angevine, à l' *(ah lawʀzh-veen)* In the style of Anjou: cooked in Anjou wine. An *angevine* is a sweet grape with pale yellow flesh, the earliest to ripen.

anguille *(awʀ-gwee . . .)* Stuffed eel with bacon in a creamy crayfish sauce.

anglaise, à l' *(ah lawʀ-glez)* In the English style: poached, boiled or steamed; for fish, it can also mean fried in a coating of egg and breadcrumbs.

assiette *(ass-yet . . .)* Mixed cold meats.
crème *(krem . . .)* Egg custard.
foie de veau *(fwah de vō . . .)* Calf's liver and

bacon, grilled.
œuf frit *(ef free . . .)* Egg fried, then baked.

anguille *(awʀ-gwee)* Eel.

anguille de mer *(awʀ-gwee de mair)* Conger eel: see *congre*.

anguillette *(awʀ-gwee-yet)* Baby eel.

animelles *(a-nee-mel)* Testicles, usually ram's.

anis *(a-nee)* Anise or aniseed.

anisette *(a-nee-zet)* Liqueur made from aniseed.

Anna, pommes *(pom ah-nah)* Sliced potatoes baked in butter.

Annette, pommes *(pom a-net)* Potato strips baked in butter.

antiboise, à l' *(ah lawn-tee-bwahz)* In the style of Antibes on the Côte d'Azur: with cheese, garlic and, frequently, tomatoes and sardines too.

œufs *(ef . . .)* Baked eggs with cheese, garlic and tiny fried fish.
tomates *(to-mat . . .)* Oven-browned tomatoes with tuna and anchovies, seasoned with garlic.

antillaise, à l' *(ah lawn-tee-yez)* 'Caribbean style': cooked in or served with rum.

anversoise, à l' *(ah lawʀ-vairz-wahz)* In the style of Antwerp (Anvers) in Belgium: garnished with hop stalks in cream or butter.

filet d'Anvers *(fee-lā dawn-vair)* Stuffed ham cornet.

apéritif *(a-pā-ree-teef)* Any drink taken before lunch or dinner: usually alcoholic, but not necessarily.

appétit *(a-pā-tee)* Appetite: taste, passion or gusto.

bon appétit *(bō nah-pā-tee)* 'Have a good meal', 'Enjoy your meal'.

arachide (a-ra-sheed)
Peanut, in its natural state; salted, roasted, dry-roasted or otherwise prepared peanuts are called *cacahouettes*.
  pâté d'arachide (pa-tā . . .) Peanut butter.

araignée de mer (a-ren-yā də mair) Spider crab.

arapède (a-ra-ped) Limpet: see *patelle*.

arc-en ciel, truite (trwee ar-kawн-syel) Rainbow trout.

archiduc, à l' (ah lar-shee-dəək) 'As the archduke likes it': with cream, and seasoned with paprika.

ardennaise, à l' (ah lar-den-nez) In the style of the Ardennes region of N France: with juniper berries.
  endive (awн-deev . . .) Braised chicory (US: endive) with ham and pork.
  marcassin (mar-kass-aн . . .) Young wild boar roasted with bacon and celeriac in red wine sauce with juniper berries.

argenteuil (ar-zhawн-təy) With asparagus.
  crème (krem . . .) Cream of asparagus soup.

ariégeoise, à l' (ah la-ryā-zhwahz) With cabbage, salt pork, potatoes and kidney beans.
  poitrine de mouton farcie (pwah-treen . . .) Mutton breast stuffed with ham, breadcrumbs and garlic, served in a reduction of the cooking liquid.
  poulet farci (poo-lā . . .) Chicken stuffed with ham, liver and garlic, cooked in stock which is first served as a soup.

arlésienne, à l' (ah lar-lā-zyen) In the style of Arles (S France): this covers lots of dishes garnished variously with aubergine (eggplant), olives, onions, potatoes, rice and tomatoes.
  salade (sa-lahd . . .) Salad of potatoes,

artichokes, olives, anchovies and tomatoes.

armagnac (ar-mahn-nyak) Brandy made in the Armagnac region of SW France—the only rival to Cognac.

arménienne, à l' (ah lar-mān-yen) In the Armenian style:
  aubergine farci (o-bair-zheen far-see . . .) Baked aubergine (eggplant) stuffed with lamb.

armoricaine, à l' (ah lar-mor-ee-ken)
  homard—see under *américaine*.
  moules (mool . . .) Mussels with tomatoes and onions.
An *armoricaine* is a cultured oyster, much prized for its delicate taste.

arpajonnaise, à l' (ah lar-pa-zho-nez) With haricot beans.

arrosé(e) (a-ro-zā) Sprinkled, moistened or basted (e.g. with stock).

artésienne, à l' (ah lar-tā-zyen) In the style of Artois in N France: cooked in beer, or with beer.

artichaud (ar-tee-shō) Globe artichoke.
  fond d'artichaud (fawн . . .) Artichoke heart.

artichaud d'hiver (ar-tee-shō dee-vair) 'Winter artichoke': a colloquial name for the Jerusalem artichoke (*topinambour*).

asperge(s) (as-pairzh) Asparagus.

aspergé (as-pair-zhā) Sprinkled; sprinkled with.

aspergille (as-pair-zhee) A type of snail.

assaisonné (ah-sā-zō-nā) Seasoned; seasoned with.

assiette (as-yet) Plate or dish.
  à potage (. . . ah po-tahzh) Soup plate.
  à salade (. . . ah sah-lahd) Salad plate.

assiette anglaise (as-yet

awʀ-glez) Assorted cold meats, usually served as a first course.

athérine *(a-tā-reen)* Sandsmelt: a small sea fish, usually served fried.

attendri *(ah-tawʀ-dree)* Tenderized.

au *(ō)* See *à.*

auberge *(ō-bairzh)* Inn.

aubergine *(ō-bair-zheen)* Eggplant or aubergine.

aulx *(ō)* Plural of *ail* (garlic).

aumonière *(ō-maw-nyair)* 'Purse': a descriptive term for dishes in which the ingredients are rolled into a pancake.

aurore *(ō-ror)* 'Dawn':
  consommé *(kon-som-ā . . .)* Clear chicken and tomato soup.
  œufs durs à l' *(ef deer ahl . . .)* Stuffed hard-boiled eggs coated in *Mornay* sauce and grated cheese, served with tomato sauce.
  sauce *(sōs . . .)* Creamy *béchamel* sauce with tomato purée.

autrichienne, à l' *(ah lo-tree-shyen)* Austrian style: seasoned with paprika; also with fried onions, fennel or sour cream.
  œufs *(ef . . .)* Poached eggs with cabbage and sausages.

aux *(ō or ōz)* See *à.*

avec *(a-vek)* With.

aveline *(av-leen)* Filbert, hazelnut.

avesnoise, carpe à l' *(karp ahl ah-ven-wahz)* Carp stuffed with roes, served in a wine and cream sauce with crayfish tails.

avocat *(a-vō-kah)* Avocado, avocado pear.

avocette *(a-vō-set)* Avocet: a pigeon-sized wading bird similar to a wild duck, which often has a rather fishy taste.

avoine *(av-wahn)* Oats.

farine d' *(fa-reend . . .)* Oatmeal.

aziminu *(a-zee-mee-noo)* Corsican fish soup similar to *bouillabaisse.*

azyme, pain *(paʀ a-zeem)* Unleavened bread.

B

baba *(ba-ba)* Sponge cake steeped either in rum or in kirsch.

backenoff *(ba-kǝ-nof)* Marinated beef, mutton and pork, stewed in wine with potatoes and onions.

bacon *(ba-kawʀ)* Sliced, packaged streaky or back bacon. A side of bacon from which slices are cut in a shop is called *poitrine fumée.* Bacon used in cooking is called *lard.*

badèche *(ba-desh)* Sea bass: see *bar.*

bagration *(ba-gra-syawʀ)*
  salade *(sah-lahd . . .)* Salad of macaroni and artichoke hearts, with tomato mayonnaise, hard-boiled eggs and truffles.
  soupe *(soop . . .)* Veal or fish soup with macaroni and grated cheese.

baguette *(ba-get)* 'Stick': a long, slender loaf of traditional French white bread.

bajou *(ba-zhoo)* Cheek of an animal, usually referring to pork.

ballon *(ba-lawʀ)* A cut of meat, usually mutton or lamb, which has been boned and rolled.

ballottine *(ba-lo-teen)* Any meat, fowl or fish that has been boned and rolled; *ballotines* may be served hot or cold, and are usually not stuffed, but there are exceptions.

balvet, potage *(pō-tazh bal-vā)* Soup of puréed peas, with various other vegetables.

bambou *(bawʀ-boo)* Bamboo, bamboo shoots.

banane *(ba-nan)* Banana.

banquière, à la *(ah lah bawn-kyair)* 'As the bank-manager likes it': a garnish for sweetbreads, chicken etc. consisting of mushrooms, truffles, *quenelles* (little mousses) and sometimes larks, with madeira sauce: very rich.

bar *(bar)* Bar, café or drinks bar; also the French name for the sea bass or sea perch.

baraquille *(ba-ra-kee-yə)* Triangular pastry with a rich filling of game or sweetbreads and *foie gras*; eaten hot.

barbadine *(bar-ba-deen)* Passion fruit.

barbeau *(bar-bō)* Barbel: a common freshwater fish, used mainly in stews.

barbe de capucin *(barb də ka-pəə-san)* Wild chicory (US: endive); the term also refers to a winter salad made from the roots of this plant.

barbillon *(bar-bee-yawn)* Small barbel *(barbeau)*.

barboteur *(bar-bo-tər)* Common name for a domestic duck *(canard)*.

barbotine *(bar-bo-teen)* The aromatic herb, tansy.

barbouillade *(bar-bwee-yahd)* Two very different dishes bear this name: the first is a concoction of artichokes and broad beans, and the second is stuffed eggplant or aubergine.

barbouille, poulet en *(poo-lā awn bar-bwee)* Chicken in a blood-thickened wine sauce.

barbue *(bar-bəə)* Brill.

bardane *(bar-dan)* Burdock, whose leaves are used in salads.

bardatte *(bar-dat)* Cabbage stuffed with hare or rabbit, cooked in white wine and served with chestnuts.

bardé *(bar-dā)* Larded: covered with strips of un-cured bacon.

barigoule, artichaut à la *(ar-tee-shō ah lah bar-ee-gool)* Artichoke stuffed with mushrooms, ham, sausage-meat and garlic.

baron *(ba-rawn)* Large joint of mutton or lamb comprising the saddle and both hind legs.

barquette *(bar-ket)* Boat-shaped pastry shell, variously stuffed.

basilic *(ba-zee-leek)* The herb, sweet basil.

basquaise, à la *(ah lah bas-kez)* In the Basque style: a garnish for meat consisting of Bayonne ham, potatoes and fried *cèpes*.
  gâteau *(ga-tō . . .)* Pastry filled with custard or fruit, e.g. cherries or plums.
  pommes *(pom . . .)* Baked potatoes stuffed with ham, sweet peppers, tomatoes and garlic.

bastardeau *(bas-tar-dō)* Local name for the bustard: see *outarde*.

bat *(ba)* The tail of a fish, or the length of a fish from eye to tail.

bâtarde *(bah-tard)* 'Bastard'! The name for a traditional white loaf slightly larger than a *baguette*.
  sauce *(sōs . . .)* A kind of thick butter sauce.

batavia *(ba-tav-yah)* A type of lettuce.

batelière, à la *(ah lah ba-təl-yair)* A garnish for fish dishes consisting of fried eggs, mushrooms and onions; the name also refers to pastry shells with a rich seafood filling.

bâton or **bâtonnet** *(ba-tawn, ba-tawn-nā)* 'Baton': a white loaf, smaller than a *baguette*; the name is also applied to various small pastries and cakes shaped like little sticks, and often stuffed with delicious things.

baudroie *(bō-drwah)* Monkfish: see *lotte*.

baume *(bōm)* Balm, a mint-like herb.

bavarois *(ba-var-wah)* Bavarian cream: one of several cold desserts containing whipped cream and egg-custard, often served with fruit.

bavaroise *(ba-var-wahz)* A beverage based on either coffee or tea mixed with syrup, milk and eggs, and sometimes including liqueur: a kind of French egg-nog.

bavette *(ba-vet)* Cut of beef equivalent to the skirt or flank: see *bœuf*.

baveuse *(ba-vəz)* A sea blenny; also, a method of cooking an omelette so that it is moist and juicy.

bayonnaise, à la *(ah lah bah-yō-nez)* In the style of Bayonne in SW France: with Bayonne ham.
  jambon *(zhawn-boʀ . . .)* Bayonne ham cooked in madeira wine with sausages, tomatoes, rice and mushrooms.
  poularde *(poo-lard . . .)* Roasting hen with lemon-steeped onions.

béarnaise, à la *(ah lah bair-nez)*
  daube *(dōb . . .)* Pieces of beef marinated in red wine, then braised in the marinade with ham and fried onions.
  sauce *(sōs . . .)* A rich creamy sauce made with egg-yolks, vinegar, shallots, butter, white wine and tarragon; *sauce béarnaise* is one of the classic French sauces.

beatilles *(bā-ah-tee-yə)* Titbits: cockscombs, kidneys, lamb's sweetbreads and mushrooms in a white sauce; used to garnish various pastry dishes, particularly *bouchées*, *vol-au-*

vents and *tourtes*.

beaucaire, à la *(ah lah bō-kair)*
  anguille *(awʀ-gee . . .)* Stuffed, braised eel in wine and brandy.
  carré *(kar-rā . . .)* Baked rack of lamb with artichokes.

beauceronne, à la *(ah lah bō-sə-ron)*
  omelette *(om-let . . .)* Bacon, potato and sorrel omelette.
  culotte de bœuf *(kөө-lot də bəf . . .)* Braised beef rump with onions, bacon and potatoes.

beauharnais, à la *(ah lah bō-ar-nā)* A traditional method of preparing small cuts of meat, especially *tournedos*, with *béarnaise* sauce mixed with puréed tarragon, plus a garnish of artichoke hearts and little potato balls or stuffed mushrooms.

beaulieu, poulet *(poo-lā bōo-lyə)* Chicken with artichokes, potatoes and olives, in a white wine sauce.

beauvilliers *(bō-veel-yā)* A very *haute-cuisine* garnish for braised meat, comprising spinach *cromesquis*, tomatoes stuffed with puréed brain, and sautéed salsify.

bécasse *(bā-kas)* Woodcock.

bécasseau *(bā-ka-sō)* Young woodcock.

bécassine *(bā-ka-seen)* Snipe.

bécau *(bā-kō)* Young snipe.

becfigue or **becfin** *(bek-feeg, bek-faʀ)* Figpecker: a small bird of SW France, usually cooked by roasting it or by grilling it on a skewer.

béchamel *(bā-shah-mel)* Bechamel sauce: a creamy white sauce made with flour, butter and milk; often the base for other, more elaborate sauces.

bec-plat *(bek-pla)*
Spoonbill duck.

beignet *(ben-yā)* A fritter; the term is applied to various ingredients—sweet or otherwise—which are dipped into batter and then deep-fried.
  soufflé *(soo-flā . . .)* Stuffed *choux*-pastry ball deep-fried in hot oil.
  viennois *(vyen-wah . . .)* Deep-fried *brioche*-pastry ball filled with cream, custard or jam; also called a *dauphine beignet*.

belle-angevine *(bel awʀzh-veen)* A winter pear.

belle comtoise, escalope de veau *(es-ka-lop də vo bel kawʀ-twahz)* Veal escalope coated with breadcrumbs, then baked with slices of cheese and ham.

belle-dijonnaise, à la *(ah lah bel dee-zhawʀ-nez)* With blackcurrants.

belle-garde *(bel-gahrd)* A variety of peach used in pastries and *compôtes*.

belle-hélène *(bel ā-len)* Garnished with asparagus, mushrooms and truffles.
  œuf *(əf . . .)* Poached egg served on a chicken croquette in cream sauce with asparagus tips.
  poire *(pwahr . . .)* Dessert of cold, poached pear with ice-cream and hot chocolate sauce.

bellevilloise, œufs à la *(əf ah lah bel-vee-wahz)* Eggs baked with chopped onions and served in a creamy onion sauce with grilled slices of *andouillette* (a kind of sausage).

belon *(bə-lawʀ)* Flat oyster renowned for its excellence.

béluga *(ba-lөө-gah)* Caviar from the beluga sturgeon: highly prized and very expensive.

bénédict, œufs *(əf bā-nā-dict)* Poached eggs with ham and *hollandaise* sauce.

bénédictine *(bā-nā-dik-teen)* The liqueur benedictine; also, a garnish for poached eggs or fish, which consists of salt cod pounded to a cream with garlic and truffles.
  morue *(mo-rөө . . .)* Pounded salt cod blended with mashed potato.

berawecka *(bə-rah-wee-kah)* Fruit cake containing dried pears, prunes, figs or dates; also spelled *birewecka*.

bercy *(bər-see)*
  œufs *(əf . . .)* Baked eggs served with sausage and tomato sauce.
  sauce *(sōs . . .)* Sauce made with butter, shallots, bone-marrow and wine.

bergamote *(bər-gah-mot)* Bergamot: a name for both a variety of pear and of orange.

berger or **bergère** *(bair-zhā, bair-zhair)* 'Shepherd' or 'shepherdess': various ways of preparing dishes as shepherds do or might; the details vary from one region to another, so you must ask.
  soupe *(soop . . .)* Onion and garlic soup, which may also include leeks, tomatoes and cheese.

berlingot *(bər-laʀ-gō)* Peppermint candy or hard sweet.

berrichonne, à la *(ah lah bair-ee-shon)* In the style of Berry: this often means meat cooked in blood, or served in a blood-thickened sauce; also, a garnish for large cuts of meat—particularly mutton—featuring braised cabbage, little onions, chestnuts and streaky bacon.
  flan de poireaux *(flawʀ də pwah-rō. . .)* Open tart filled with chopped ham and leeks in cream.
  princesse *(praʀ-ses . . .)* Almond pastry.
  terrine *(tai-reen . . .)*

Rabbit and calf's foot terrine.

besi (*bə-see*) Salted, dried cow's meat, similar to beef jerky; also a name applied to several kinds of winter pear.

bête rousse (*bait roos*) Young wild boar, six months to one year old.

betterave (*bet-rahv*) Beetroot; beet.

beugnon (*ben-yawʀ*) Sweet fritter shaped like a ring.

beurre (*ber*) Butter. The French make scores of different kinds of butter to accompany their dishes, e.g. *beurre de persil*, parsley butter; for these, see under the various types.
    beurre demi-sel (*. . . də-mee sel*) Salted butter (less salty than English or us salt butters).
    beurre douce (*. . . doos*) Unsalted butter.

beurré (*bə-rā*) Buttered; also the name of a family of juicy dessert pears.

beursaudes (*ber-sōd*) Pieces of bacon or pork which are first fried and then baked, and served as *hors d'œuvres* or snacks; also called *grillaudes*.

biarrotte, à la (*ah lah byah-rot*) In the style of Biarritz: with *cèpe* mushrooms and potato cakes.

biche (*beesh*) Doe: a deer, a female deer.

bière (*byair*) Beer.
    soupe à la (*soop ah lah . . .*) Beer and onion soup enriched with cream.

bifteck (*bif-tek*) Beef or beefsteak—but sometimes this turns out to be horse-meat (*cheval*): ask if in doubt. In any event, *bifteck* is normally an inexpensive cut of meat, most frequently made up into a hamburger or pan-fried.

bigarade (*bee-gha-rahd*) Bitter orange; also, an orange garnish for duck.
    sauce (*sōs . . .*) Orange sauce, served with duck.

bignon (*been-yawʀ*) Sweet fritter.

bigorneau (*bee-gor-nō*) Winkle.

bigoudenn, à la (*ah lah bee-goo-den*) In the style of Bigouden in Brittany:
    pommes (*pom . . .*) Baked slices of unpeeled potato.
    ragoût (*ra-goo . . .*) Sausage stewed with bacon and potato.

bijane (*bee-zhan*) Red wine and bread soup, served cold.

birewecka (*beer-wee-ka*) See *berawecka*.

biscotin (*bees-ko-taʀ*) Sweet biscuit.

biscotte (*bees-kot*) Rusk, or melba toast: a crisply-baked slice of bread, rarely served in restaurants but sold in packs in any food shop, for snacks and picnics.

biscuit (*bees-kwee*) As in English, a biscuit, cookie or cracker, but in French it can also be a light, dry sponge-cake, or a delicate mousse-like pâté, usually of puréed fish or vegetables.

bisque (*beesk*) Thick soup, usually of puréed seafood, sometimes of game.

bistorto (*bees-tor-tō*) Bun or *brioche* containing saffron and aniseed, baked in a ring shape.

bistouille (*bees-twee-yə*) Coffee laced with spirits.

bitok (*bee-tok*) Cake of minced meat or minced poultry, fried and then simmered in sour cream.

blanc or **blanche** (*blawʀ, blawʀsh*) White. The word is often used to describe the white meat or breast of chicken (*blanc de poulet*), or a fillet of fish (e.g. *blanc de turbot*). The English colloquialism 'plonk' for inexpensive wine may derive from *vin blanc*.

beurre blanc *(bər . . .)* Butter whipped up with vinegar or white wine and chopped shallots.

blanc-cassis *(blawн-ka-sees)* An aperitif of *crème de cassis* (a blackcurrant liqueur) mixed with dry white wine; short for *vin blanc-cassis*.

blanchaille *(blawн-shī)* Whitebait, usually fried.

blanche-neige *(blawнsh-naizh)* 'Snow-white': cold chicken or fish served in a creamy white sauce.

blanc-manger *(blawн-mawн-zhā)* Blancmange: almond milk mixed with gelatine and then chilled.

blanquette *(blawn-ket)* Stew made of veal, lamb, chicken or seafood which is first simmered—not sautéed, as in a fricassée —and then served 'blanketed' in creamy sauce thickened with egg-yolks.

blé *(blā)* Wheat; wheat-flour.

blennie cagnette *(blai-nee kan-yet)* Blenny, a freshwater fish.

blette *(blet)* Swiss chard.

bleu(e) *(blə)* Blue: the rarest possible cooking for a steak.

truit au bleu *(trweet ō blə)* Freshly-caught trout poached briskly in vinegar *court-bouillon*, causing the flesh to turn faintly blue.

blini *(blee-nee)* Russian pancake, eaten with caviar.

bœuf *(bəf)* Beef; the principal cuts are:
aiguillette *(ā-gee-yet)* UK: silverside or top rump, US: rump roast; also called *culotte* or *pièce de bœuf*.
aloyau *(ahl-wah-yō)* UK: sirloin and fillet joint, US:

tenderloin and loin joint.
bavette *(bah-vet)* Flank or suet; also called *flanchet*.
chateaubriand *(sha-tō-bree-yawн)* Chateaubriand (part of the fillet).
contre filet *(kawн-trə fee-lā)* Sirloin steak, porterhouse steak, club steak, sirloin roast or T-bone steak; also called *faux filet*.
côtes *(kot)* Rib, rolled rib or standing rib.
crosse *(kors)* Shin or shank.
culotte *(kөөlot)* See *aiguillette*.
entrecôte *(awn-trə-kot)* Rib steak or sirloin steak.
faux filet *(fō fee-lā)* See *contre filet*.
filet *(fee-lā)* Fillet, or fillet steak; see also under *filet*.
flanchet *(flawн-shā)* See *bavette*.
gîte de devant *(zheet də də-vawн)* UK: shin, US: shank.
gîte de derrière *(zheet də dair-yair)* UK: shin, US: soup bone.
macreuse *(ma-krөz)* Neck.
onglet *(awн-glā)* Flank or loin.
paleron *(pal-ө-rawн)* Shoulder, chuck, chuck roast or pot roast.
pièce de bœuf *(pee-es də bef)* See *aiguillette*.
plat de côte *(pla də kot)* Rib chops, short ribs.
poitrine *(pwah-treen)* Brisket; corned beef.
romstek *(rawm-stek)* Rump steak, sirloin steak or New York steak.
tende de tranche *(tawнd də trawнsh)* Topside or round steak.

bohémienne, à la (ah lah bo-wa-myen) Gypsy style; with rice, tomatoes, sweet peppers, onions and paprika in various combinations.
œufs *(ef . . .)* Poached eggs on *foie gras*, cooked in a cream sauce and topped with strips of ham.

pommes (*pom . . .*)
Baked potatoes filled with
sausage-meat.

poulet sauté (*poo-lā sō-tā*)
Chicken seasoned with
paprika and sautéed with
tomatoes, garlic, pimen-
tos, onions and fennel.

boisson (*bwah-sawʀ*)
Drink; a beverage of any
kind, whether alcoholic or
not.

boivin, poulet (*poo-lā
bwah-vaʀ*) Sautéed chick-
en with artichokes, baby
onions and new potatoes.

bolet (*bo-lā*) The boletus
mushroom: see *cèpe*.

bombe (*bom*) Vessel for
making ice-cream, orig-
inally spherical in shape, as
were the bombs of the
period—hence the name,
which is also applied to
dozens of different ice-
cream desserts made in
bombes. These should always consist of two dif-
ferent ice-cream (or water-
ice) mixtures: an outer lining and an inner filling.
Some of them have
wonderfully romantic
names, e.g. *bombe Aida*
(tangerine ice filled with
vanilla-and-kirsch ice),
bombe dame-blanche
(vanilla outside, almond
within), and so on.

bonbon (*bawʀ-bawʀ*) A
candy or sweet.

bon-chrétien (*bawʀ-krā-
tyeʀ*) A kind of pear
which is usually served
cooked.

bonite (*bo-neet*) Small
cousin of the tuna.

bonne-bouche (*bon boosh*)
'Tasty little bite': a general
term for an *hors d'œuvre*,
titbit, snack or similar small
temptation.

bonne-femme (*bon-fam*)
'Good woman':
  pommes (*pom . . .*)
  Baked apples.
  potage (*pō-tahzh . . .*)
  Potato and leek soup.

poulet (*poo-lā . . .*)
Chicken baked with
bacon, onions and
potatoes.
  sole (*sol . . .*) Sole with
  chopped onions and
  mushrooms in a white
  wine sauce.

bonvalet (*bawʀ-va-lā*)
Almond cake with ice-
cream and kirsch icing.

bordelaise, à la (*ah lah
bord-lez*) In the regional
style of Bordeaux, and often meaning that the dish
is cooked in wine with
mirepoix (diced mixed vegetables); the name is also
given to the following
dishes:
  cèpes (*sep . . .*) Cèpe
  mushrooms sautéed in
  butter with garlic, parsley
  and—sometimes—grape
  juice.
  écrevisses (*ā-krø-
  vees . . .*) Crayfish flamed
  in brandy, cooked with
  mirepoix and served in a
  white wine sauce.
  lamproie (*lawʀ-
  prwah . . .*) Lamprey in
  a red wine and blood
  sauce, with leeks.
  sauce (*. . . sōs*) Red
  wine sauce incorporating
  shallots and
  bone-marrow.

bordé de (*bor-da dø*) Bor-
dered or ringed with . . . A
traditional method of serving one principal item of
food surrounded by others
that complement it.

bortsch (*borsh*) Beetroot
soup with sour cream; of
Russian origin.

boston, filet (*fee-lā boz-
tawʀ*) Fried beef fillets in
oyster sauce.

bouc (*book*) A male goat,
or ram; also a name for a
shrimp: see *crevette*.

bouchée (*boo-shā*)
'Mouthful': a small, hollow
puff-pastry case which can
be filled with various mixtures: see also *vol-au-vent*.

bouchère, à la (*ah lah boo-
shair*) 'Butcher's style':

consommé *(kawʀ-som-ā . . .)* Clear beef soup with bone-marrow and cabbage, served on bread.
salade *(sa-lahd . . .)* Salad comprising boiled beef, potatoes, tomatoes, and hard-boiled eggs.

boudin *(boo-daʀ)* Large cooking sausage or meat pudding, which can be made in one of two ways:
boudin blanc *(. . . blawʀ)* White pudding, made from white meat, eggs and cream (but no blood) in a casing; this is served grilled with scrambled eggs and truffles as a traditional Christmas breakfast.
boudin noir *(. . . nwahr)* Black pudding: pork meat and suet with pig's blood, in an intestine casing.

bouffi *(boo-fee)* Term for a kipper: see *hareng saur*.

bougras *(boo-grah)* Soup of potatoes, leeks, cabbage and onions, which is cooked in the stock left over from making *boudin*.

bouïdo—see *aïgo bouïdo*.

bouillabaisse *(bwee-yah-bes)* Provençal fish soup/stew made from a great variety of fish—the more the merrier, in a sense, but *rascasse* (scorpion fish), conger and gurnard will usually be there; *bouillabaisse* is made all over France, however, so the ingredients will vary with the locality. It is often served in two dishes, one for the fish and the other for the broth.
épinards en bouillabaisse *(ā-peen-ar . . .)* A spinach soup containing potatoes, garlic, oil and saffron, which is served on a slice of bread with poached eggs.

bouillade *(bwee-yahd)* A sauce to accompany snails or fish, which is made with sweet peppers, garlic and wine.

bouillant *(bwee-yawʀ)* 'Boiling hot': a puff-pastry patty filled with *salpicon* of chicken and served very hot as an *hors d'œuvre*.

bouilleture *(bwee-yə-teer)* A stew of eels and fresh-water fish with red wine, kneaded butter, mushrooms, little onions and prunes, served on toast.

bouilli *(bwee-yee)* Boiled: short for boiled beef.

bouillinade *(bwee-nahd)* Fish stew with onions, peppers, garlic and potatoes.

bouillon *(bwee-yawʀ)* Stock, broth.

boulangère, à la *(ah lah boo-lawʀ-zhair)* 'Baker's style': a garnish of thinly-sliced potatoes and onions cooked with the dish they accompany: usually mutton or lamb, sometimes poultry.

boule *(bool)* 'Ball': a large, round loaf of white bread; also called *miche*.

boule-de-neige *(bool də naizh)* 'Snowball': this can mean three quite different things: the edible fungus *agaric*, a sponge-cake ball dipped in whipped cream, or an ice-cream ball covered with whipped cream.

boulette *(boo-let)* Ball-shaped portion of some foodstuff (minced meat, chicken, fish etc.), either dipped in batter and deep-fried, or brushed with butter and baked.

boulonnaise, maquereau à la *(ma-kə-rō ah lah boo-lo-nez)* Poached mackerel with mussels in a rich butter sauce.

boulot *(boo-lō)* A whole apple baked in pastry.

boumiane *(boo-mee-an)* Stewed tomatoes and aubergines (eggplants) garnished with anchovies.

151

bouquet *(boo-kā)* A sprig or bunch; also a term used to describe the smell or 'nose' of wine.

bouquet garni *(boo-kā garnee)* Little bag of mixed herbs which is dropped into a stew, soup etc. while it cooks.

bourdane *(boor-dan)* Apple dumpling.

bourdaloue *(boor-da-loo)* Dessert of hot poached fruit with vanilla custard.

bourgeoise, à la *(ah lah boor-zhwahz)* A method of presenting braised meat, with onions, carrots and sometimes braised lettuce and celery, plus diced bacon.

bourguignonne, à la *(ah lah boor-geen-yon)* In the style of Burgundy: a way of casseroling meat—notably beef and chicken—in a red wine sauce with onions, mushrooms and sometimes bacon.

  escargots *(es-kar-gō . . .)* Snails grilled in parsley and garlic butter.
  omelette *(om-let . . .)* A pig's blood omelette; also called *omelette au sang*.
  potée *(po-tā . . .)* Thick soup or stew of vegetables, salt pork and sometimes chicken, beef or garlic sausage.

bourrache *(boo-rash)* The herb borage.

bourride *(boo-reed)* Fish stew served with *aïoli* and accompanied by bread or toast; similar—but by no means identical to—*bouillabaisse*, and popular all down the Mediterranean coast.

boutargue *(boo-targ)* A salty paste made from the dried roes of tuna or mullet, mashed with oil; also spelled *poutargue*.

brabançonne, à la *(ah lah bra-baн-son)* A garnish for meat, consisting of chicory and potato croquettes.

braisé(e) *(bre-zā)* Braised; cooked in a braising-pan.

branche, en *(awн brawнsh)* Term describing vegetables which are served whole rather than chopped up, or served only in part, e.g. asparagus or spinach served whole, rather than as tips alone or chopped leaves.

brandade *(brawн-dahd)* Method of preparing *morue* (salt cod) by pounding it with oil, milk and garlic until it becomes creamy.

braou *(broo)* Soup of cabbage and rice; also known as *brou bouffat*.

brasserie *(bras-ree)* Café-restaurant with an extensive *à la carte* menu, and frequently a fixed-price menu too, which keeps café hours and so can usually provide meals from 7 or 8 a.m. until the small hours.

brayaude *(brah-yod)*
  omelette *(om-let . . .)* Omelette filled with ham, potato, cheese and cream.
  gigot *(zhee-gō . . .)* Leg of lamb or mutton studded with garlic, and stewed in white wine, vegetables and herbs.

brebis *(brā-bee)* Ewe sheep.

brème *(brem)* Freshwater bream
  de mer *(. . . də mair)* Sea bream.
  de rochers *(. . . də ro-shā)* Black bream.

brési *(brā-see)* Thin slices of smoked, salted and dried beef or veal.

bresolles *(brə-sol)* Thinly-sliced beef, veal or mutton baked in alternating layers with a forcemeat of chopped ham, onions, garlic and olive oil; served with braised chestnuts and madeira sauce.

bressane, à la *(ah lah bresan)* In the style of Bresse, a province famous for its fine chickens:

chapon (sha-pawn . . .) Capon baked in rock salt with truffles.

grenouilles (gren-wee-ye . . .) Frogs' legs with a butter, cream and herb sauce.

breton (bre-tawn)

far (fah . . .) Sweet batter pudding with raisins or prunes.

gâteau (ga-tō . . .) Large, plain (but rich) cake.

bretonne, à la (ah lah bre-ton) In the style of Brittany: often indicating a garnish of fresh white haricot beans.

purée (pee-rã . . .) Puréed haricot beans served as a vegetable or, thinned down, as a soup.

sauce (sōs . . .) A creamy white sauce containing strips of mixed vegetables, served with eggs, fish and white meat.

bretzel (bret-sel) Pretzel.

brigne (breen-ye) Provençal sweet fritter.

brignole (breen-yol) Dried plum.

Brillat-Savarin (bree-yah sa-va-ran) The famous gourmet of 250 years ago, whose name is given to a number of dishes, many of which include *foie gras* and truffles:

noisettes (nwah-zet . . .) Boned lamb cutlets with *foie gras*, truffles, asparagus tips and *duchesse* potatoes.

consommé (kawn-so-mã . . .) Chicken consommé thickened with tapioca and garnished with strips of chicken, lettuce, sorrel and chervil.

poire (pwahr . . .) Rum-steeped sponge-cake topped with poached pears and an apricot glaze.

brilloli (bree-yō-lee) Corsican chestnut porridge; also spelled *brioli*.

brioche (bree-yosh) A bun or small cake made from a rich yeast dough incorporating butter and eggs; they come in various shapes and sizes, and some have cream fillings.

brioli—see *brilloli*.

broccana (brō-kah-nah) Sausage-meat and veal pâté.

broche, à la (ah lah brosh) Spit-roasted.

brochet (bro-shã) Freshwater pike.

brocheton (brosh-tawn) Small pike.

brochette (bro-shet) A grilling skewer: anything grilled on a skewer, e.g. *shish kebabs*.

brocoli (bro-co-lee) Broccoli; also called *choux brocolis*.

brou (broo) The husk of a nut; also, a soup made from cabbage and rice (also spelled *braou*).

brou de noix (broo de nwah) Sweet walnut liqueur.

broufado (broo-fah-dō) Marinated beef and onions in a stew with anchovies, capers and vinegar.

brouillade (brwee-yahd) A general term for a mixture of ingredients, as in a stew or soup; also, a term for scrambled eggs.

brouillard (brwee-yahr) 'Fog': a colloquial name for a thick soup.

brouillé (brwee-yã) Scrambled or mixed.

broutes or **brouton** (broot, broo-tawn) Boiled leeks and cabbage (or cabbage alone) in an oil and vinegar sauce; a rustic Lenten dish.

broye (brwah) Maize-flour porridge.

brugnon (breen-yawn) Nectarine.

brûlé(e) (bree-lã) Burnt, roasted.

153

crème *(krem . . .)* Rich cream and egg custard topped with caramel.

brun or **brune** *(braн, brөөn)* Brown; also a term for brown ale.
   sauce brune *(sōs . . .)* Brown sauce, based on meat stock and *sauce espagnole*.

brunoise *(brөөn-wahz)* Finely diced or chopped vegetables, used as a base for various soups, sauces and stuffings.

brut *(brөө)* Very dry, or sugarless—specifically in reference to champagne.

bruxelloise, à la *(ah lah brөөk-sel-wahz)* In the style of Brussels in Belgium: with Brussels sprouts and tiny buttered potatoes.
   potage *(po-tahzh . . .)* Brussels sprout soup.

bûche *(bөөsh)* 'Log': a rolled sponge-cake.
   de Noël *(. . . dө nō-el)* A Christmas log: a chestnut and chocolate sponge log.

buffet *(bөө-fã)* Buffet; refreshment room; station restaurant; bar/restaurant in a hotel or public building; also, a buffet meal in the English sense.

buglosse *(bөө-glos)* A flower, thought to be tonic, which is eaten in salads.

bugne *(bөө-nyө)* Sweet pastry fritter from Lyon.

buisson *(bwee-sawн)* 'Bush': fish or vegetables served heaped up on the dish in the approximate shape of a bush, albeit a rather flat one.

bullido *(bөө-lee-do)* See *aïgo bouïdo*.

byrrh *(beer)* Aperitif of red wine and quinine.

C

cabassol(le)s *(ka-ba-sol)* Lamb's tripe, trotters and head, boiled with ham and vegetables.

cabessal *(ka-bө-sal)* Boned, stuffed hare in a blood-thickened red wine sauce.

cabillaud *(ka-bee-yō)* Fresh cod; salt cod is *morue*.

cabiros *(ka-bee-ros)* Young goat (Corsican).

cabri *(ka-bree)* Young goat.

cacao *(ka-ka-o)* Cocoa; powdered cocoa.
   crème de *(krem dө . . .)* Cocoa liqueur.

cacahouete or **cacahuète** *(ka-ka-wet)* Prepared peanuts—salted, roasted, dry-roasted or whatever; another spelling is *cacouete*. (The peanut in its natural state is *arachide*.)

caccavelli *(kah-kah-vel-ee)* Corsican lemon cheesecake.

cachir *(ka-sheer)* Kosher.

cachuse *(ka-shooz)* Pork braised with onions; also spelled *caqhuse*.

cacouete—see *cacahouette*.

caen, tripes à la mode de *(treep ah lah mod dө kawн)* Tripe cooked slowly in cider and Calvados with trotters, onions, carrots and herbs.

cadurcienne, tripes à la *(treep ah lah ka-dө-syen)* Tripe cooked with saffron.

café *(ka-fã)* Coffee; also, of course, a café—see Section One.
   au lait *(. . . ō lã)* Coffee with milk, which will be hot unless you specifically ask for it to be cold.
   crème *(. . . krem)* Coffee with milk (not cream).
   décaféiné *(. . . dã-ka-fã-nã)* Decaffeinated coffee.
   express *(. . . eks-pres)* Espresso coffee.
   glacé *(. . . gla-sã)* Iced coffee.
   grand café *(grawн . . .)* A large cup of whichever kind of coffee you want.

noire *(. . . nwahr)* Small black coffee.

cagouille *(ka-goo-yee)* A type of snail.

cafeine *ka-fā-een)* Caffeine.

caïeu *(kah-yə)* Variety of giant mussel *(moule)*.

caille *(kah-ee)* Quail.

caillé *(kah-yā)* Clotted, curdled; curds of milk.

caillette *(kah-yet)* Pork liver and bacon rissole.

caion *(kah-yawн)* Term for pig or pork.

caisse *(kes)* Cash desk; cash register.

cajasse *(ka-zhas)* Sweet, rum-laced pastry or cake.

cajou *(ka-zhoo)* Cashew nut; also known as *ana-carde* and *acajou*.

cake *(kek)* Fruit-cake.

caladon *(ka-la-dawн)* Almond cake.

calamar *(ka-la-mahr)* Squid.

calisson *(ka-lee-soн)* Boat-shaped marzipan sweet; also known as *canissoun*.

calvados *(kal-va-dos)* Famous cider brandy from Normandy.

calvaise, homard à la *(o-mar ah lah kal-vez)* Lobster with a spicy tomato sauce; *langouste à la calvaise* is crawfish prepared in the same way.

camomille *(ka-mo-mee-yə)* Camomile; camomile tea.

campagnard or **de campagne** *(kawн-pan-yar, də kawн-pan-yə)* Country-style, rustic: in general, this means that the dish or garnish is simple and unsophisticated. More specifically, it refers to rough-cut pâtés and terrines, often containing mushrooms, herbs and pepper. See also *jambon* and *pain*.

   saucisson *(sō-see-sawн)*

Coarsely-chopped pork sausage.

canapé *(ka-na-pā)* Little pastries or rounds of bread stuffed or spread with a tasty filling and eaten as a cocktail snack or starter.

canard *(ka-nar)* Duck; domestic duck (as opposed to wild).

canard sauvage *(ka-nar sō-vahzh)* Wild duck; more specifically, the mallard.

cancalaise, à la *(ah lah kawн-ka-lez)* With oysters and shrimps in a cream and white wine sauce.
   consommé *(kawн-so-mā . . .)* Fish consommé garnished with pike *quenelles* (little mousses), oysters and chervil.

caneton *(kan-tawн)* Duckling.

canette *(ka-net)* Female duckling.

canistrelli *(ka-nees-trel-ee)* Almond and hazelnut cake flavoured with aniseed.

canissoun *(ka-nee-soon)* Type of marzipan sweet, also known as *calisson*.

canneberge *(kan-bairzh)* Alternative name for the cranberry *(airelle rouge)*.

cannelle *(ka-nel)* The spice cinnamon; also, a fruit tart with cinnamon pastry.

cannelon *(ka-nə-lawн)* Cone-shaped puff-pastry with a forcemeat or creamy shellfish filling.

canotière, matelote à la *(mat-lot ah lah ka-no-tyair)* Carp and eel stew cooked 'boatman-style': with white wine, brandy, mushrooms and baby onions.

cantalou(p) *(kawн-ta-loo)* Cantaloupe melon.

capelin *(kap-laн)* Poor cod, a Mediterranean fish prepared like whiting; also spelled *caplin*.

capoun(s) *(ka-poon)* Baked cabbage or Swiss chard filled with rice and sausage meat; also called *sou fas-soun/fassum*.

capres *(kah-prə)* Capers: either pickled buds of the caper plant or pickled seed-pods of the nasturtium; the former, called 'nonesuch', are preferred.

capucine *(ca-pœ-seen)* Nasturtium: the leaves and flowers are used in salads.

caqhuse *(ka-kœ)* See *cachuse*.

carafe *(ka-raf)* Carafe, pitcher or decanter. The house wine in a restaurant is often served decanted in a carafe. A full carafe contains one litre, a *demi-carafe* half a litre, and a *quart* one quarter of a litre (not one quart).

caramote *(ka-ra-mot)* Type of large prawn.

carbonnade(s) *(kar-bo-nahd)* Term meaning meat cooked directly in flames, or by close-grilling it over coals.
  bœuf *(bœf . . .)* Stew of beef and onions in beer.

cardamome *(kar-da-mom)* The spice cardamom.

cardinal, à la *(ah lah kar-dee-nal)* Usually implies a dish that is pink or red in colour; also a garnish for fish, consisting of mush-rooms, truffles and scallops.
  sauce *(sōs . . .)* A creamy pink lobster sauce containing truffles and pieces of lobster, served with fish—most notably with lobster and sole.

cardinalizer *(kar-dee-na-lee-zā)* Method of cooking shellfish by plunging them into a boiling *court-bouillon* of salt water, thyme and bay, causing them to turn red.

cardon *(kar-dawn)* Cardoon; a relative of the globe artichoke, whose stems are cooked in a white wine *court-bouillon*.

cargolade *(kar-go-lahd)*

Snails *(escargots)* either stewed in wine or baked over charcoal.

cari *(ka-ree)* Curry, curry powder.

caroline *(ka-ro-leen)* Small éclairs eaten as a starter, also a term for Carolina rice.

carotte *(ka-rot)* Carrot.

carpe *(karp)* Carp.

carpeau or **carpillon** *(kar-pō, kar-pee-yawn)* Young carp; also, confusingly, a name for the freshwater mullet.

carré *(ka-rā)* Rack of lamb; best end of neck of lamb, pork or veal.

carrelet *(ka-rə-lā)* Dab or plaice.

carte *(kart)* Menu, which usually includes one or more set meals *(menu prix fixe)* varying in cost accord-ing to the choice and num-ber of courses offered, as well as a selection of *à la carte* dishes:
  à la carte *(ah lah kart)* Dishes chosen from a restaurant's full list of of-ferings, and charged for individually.
  carte conseillée *(. . . kawn-sā-yā)* See *carte promotionelle*.
  carte des vins *(. . . dā van)* Wine-list.
  carte promotionelle *(. . . pro-mo-syawn-nel)* This is a restaurant's least expensive (and hence simplest) menu, which is required by French law in all establishments where fixed menus are offered; also called a *carte conseillée*.

carvi *(kar-vee)* The spice caraway; *graines de carvi* are caraway seeds.

cassade or **cassate** *(ka-sad, ka-sat)* 'Two-tone' ice-cream with Chantilly cream and crystallized fruit, from the Italian *cassata*.

casse-croûte *(kas-croot)* General term for a snack;

also a colloquial name for a snack-bar.

casse-museau *(kas-moo-zō)* Rock candy; rock cake.

casserole *(kas-rol)* General name for a saucepan; more particularly, a copper or terracotta pan with a lid. The name is also applied to various rice dishes which are moulded into a drum shape after they are cooked, and also to a one-dish meal in the American sense—although this usage is rare.

cassis *(ka-see)* Blackcurrant.
   crème de cassis *(krem də . . .)* Blackcurrant liqueur; see also *kir*.

cassissine *(ka-see-seen)* Blackcurrant stuffing; also, a blackcurrant sweet or candy.

cassolette *(kas-o-let)* An individual cooking-dish, used for various fruit or cream desserts, but more often for starters—purées and *salpicons*—usually with a border of piped *duchesse* potatoes.

cassonade *(ka-so-nahd)* Soft brown sugar; Demerara sugar.

cassoulet *(kas-soo-la)* Famous stew of SW France featuring white haricot beans, pork and sausages, and including preserved goose or duck *(confit)*, or mutton, depending on local tradition or the whim of the cook.

castagnaci *(kas-tan-yah-see)* Corsican chestnut-flour fritters or thick pancakes.

castiglione, à la *(ah lah kas-teel-yon)* Garnish for meat, consisting of mushrooms stuffed with rice, bone-marrow and aubergine (eggplant) sautéed in butter.

catalane, à la *(ah lah ka-ta-lan)* Refers to the cooking style of both Spanish Catalonia and of Roussillon in SW France, and often signals the presence of garlic and/or bitter oranges, as well as various combinations of the following: eggplant (aubergine), tomatoes, onions, peppers, rice and chick-peas.
   mouton *(moo-tawn . . .)* Mutton braised in white wine with ham and vegetables and fifty cloves of garlic; also known as *mouton en pistache*.
   saucisse *(sō-sees . . .)* Sausage fried with garlic, orange peel and herbs.
   soupe *(soop . . .)* Tomato and onion soup with ham.

catigau or **catigou** *(ka-tee-gō* or *ka-tee-goo)* Eel *(anguille)* stewed in oil and red wine with tomatoes, garlic, potatoes and onions. Also, cold topside of veal *(noix)* with tomato jelly and anchovy butter.

cauchoise, à la *(ah lah kō-shwahz)* In the style of Caux in Normandy and often referring to white meat in cream and Calvados sauce with apples.
   salade *(sa-lahd . . .)* Salad of chopped ham, celery and potato in a cream dressing.

caudière or **caudrée** *(kō-dy-air, kō-drā)* Sea fish stew-cum-soup with onions and mussels.

caviar *(kav-yahr)* Caviar: sturgeon roes.
   blanc *(. . . blawn)* Mullet roes.
   malossol *(. . . ma-lo-sol)* Fresh, lightly-salted roes.
   niçois *(. . . nee-swah)* Paste of anchovies, oil, herbs and olives.

cavour, à la *(ah lah kah-voor)* A garnish of pasta; also a garnish—for sweetbreads and veal escalopes in particular—of large mushrooms stuffed with puréed chicken's liver and sliced truffle.

cayenne *(ka-yen)* Cayenne

157

pepper; ground, hot red pepper.

cédrat *(sā-drah)* Citron: a large, sour citrus fruit of S France and Corsica, similar to a lemon.

céleri (en branche) *(sā-lə-ree (awʀ brawʀsh))* Celery.

céleri-rave *(sā-lə-ree rahv)* Celeriac; celery root.

Célestine *(sā-lā-steen)* The name of one of Napoleon's cooks, whose name is given to the following:
  potage *(po-tahzh . . .)* Puréed soup of celery, leeks, potatoes and rice.
  poularde *(poo-lahrd . . .)* Sautéed chicken with mushrooms and tomatoes in a wine and cream sauce.

cendres, sous les *(soo lā sawnd)* Method of cooking in hot ashes:
  truffes *(trøf . . .)* Truffles wrapped in a slice of pork and baked in ashes.

cèpe *(sep)* Cep or boletus mushroom, also known as *bolet*; very fleshy, with a strong flavour sometimes described as 'nutty'. Delicious in omelettes.

céréale *(sā-rā-yahl)* Cereal; farinaceous grain and foodstuffs in general.

cerf *(sair)* Stag; deer; red deer.

cerfeuil *(sair-føy)* The herb chervil.

cerise *(sə-reez)* Cherry.

cerneau *(sair-nō)* Marinated green walnuts, served as a starter.

cervelas *(sair-və-lah)* A mildly garlicky smoked-pork sausage which is served sliced, either hot or cold, as an *hors d'œuvre*; the word has also come to mean a fish terrine or loaf.

cervelle(s) *(sair-vel)* Brains, usually calf's.

cévenole, à la *(ah lah sā-və-nol)* In the style of Cevennes: with chestnuts and/or mushrooms.

chablisienne, à la *(ah lah shah-blee-zyen)* In the style of Chablis: cooked in the famous white wine of Chablis, or served in a white wine sauce.

chabot *(sha-bō)* Mediterranean fish used in *bouillabaisse*.

chabrol, chabrot or **champereau** *(shabrol, sha-brō, shawʀ-pə-rō)* The final step in enjoying a *garbure* soup, which involves pouring wine into the bottom of the bowl, mixing it around with all the remaining bits, and drinking it.

chachlik *(shash-leek)* Shashlik: bits of marinated lamb grilled on a skewer, sometimes with onions and peppers; Russian in origin.

chair *(shair)* Flesh; meat; animal flesh.

chalonnaise, à la *(ah lah sha-lawʀ-nez)* Garnish for poultry or sweetbreads, consisting of tartlets filled with puréed kidney plus mushrooms, cockscombs and truffles in white sauce.

chambord, à la *(ah lah shawʀ-bor)* Garnish for fish, notably carp, consisting of roes, *quenelles* (small mousses), truffles, mushrooms and crayfish in red wine.

chamois *(sham-wah)* Chamois, a wild mountain antelope.

champagne *(shawʀ-pan-yə)* Champagne; also a classification term applied to the best cognac brandy.

champenoise, à la *(ah lah shawʀ-pən-wahz)* In the style of Champagne:
  potée *(po-tā . . .)* Stew of ham, bacon and sausage, with cabbage.

champignon *(shawn-peen-yawn)* Mushroom.

champigny *(shawn-peen-yee)* Puff-pastry with apricot jam filling.

champvallon, côtelette d'agneau *(kōt-let-dan-yō shawn-va-lawn)* Lamb chops baked in alternating layers of onions and potatoes.

chanciau *(shawn-syō)* Thick pancake, either sweet or savoury; also called *sanciau*.

chanoinesse, à la *(ah lah shawn-wah-nes)* 'As the canoness likes it': a garnish of tartlets filled with tiny carrots and chopped truffles in cream.

chanterelle *(shawn-trel)* Orange/yellow mushroom also known as *girolle*, which looks like an umbrella blown inside out; flourishes late in the year, and is particularly good to eat.

chantilly *(shawn-tee-yee)* Cream whipped with sugar and, often, with vanilla.

chapelure *(shap-leer)* Breadcrumbs.

chapon *(sha-pawn)* Capon; a castrated cock; the word can also refer to French bread seasoned with garlic, oil and vinegar (principally a salad ingredient).

charbon de bois, au *(ō shar-bawn de bwah)* Charcoal-grilled.

charcuterie *(shar-kee-tree)* 'Pork butchery': in general, the preparation and serving of cold meats, usually pork but also including dishes made from other meats; a *charcuterie* is a shop selling these meat products or, more generally, a delicatessen.

charentais *(sha-rawn-tā)* Variety of sweet melon.

charentaise, à la *(ah lah sha-rawn-tez)* In the style of Charente, the region in western France producing cognac, probably the finest brandy in the world.

   homard *(o-mar . . .)* Lobster in a sauce of cream blended with *Pineau des Charentes*, a mixture of cognac and fresh grape-juice.

   merveilles *(mair-vā . . .)* Sweet fritters spiked with cognac.

chargouère *(shar-gwair)* Turnover, a pastry with either plums or prunes.

chariot *(sha-ryō)* Chariot: a restaurant trolley used to display various dishes at table—particularly *hors d'œuvres*, cheeses and desserts.

charlotte *(shar-lot)* A name referring to two types of dessert: the first is a baked fruit pudding (usually with apples) in a breadlined mould, which is generally served hot; the second is a sponge lining containing a cream filling, of which the following is the prototype:

   charlotte russe *(shar-lot roos)* Bavarian cream custard in a mould lined with sponge-fingers; served cold.

charollais *(sha-ro-lā)* Burgundian beef cattle noted for their excellence.

Chartres, pâté de *(pa-tā de shart)* Partridge pâté wrapped in pastry.

chartreuse *(shar-trez)* Type of herb-flavoured liqueur, which may be green or yellow, made by monks near Grenoble; the word also implies a dish that is presented in a mould:

   œufs *(ef . . .)* Eggs cooked in a vegetable mould with slices of sausage.

   perdreau en *(pair-drō awn . . .)* An elaborate dish composed of partridge—or sometimes pheasant *(faisan)*—

arranged in a mould with cabbage, bacon, sausage and various other vegetables.

chasseur *(sha-ser)* 'Hunter' or 'hunter's style': a garnish of sautéed mushrooms and shallots.
  consommé *(kawʀ-so-mā . . .)* Game consommé with madeira and thin slivers of mushroom.
  sauce *(sōs. . .)* White wine sauce containing chopped, sautéed mushrooms and shallots with herbs.

chasse royale *(shas ro-yal)* Mixed roast game served in the shape of a pyramid.

châtaigne *(sha-tān-yə)* Chestnut, better known by the name *marron*.

châtaigne d'eau *(sha-tān-yə dō)* Water chestnut.

château *(sha-tō)*
  entrecôte *(awʀ-trə-kot . . .)* Thick slice of sirloin steak.
  pommes *(pom . . .)* Potatoes cut into strips or olives and cooked in butter.

chateaubriand *(sha-tō-bree-yawʀ)* Thick middle cut of beef fillet (usually for two), grilled and served with *château* potatoes and either *chateaubriand* sauce (shallots, herbs and white wine) or *béarnaise* sauce.

châtelaine, à la *(ah lah shat-len)* 'As the lady of the manor prefers it': an elaborate garnish of braised lettuce, plus artichoke hearts filled with puréed chestnuts and rice then browned with breadcrumbs, and potato balls browned in butter.

chatouillard, pommes *(pom sha-twee-yahr)* Deep-fried ribbon potatoes.

chauchat, sole *(sol shō-sha)* Sole, which is poached, then coated in *Mornay* sauce, and served ringed with fried potatoes.

chaud(e) *(shō(d))* Hot, heated or warmed.

chaudé *(shō-dā)* Kind of plum tart.

chaudeau *(shō-dō)* Orange tart.

chaud-froid *(shō-frwah)* 'Hot-cold': cooked game or game fowl served cold in white sauce and aspic.

chaudrée *(shō-drā)* Stew-cum-soup of seafish usually containing conger eel, plus other white fish, plus wine, onions and potatoes.

chausson *(shō-sawʀ)* Name for various puff-pastry turnovers with sweet or savoury fillings.

chayot(t)e *(shah-yot)* Type of edible gourd: a custard marrow, also called a *brionne*.

cheddar *(shā-dar)* English Cheddar cheese, also called *chester* by the French for no very obvious reason; *Cheddar* is also the name of a commercially-manufactured French version of English Cheshire cheese.

chemisé(e) *(shə-mee-zā)* 'Wearing a shirt': a menu term describing any ingredient or dish which is served coated or wrapped in something else—pastry, aspic, vine leaves or whatever; also called *en chemise*.

chester—see *cheddar*

chevaine *(shə-ven)* Chub, also called *chavanne*.

cheval *(shə-val)* Horse; horse-meat.

chevalière, poularde à la *(poo-lard ah lah shə-val-yair)* Chicken pieces wrapped in pastry with mushrooms and truffles.

cheveux d'ange *(shə-və-dawʀzh)* 'Angel's hair': grated carrots; with grated carrots. Also a term for carrot jam or marmalade, and for vermicelli: very fine pasta, used mainly in soups.

chèvre *(shev-rə)* Goat; also short for goat's-milk cheese.

chevreau *(shə-vrō)* Kid; young goat.

chevreuil *(shə-vrəy)* Roebuck or roedeer; also a name for venison.

chez nous *(shā-noo)* 'Our way' or 'home-made': a speciality of the house.

chicorée *(shee-ko-rā)* Salad green resembling a frizzy lettuce, called chicory in the us but known as 'curly endive' in Britain. The vegetable which the French call *endive* is something entirely different (see under that heading). *Chicorée* also denotes chicory as a coffee-substitute.

chien de mer) *(shyen də mair)* Dogfish, also called *roussette*.

chiffonnade *(shee-fo-nahd)* Leaves such as lettuce and sorrel, cut into thin strips *(juliennes)*, usually for inclusion in soups.

chilienne, à la *(ah lah sheel-yen)* 'Chile style': with rice and sweet peppers.

chinonaise, à la *(ah lah shee-nawn-nez)* In the style of Chinon in Central France: garnished with potatoes and sausage-stuffed cabbage.

chipiron(e)s *(shee-pee-rawn)* Colloquial name for a squid *(calamar)*.

chipolata *(shee-po-lah-tah)* A chipolata sausage: also, a garnish of braised chestnuts, chipolatas, diced pork, little glazed onions and sometimes glazed carrots.

chips, pommes *(pom sheep)* UK: potato crisps; US: potato chips.

chivry *(shee-vree)*
    beurre *(bər . . .)* Butter mixed with tarragon, chervil, and other herbs.
    sauce *(sōs . . .)* White wine sauce containing shallots, tarragon and chervil.

chocolat *(shō-kō-lah)* Chocolate.
    au lait *(. . . ō lā)* Milk chocolate.
    chaude *(. . . shōd)* Cup of hot chocolate.
    en poudre *(. . . awn poo-drə)* Powdered chocolate; cocoa.

choix *(shwah)* Choice, selection or preference. *Aux choix* is a menu term meaning 'customer's choice', so that *omelette aux choix* means that you can choose your own filling or seasoning.

chope *(shop)* Slang term for a beer glass or mug holding about twelve ounces; see also *demi*.

chorizo *(sho-ree-zō)* Highly-spiced Spanish sausage.

choron *(sho-rawn)* Garnish of potato-balls and artichoke hearts stuffed with peas or asparagus tips.
    sauce *(sōs . . .)* *Béarnaise* sauce with puréed tomatoes added.

chou *(shoo)* Cabbage:
    de Chine *(. . . də sheen)* Chinese cabbage; Chinese lettuce.
    farci *(. . . far-see)* Stuffed cabbage.
    frisé *(. . . free-zā)* Kale.
    de mer or **marin** *(. . . də mair, ma-ran)* Sea kale.
    navet *(. . . na-vā)* Rutabaga; sweet turnip.
    rave *(. . . rahv)* Kohlrabi; turnip cabbage.

rouge *(. . . roozh)* Red cabbage.

chou, pâte à *(pat ah shoo)* Form of pastry-dough made by adding flour to boiling water and butter then whisking eggs in; used for a variety of buns such as éclairs and profiteroles, as well as for *gougère*; usually called choux pastry by English-speaking cooks.

chou(x) de Bruxelles *(shoo də brøøk-sel)* Brussels sprout(s).

choucroute *(shoo-kroot)* Sauerkraut; pickled white cabbage.
    garnie *(. . . gar-nee)* Sauerkraut with pork, sausages, sometimes goose, and potatoes.

chouée *(shwā)* Boiled cabbage with butter or cream and potatoes.

chou-fleur *(shoo-flər)* Cauliflower.

ciboule *(see-bool)* Spring onion.

ciboulette *(see-boo-let)* Chives.

cidre *(see-drə)* Cider.

cigarette *(see-ga-ret)* 'Cigarette': a slender tubular biscuit or *petit-four*, often served with ice-cream.

cimier *(seem-yā)* Haunch of venison.

cingalaise, à la *(ah lah seen-gah-lez)* Curried; with curry sauce.

citron *(see-trawʀ)* Lemon. **vert** *(. . . vair)* Lime.

citronnat *(see-tro-nah)* Candied lemon peel.

citronné(e) *(see-tro-nā)* Lemon-flavoured.

citrouillat *(see-troo-yah)* Pumpkin pie.

citrouille *(see-troo-yə)* Pumpkin: the orange pumpkin, as in American pumpkin pie; also called *potiron*.

civelles *(see-vel)* Tiny eels, deep-fried.

civet *(see-vā)* Stew or ragoût, usually of game (hare, venison) incorporating mushrooms, onions and bacon in red wine thickened with blood; the following is a speciality of the Languedoc:
    de langouste *(. . . də lawʀ-goost)* Crawfish (spiny lobster) stewed in white wine with garlic, tomatoes and onions.

clafouti(s) *(kla-foo-tee)* Thick pancake or batter cake originating in Limousin, with fruit—traditionally, black cherries.

clamart, à la *(ah lah kla-mahr)* With peas, or with a garnish of potato-balls and either artichoke hearts or pastry cases stuffed with peas.

clémentine *(klā-mawʀ-teen)* Clementine, a small citrus fruit similar to the mandarin orange.

clermont, à la *(ah lah klair-mawʀ)* In the style of Clermont-Ferrand: with stuffed cabbage rolls, sliced salt pork and potatoes.

clou de girofle *(kloo də zhee-rof-lə)* Clove.

clovisse *(klo-vees)* Variety of small clam.

clupe *(kløøp)* General term for any fish of the herring/sardine/anchovy family.

cochon *(ko-shawʀ)* Pig; also a general term for pork products.
    de lait *(. . . də lā)* Sucking pig; baby pig.

cochonnaille *(ko-sho-nī)* Term meaning anything made from pork.

cochonnet *(ko-sho-nā)* Piglet, also called *porcelet*.

cocktail *(kok-tel)* Cocktail, or any mixed drink. Also, a cocktail party: in France one attends a *cocktail*, not a cocktail party.

coco *(ko-ko)* Coconut.

cocon *(ko-kawʀ)* Liqueur-laced marzipan sweet shaped like a silkworm's cocoon.

cocotte *(co-kot)* Roasting or baking dish. Can also be a small, round, straight-sided ceramic dish in which various foods are both cooked and served; the menu term *en cocotte* refers to dishes prepared in one of these.

cœur *(kɵr)* Heart. In gastronomic terms this can mean: the heart of an animal, the centre or heart of various vegetables, or a dish prepared in the shape of a heart. *Cœur* is also a name for the best cut of certain meats.

cœur de palmier *(kɵr dɵ pal-myā)* Tender shoots of the palm tree, usually served with *vinaigrette* sauce as an *hors d'œuvre*.

cognac *(kon-yak)* The famous white wine brandy of Charente.

coing *(kwaʀ)* Quince.

cointreau *(kwaʀ-trō)* Orange liqueur.

colbert, à la *(ah lah kol-bair)* Describes fish coated in egg and breadcrumbs, then fried.
  consommé *(kawʀ-so-mā . . .)* Clear chicken soup with shredded vegetables and a poached egg.
  sauce or **beurre** *(sōs, bɵr . . .)* Sauce or prepared butter incorporating meat juices and tarragon.

colin *(ko-laʀ)* Hake, a sea fish related to the cod; also called *saumon blanc*.

colineau *(ko-la-nō)* Codling.

collerettes, pommes *(pom kol-ret)* Paper-thin slices of potato, fried.

collet or **collier** *(ko-lā, kol-yā)* Scrag of mutton: neck of mutton.

collioure, sauce *(sōs kol-yoor)* Anchovy mayonnaise.

colombe *(ko-lawʀb)* Dove.

colombine *(ko-lawʀ-been)* Deep-fried croquette consisting of a savoury interior coated with Parmesan cheese and semolina.

commander *(ko-mawʀ-dā)* To request; to order from a menu.

commodore, consommé *(kawʀ-so-mā ko-mo-dor)* Fish consommé with clams and diced tomatoes.

complet *(kawʀ-plā)* Full, full up, complete; with no more room for customers.
  café complet *(ka-fā . . .)* Term for a continental breakfast.
  pain complet *(paʀ . . .)* Wholemeal bread.

compote *(kawʀ-pot)* Compote (of fruit): stewed fruit in thick syrup, usually served cold.
  poulet en *(poo-lā awʀ . . .)* Chicken stew; game birds are also cooked in this way.

compris *(kawʀ-pree)* Complete; with no further charges; 'all in'.
  service compris *(sair-vees . . .)* on the bill indicates that service is included in the charge.
  service non-compris *(sair-vees nawʀ . . .)* means service should be added, usually 10 to 15 per cent; a further tip, called the *pourboire* may be added at the customer's discretion, whether service is included in the bill or not.

concassé *(kawʀ-ka-sā)* Coarsely chopped, crushed or ground.

concombre *(kawʀ-kawʀ-brɵ)* Cucumber.

condé *(kawn-dā)* Almond icing used to coat pastries.
  abricots or **poires** *(a-bree-kō, pwahr . . .)* Poached apricot or pear halves on rice, served hot.

potage à la *(po-tahzh ah lah . . .)* Soup of puréed red kidney beans.

conférence *(kawn-fā-rawns)* A type of pear.

confiserie *(kawn-feez-re)* Candy, sweets or confectionary; a confectioner's shop.

confit(e) *(kawn-fee(t))* Preserved. The name is used for candied or crystallized fruit, and also for potted meat: goose, duck, pork or turkey (less frequently other meats), cooked and preserved in their own fat in stoneware or similar jars.

confiture *(kawn-fee-tøør)* Conserve; fruit or berry jam.
  confiture d'oranges *(. . . dor-awnzh)* Marmalade.

congre *(kawn-grø)* Conger eel or sea eel, as distinct from the freshwater eel (*anguille*).

conseillée *(kawn-sā-yā)* Advised, recommended; see *carte*.

conserve *(kawn-sairv)* Tinned; any food preserved by tinning or bottling.

consommation(s) *(kawn-so-ma-syawn)* 'Consumption': drinks, meals, snacks etc. ordered in a café or bar. A *tarif des consommations* is a price list: the café or bar equivalent of a restaurant's *à la carte* menu, always found posted in some convenient place, but normally not available as an individual menu.

consommé *(kawn-so-mā)* General term for scores of different clear soups or broths, each made from an enriched, concentrated stock of meat, poultry or game, and usually containing added ingredients such as pasta, vegetables, herbs, bits of meat or fowl etc.; see the individual dictionary entries for specific

descriptions.

contiser *(kawn-tee-zā)* Method of garnishing chicken, game or fish fillets by encrusting them with truffles or similar ingredients.

contre-filet *(kawn-trø fee-lā)* Cut of beef (*bœuf*) equivalent to sirloin; also called *faux-filet*.

conversation *(kawn-vair-sa-syawn)* Puff-pastry tart with sugar glazing and an almond or cream filling.

copeau *(ko-pō)* 'Wood-shaving': the edible ones can be chocolate shavings for cake decoration, cheese shavings, sweet biscuits or *petit-fours* rolled into a hollow twist, or fried ribbon potatoes.

cop(p)a *(ko-pah)* Spicy Corsican smoked pork sausage.

coq *(kok)* Cock or cockerel; also used more generally for chicken and pullet.
  à la bière *(. . . ah lah by-air)* Chicken cooked in beer and juniper spirit with mushrooms.
  au vin *(. . . ō van)* Chicken cooked in wine with mushrooms, onions and herbs.

coq de bruyère *(kok dø brøø-yair)* Wood grouse; black grouse.

coque *(kok)* A *brioche* cake containing sliced citron and rum; also a cockle—a general name for a shell or sea-shell.
  œuf à la coque *(øf ah lah . . .)* Soft-boiled egg.

coquelet *(kok-lā)* Cockerel, young cock.

coquetier *(kok-tyā)* Egg-cup.

coquillages *(ko-kee-yahzh)* Shellfish in general.

coquille *(ko-kee)* Shell, scallop shell or shell-shaped bowl in which various hot *hors-d'œuvres* are served—usually *salpicons* (diced chicken or fish in a creamy sauce) topped with breadcrumbs or grated cheese, and browned.

coquille Saint-Jacques *(. . . san zhak)* Scallop (white-fleshed shellfish with 'coral'), usually served hot in the shell as described above.

corbeau *(kor-bō)* Name for both the crow and the raven in Normandy, where they are said to be eaten.

corbeille *(kor-bā)* Basket; fruit-basket.

corde *(kord)* Type of sweet pastry.

cordial *(kor-dyal)* Cordial; a stimulating drink.

cordon *(kor-dawʀ)* Literally, a rope or cord: a band of gravy or thick sauce surrounding the food on its serving-dish.

cordon bleu *(kor-dawʀ blə)* 'Blue ribbon': the French culinary prize traditionally awarded to female cooks.
  escalope *(es-ka-lop . . .)* Veal escalope filled with ham and cheese.

coriandre *(ko-ryan-drə)* Coriander, the spice.

corne d'abondance *(korn dab-awʀd-awʀs)* 'Horn of plenty': a brown, horn-shaped mushroom, also known as *craterelle* and, less encouragingly, as *trompette de la mort*. It smells and tastes rather like a truffle, and grows late in the year.

cornet *(kor-nā)* Cornet, cornet-shaped: a slice of ham or tongue rolled conically and stuffed with one of several kinds of filling; can also mean an ice-cream cone, or a cream horn: a conical pastry filled with cream.

cornichon *(kor-nee-shawʀ)* Gherkin: cucumber pickle.

correzienne, galette *(gah-let ko-rā-zyen)* Walnut and chestnut filled pastry.

côte *(kōt)* Chop or cutlet of meat; also, rib of beef.

côtelette *(kōt-let)* Chop or cutlet of any kind of meat, particularly lamb or mutton.

cotignac *(ko-teen-yak)* Quince paste, also called *pâté de coing*, which is made into sweets and candies.

cotriade *(ko-tryahd)* Breton fish stew of various fish, usually including conger eel and shellfish, with onions, potatoes and herbs.

cou *(koo)* Neck of animal or fowl.
  cou d'oie farci *(koo dwah far-see)* Goose neck stuffed with *foie gras*, minced pork and truffles; served cold in slices.

coudenat or **coudenou** *(kood-nah, kood-noo)* Large pork sausage, served hot, in slices.

coukebootram *(kook-boo-tram)* *Brioche* (bun or cake) with raisins; also spelled *kokeboteram*.

coulemelle *(kool-mel)* Parasol mushroom, so called because of its shape when fully grown; pale grey/brown, flourishing late in the year.

coulibiac *(koo-lee-byak)* Puff-pastry pie filled with a *salpicon* of salmon or chicken, served as a hot entrée; Russian in origin.

coulis *(koo-lee)* General term for a thick sauce or purée; also used to describe puréed shellfish soups.

coupe *(koop)* A cup, glass or small bowl; one portion of something; one helping; one scoop of ice-cream. Also the name of a dessert of ice-cream with liqueur-steeped fruit.

coupe jacques *(koop zhak)* Two kinds of ice-cream with fruit steeped in kirsch; nowadays, all but the very best restaurants will serve a commercially-packaged version of the original.

couque *(kook)* 'Cake' in Dutch: a sweet Flemish *brioche*. Also a term for gingerbread *(pain d'épices)*.

courge *(koorzh)* General term for gourd vegetables, also often used for marrow.

courgette *(koor-zhet)* Courgette, or Italian zucchini; similar to the English baby marrow.

court-bouillon *(koor bwee-yawn)* General term for a wide variety of broths based on vegetable stock (and sometimes white wine) seasoned with aromatic herbs; used for poaching meat, fish and vegetables.

couscous *(koos-koos)* Popular North African dish featuring a ragoût of lamb or chicken with vegetables in a spicy sauce with steamed semolina.

cousinat *(koo-see-nah)* Chestnut soup with apples or prunes and cream.

cousinette *(koo-zee-net)* Soup with spinach, lettuce and sorrel.

coussinet *(koo-see-nā)* Cranberry, much better known as *canneberge*.

couvert *(koo-vair)* 'Cover': a table-setting or place at table; also, a cover charge.

crabe *(krab)* Crab.

cramique *(kra-meek)* Flemish bread or bun with raisins or currants.

crapaud *(kra-pō)* Toad: a colloquial name for *rascasse* (scorpion fish).

crapaudine *(kra-pō-deen)* Spatchcock: a method of cooking a fowl by splitting it down the centre, then flattening and grilling it.

craquelin *(krak-lan)* A crisp biscuit or cracker; also a type of *brioche* (bun), and a light Breton pastry filled with apple.

craquelot *(krak-lō)* Small,

smoked, salted herring *(hareng saur)*.

craterelle *(krat-rel)* Mushroom: see *corne d'abondance*.

crécy, à la *(ah lah krā-see)* With carrots.
  potage *(po-tahzh . . .)* Puréed carrot soup.

crème *(krem)* Cream.
  aigre *(. . . ā-grə)* Sour cream.
  anglaise *(. . . awn-glez)* Light egg-custard.
  brûlée *(. . . brөө-lā)* Rich cream custard with a topping of burnt brown sugar.
  caramel or **renversée** *(. . . ka-ra-mel, rawn-vair-sā)* Vanilla custard with caramel sauce; also called a *flan*.
  chantilly *(. . . shawn-tee-yee)* Whipped cream containing sugar and vanilla.
  épaisse *(. . . ā-pes)* Thick cream; double cream.
  fouetté *(. . . fwā-tā)* Whipped cream.
  fraîche *(. . . fresh)* Lightly soured cream.
  pâtissière *(. . . pa-tee-sy-air)* Pastry cream.
  renversée—see *caramel* above.

créole, à la *(ah lah krā-yol)* Creole style: with rice, sweet peppers and tomatoes; also, desserts and puddings with rice.
  chayot(t)e *(shah-yot . . .)* Custard marrow stewed with sautéed onions, tomatoes and garlic, and served with rice.

crêpe *(krep)* Large, thin, wheat-flour pancake, either sweet or savoury; see individual entries for the various toppings and fillings.

crépinette *(krā-pee-net)* Small sausage of minced pork, lamb, veal or chicken, sometimes with truffles *(truffe)*, coated in butter and breadcrumbs, which

crête de coq *(krait də kok)* Cockscomb.

cresson *(kres-sawн)* Watercress; cress.

cretons *(krə-tawн)* Crackling, frizzled fat.

creuse *(krөz)* Type of oyster with a rough shell.

crevette *(krə-vet)* General word for a shrimp or prawn.
   rose *(. . . roz)* Prawn.
   grise *(. . . greez)* Shrimp.

croissant *(krwah-sawн)* Crescent-shaped breakfast roll made from yeast dough, or from puff-pastry dough; deliciously light and crispy when fresh, but it quickly goes limp.

croissant beurre *(krwah-sawн bər)* Richer version of the traditional croissant, made with butter.

cromesqui *(kro-mes-kee)* Any foodstuff rolled into a ball, dipped in batter and fried; also the name of a hot *salpicon* starter cooked in this fashion.

croquant *(kro-kawн)* Crispy or crunchy; also the name of a crisp, almond *petit-four* biscuit.

croque au sel, à la *(ah lah krok ŏ sel)* Served raw, with salt.

croquembouche *(krok-awн-boosh)* Any crisp, sweet dish with a sugar glaze that crunches in the mouth, especially *choux profiteroles* filled with cream and coated with a sugar glaze; these are served in a conical tower at wedding parties.

croque-madame *(krok ma-dam)* Sandwich of toasted cheese and fried egg; variations include toasted cheese with bacon, and toasted cheese with Strasbourg sausage, plus or minus the fried egg.

croque-monsieur *(krok mo-*

**syər)* Toasted ham-and-cheese sandwich.

croquet *(kro-kā)* A dry *petit-four* biscuit; also a crisp almond biscuit.

croquette *(kro-ket)* A small sausage-shaped preparation, coated in egg and breadcrumbs and deep-fried; it can be based on puréed potato or some other vegetable, pasta, rice, or on a *salpicon* of meat or fish bound with a thick sauce.
   Sweet *croquettes*, often made of stewed fruit and rice bound with a pastry cream, are coated and cooked in a similar fashion.

croustade *(kroos-tahd)* Deep pastry case or shell, made either of flaky or puff-pastry dough, stuffed with *ragoût*, *salpicon* or some other savoury filling. *Croustade* may also be fashioned from puréed potato, pasta or hollowed-out bread which is brushed with egg and deep-fried before it is filled.

croustillant *(kroos-tee-yawн)* Crunchy, crisp or crusty.

croustille *(kroos-tee-yө)* Game chip, or home-made potato crisp.

croûte *(kroot)* A 'crust', which may be a slice of fried bread or a pastry case, which is topped or filled with a *salpicon* or meat, fish or vegetables and served hot as an *hors-d'œuvre*, or with stewed fruit and/or pastry cream as a dessert. *En croûte* describes something cooked inside a pastry case.

croûte-au-pot *(kroot ŏ pŏ)* Soup made from *pot-au-feu* liquid; also called *consommé à l'ancienne*.

croûtons *(kroo-tawн)* Tiny cubes of crisp-fried or toasted bread used to garnish soups, salads etc.

cru *(kroo)* Raw or

uncooked; also a term used in the classification of top-ranking vineyards.

jambon cru (*zham-bawн . . .*) Smoked, uncooked ham.

cruchade (*kroo-shahd*) Fritter or pancake made of maize-meal porridge.

crudités (*kroo-dee-tā*) Selection of raw, in-season vegetables offered as a starting course, often with cold sauces and dips.

crustacé (*kroo-sta-sā*) Crustacean or shellfish: crab, lobster, shrimp and so on.

cubat, sole (*sol koo-bah*) Poached fillet of sole with puréed mushrooms in *Mornay* sauce.

cuiller or **cuillère** (*kwee-yā, kwee-yair*) Spoon.

cuisine (*kwee-zeen*) Cooking in general; also, the kitchen.

    bourgeoise (*. . . boor-zhwahz*) 'Middle-class': descriptive of wholesome casseroles etc.; good food without frills.

    haute (*ōt . . .*) Fine, classical French cooking; usually very rich and, in restaurants, very expensive.

    maigre (*. . . mā-grə*) Meatless, semi-vegetarian cooking.

    minceur (*. . . maн-ser*) Low-fat or diet cooking; meals prepared with smaller quantities.

    nouvelle (*noo-vel . . .*) 'The new cooking': a conscious reaction to traditional *haute cuisine*, this features small portions of exquisitely-prepared, first-quality ingredients, emphasizing individual and complementary tastes, natural flavours, lightness and the appearance of the food on the plate.

    régionale (*. . . rā-zhon-al*) The style of cooking particular to an individual region of France.

végétarienne (*. . . vā-zhā-ta-ryen*) Strict vegetarian cooking.

cuisse (*kwees*) Leg or thigh.

    de grenouille (*. . . də grən-wee-yə*) Frog's leg.

cuisseau (*kwee-sō*) Leg of veal.

cuisson (*kwee-sawн*) Cooking stock; also means the act of cooking, or the cooking time.

cuit(e) (*kwee(t)*) Cooked. The word is also used to mean the opposite of uncooked (*cru*), so *jambon cuit* is cooked or boiled ham, while *jambon cru* is smoked uncooked ham; see also *cru*.

culotte (*koo-lot*) Silverside of beef; rump of beef.

cumin (*koo-maн*) The spice cumin.

curaçao (*koo-rah-sō*) Orange liqueur of Dutch origin.

curcuma (*koor-koo-mah*) The spice turmeric, a basic ingredient in curry seasoning.

cussy, à la (*ah lah koo-see*) A garnish of artichoke hearts filled with mushroom purée, sliced truffles and cock's kidneys.

custine, veau à la (*vō ah lah koos-teen*) Veal chops with a mushroom coating or stuffing, dipped in egg and breadcrumbs, fried, and served with a tomato sauce.

D

d' is the form of *de* (meaning 'of') that is used when a vowel-sound follows.

dagh kebab (*dag kā-bab*) Turkish shish kebab: veal, onions and tomatoes grilled on a skewer with thyme, and served with rice pilaf and okra.

daïkon *(dee-kawn)* Japanese radish, eaten raw or cooked like turnips.

dame-blanche, bombe *(bom dam blawnsh)* Vanilla ice-cream case filled with almond-milk egg mousse.

darblay, potage *(po-tahzh dar-blā)* Cream of potato soup with vegetables in thin strips.

dard *(dar)* Freshwater dace.

dariole *(dar-yol)* Pastry-mould shaped like a flower-pot; also the name of various sweet or savoury pastries and custards baked in a *dariole*.

darne *(darn)* Thick slice or steak of a large fish such as salmon.

d'artagnan, à la *(ah lah dar-tan-yawn)* Garnish of stuffed tomatoes, mushrooms and potato croquettes.
　consommé *(kawn-so-mā . . .)* Beef and game consommé with peas.

dartois *(dar-twah)* Puff-pastry rectangles layered with an almond-cream filling and served as a dessert, or stuffed with meat or fish and eaten as an *hors-d'œuvre*.

datte *(dat)* Date; date palm *(dattier)*.

daube *(dōb)* Method of cooking meat, fowl or game by braising it slowly in wine and meat stock with vegetables and herbs; fish too can be cooked this way, but the classic *daube* is made with beef.

dauphine *(dō-feen)*
　pommes *(pom . . .)* Deep-fried croquettes of puréed potato mixed with *choux* paste.
　sole *(sōl. . .)* Deep-fried fillets of sole garnished with a ragoût of crayfish tails, truffles, pike *quenelles* (mousses) and mushrooms.

dauphinoise, gratin de pommes à la *(gra-tan de pom ah lah dō-fee-nwahz)* Layers of paper-thin sliced potatoes baked in milk, with grated cheese and a little nutmeg.

daurade *(dō-rahd)* Gilt-headed sea bream.

de *(de)* Of.

deauvillaise, à la *(ah lah dō-vee-lez)* In the style of Deauville on the English Channel: a method of preparing fish, usually sole, by poaching it with onions and cream.

défarde *(dā-fahrd)* Lamb's feet and tripe stew.

déjeuner *(dā-zhe-nā)* Lunch.

délice *(dā-lees)* 'Delectable': a type of light pastry for desserts and sometimes starters. Note: the word *délice* is often misused in menus written by restaurateurs of the upwardly aspiring sort. The dish it describes may be perfectly fine, but suspect pretension nonetheless; the term properly applies only to the pastry mentioned above.

demi *(de-mee)* Half. Also refers to a glass or mug, which once held half a litre but nowadays holds only about a third.

demi-bouteille *(de-mee boo-tā)* Half-bottle of wine, containing roughly 35 to 37 centilitres.

demi-carapace *(de-mee ka-ra-pas)* Half-shell.

demi-deuil, à la *(ah lah de-mee-dey)* A garnish for poultry or veal of a creamy, white *suprême* sauce with sliced truffles.
　poularde *(poo-lard . . .)* Stuffed chicken cooked with sliced truffles inserted beneath the skin, and served in a creamy sauce; also known as *poularde à la mère Fillioux*.

demidoff *(de-mee-dof)*

Chicken cooked with puréed vegetables, served with sliced truffles and madeira sauce.

demi-glace *(də-mee-glas)* Brown sauce made of meat stock, with vegetables and (usually) madeira or sherry.

demi-sel *(də-mee sel)* Lightly salted; a term used to describe slightly salty butter, as well as lightly smoked herrings and boiling ham. It is also the name of a popular soft fresh cream-cheese.

demi-tasse *(də-mee-tas)* Small cup: an after-dinner coffee cup; also, a small dessert glass.

demoiselle *(də-mwah-zel)* Very small type of lobster fished around Cherbourg.

dentelle, crêpe *(kraip dawn-tel)* Large, lace-thin pancake with a sweet filling.

dents-de-lion *(dawn-də-lyawn)* Name for a dandelion *(pissenlit)*, which is sometimes used in salads.

derby, poularde à la *(poolard ah lah dair-bee)* Chicken stuffed with rice and truffles, served with *foie gras* and truffles in a port wine sauce.

dérobé *(dā-ro-bā)* 'Undressed': blanched, skinned, shelled or peeled.

des *(dā)* 'Of the', a contraction of *de les*.

dés *(dā)* 'Dice': a general term for diced ingredients.

désossé *(dā-zo-sā)* Boned; with the bones removed.

dessert *(dā-sair)* The dessert or sweet course. In France the dessert follows the cheese course and precedes the fruit, and it will require a good deal of convincing argument to have coffee served *with* dessert; this is considered immoral in French culinary ethics.

diable, à la *(ah lah dyah-ble)* Devilled: a method of preparing poultry. The bird is slit open along its back, flattened out, grilled and finally breadcrumbed and browned under the grill; served with *sauce diable*.

  artichauts *(ar-tee-shō . . .)* Sautéed artichokes stuffed with breadcrumbs, garlic and capers.

  œuf *(əf . . .)* Fried egg sprinkled with vinegar.

  sauce *(sōs . . .)* Sauce based on stock and concentrated vinegar, with chopped shallots and pepper; the English version adds cayenne pepper and worcester sauce.

diable de mer *(dyah-ble də mair)* Monkfish *(lotte)*; also a colloquial name for *rascasse* (scorpion fish).

diablotin *(dyah-blo-tan)* Slice of bread spread with thick cheese sauce, sprinkled with Parmesan and browned; normally served with soup. Also a type of chocolate sweet.

diane, sauce *(sōs dyahn)* Peppery cream sauce for beef, venison and other game (e.g. *steak diane*).

Diane de Châteaumorand, civet de lièvre de *(see-vä də lyev-rə də dyahn də shah-tō-mo-rawn)* Hare stewed in red wine with onions and mushrooms.

dieppoise, à la *(ah lah dyep-wahz)* In the style of Dieppe, on the English Channel: fish, usually sole, poached in white wine with mussels and crayfish tails, and served with mushrooms and a cream sauce; also a fish and shellfish stew *(marmite)* with leeks, cream and white wine.

digestif *(dee-zhes-teef)* General term for spirits served after dinner, e.g. *cognac, marc* etc.

dijon *(dee-zhawn)* Type of mustard made in Dijon.

dijonnaise, à la *(ah lah*

dee-zhawʀ-nez) In the Dijon style: with blackcurrants or blackcurrant liqueur.

dinatoire *(dee-nah-twahr)* French equivalent of high tea: a substantial late lunch or early-evening dinner.

dinde *(daʀd)* Turkey; hen turkey.

dindon *(daʀ-dawʀ)* Turkey: originally *coq d'Inde* (Indian cock), as the bird was brought to France from the Spanish territories in America which were known as the 'Spanish Indies', and later corrupted to *dinde* and *dindon*. The English name for the same bird comes from a similar confusion: it was imported to England by so-called 'Turkey merchants' from the Levant, and by association acquired the name 'Turkey bird'.

dindonneau *(daʀ-do-nō)* Young turkey.

dîner *(dee-nā)* To dine; dinner; a full evening meal.

diot *(dyō)* Preserved pork and vegetable sausage, prepared by cooking in white wine.

diplomate, à la *(ah lah dee-plo-mat)* A garnish of cockscombs, kidneys, sweetbreads and mushrooms, with madeira sauce.
   sauce *(sōs . . .)* Rich creamy sauce with lobster butter and diced truffles, served with fish.
   sole *(sōl . . .)* Fillets of sole stuffed with whiting forcemeat, served with *sauce diplomate*, sliced truffles and a *salpicon* of lobster.

dodine *(do-deen)* Method of preparing poultry or a joint of meat by boning, stuffing and braising it; a small *dodine* is called a *dodinette*.

dorade *(do-rahd)* Red sea-bream, not to be confused with the nearly identical-sounding *daurade*, the gilt-

headed sea bream, which is considered much finer.

doré(e) *(do-rā)* Golden, lightly browned; glazed with egg or egg-yolk.

dorure *(do-reer)* Egg-yolk glaze.

doria *(do-ryah)* With cucumber.

double *(doo-ble)* Double: strong or fortified; also, a large cut of meat, including both hind legs.

double-crème *(doo-ble krem)* Cream cheese: not English double cream, which is called *crème épaisse*.

douce or **doux** *(doos, doo)* Sweet, fresh, mild, soft.

doucette *(doo-set)* Dragonet or corn salad: another name for lamb's lettuce *(mâche)*.

douillon *(dwee-yawʀ)* 'Snug' or 'cozy': a whole pear cooked in a pastry coating.

doux—see *douce.*

doyenné de comice *(dwah-nā de ko-mees)* Highly-prized variety of table pear from Angers in W France.

dragée *(dra-zhā)* A general term for a pastille or sweet; also, a sugar-coated almond, or a preserved plum.

du *(dee)* 'Of the', a contraction of *de le.*

Dubarry, à la *(ah lah dee-ba-ree)* Garnish of cauliflower with cheese sauce.

dubonnet *(dee-bo-nā)* Brand name of a popular, bitter-sweet, wine-based aperitif, either red or white.

duchesse, à la *(ah lah dee-shes)* Garnished with *duchesse* potatoes:
   pommes *(pom . . .)* A smooth blend of mashed potatoes, eggs and butter which is piped around a dish or moulded into a shape, then baked.

171

A *duchesse* is a *petit-four* biscuit made with chocolate, almonds and hazelnuts; it is also the name of an excellent type of winter pear.

dugléré, sole *(sōl dǝǝ-glā-rā)* Sole baked with tomatoes, onions and herbs in white wine, served in a white wine sauce.

dumas, entrecôte *(awʀ-trǝ-kot dǝǝ-mah)* Rib or sirloin steak with sliced beef-marrow in a white wine and shallot sauce.

dur(e) *(dǝǝr)* Hard; cooked until hard.
  œuf dur *(ǝf . . .)* Hard-boiled egg.

duroc *(dǝǝ-rok)* New potatoes browned in butter.

duxelles *(dǝǝ-sel)* Mixture of finely-chopped mushrooms sautéed with chopped shallots.
  sauce *(sōs . . .)* Duxelles blended with white wine, stock and tomato purée, served with meat, fish or eggs.

E

eau *(ō)* Water.
  eau de robinet—see *eau potable*.
  eau-de-vie *(ō dǝ vee)* 'Water of life': brandy, or any spirits distilled from wine, *marc*, cider or other fermented fruits.
  eau gazeuze *(ō gaz-ǝz)* Carbonated water; soda water.
  eau minérale *(ō mee-nā-ral)* Mineral water; spring water.
  eau potable *(ō po-tah-blǝ)* Drinking water; tap water. Also known as *eau de robinet*.

écaillé *(ā-kī-yā)* Opened (shell); scaled (fish).

écarlate *(ā-kar-lat)* Scarlet: a general term for pickled

or salted meat; also a term for brown aspic.

échalote *(ā-sha-lot)* Shallot; a small, tender onion.

échaudé *(ā-shō-dā)* 'Scalded': a shaped pastry made from dough which is poached in water and dried before baking, to facilitate the precise forming of the shape.

échine *(ā-sheen)* Chine (backbone) or loin of pork; also called *épine*.

éclade *(ā-klahd)* Mussels (*moules*) cooked over pine needles.

éclair *(ā-klair)* Choux pastry bun filled with cream and topped with chocolate, coffee or vanilla icing.

éclanche *(ā-klawʀsh)* Name for shoulder of mutton.

écrevisse *(ā-krǝ-vees)* Freshwater crayfish; large freshwater prawn. *Nantua* on the menu indicates the inclusion of crayfish in some form.

églefin or **égrefin** *(ā-glǝ-faʀ, ā-grǝ-faʀ)* Variations on *aiglefin* (haddock).

elzekaria *(el-zǝ-ka-ryah)* Cabbage and haricot bean soup with onions and garlic.

embrucciate *(awʀ-brǝǝ-syat)* Corsican cheese tart made with *Brocciu* cheese.

émincé *(ā-maʀ-sā)* Sliver or thin slice; also a term for various dishes featuring thinly-sliced meat, game or fowl served with a sauce.

émondé *(ā-mawʀ-dā)* Skinned by blanching, e.g. tomatoes, almonds etc.

emmenthal *(ā-mawʀ-tal)* 'Swiss cheese': a hardish, waxy yellow cheese with holes, moulded in huge drums and served in slices, wedges, cubes, or grated (*rapé*); one of France's two basic 'all-purpose' cheeses, used much as the English use cheddar (the other is *gruyère*, *emmenthal* being the less expensive).

en *(awʀ)* In.

encastré *(awʀ-cas-trā)* Embedded; set in.

encornet *(awʀ-kor-nā)* Alternative name for squid *(calamar)*.

endive *(awʀ-deev)* Plump, pale-green leaf vegetable known as chicory in Britain, endive in the USA. It is usually served raw in salads, steamed as a side dish, or braised with ham or pork (and sometimes cheese sauce) as a main dish.

entier or **entière** *(awʀ-tyā, awʀ-tyair)* Entire, whole.

entrecôte *(awʀ-trə-kot)* Rib or sirloin steak, normally cut fairly thin and either fried or grilled; what is listed on the menu as 'steak' in one of its various spellings will most frequently turn out to be an *entrecôte*.

entrée *(awʀ-trā)* The course preceding the roast; in shorter menus, the *entrée* may be the main course.

entremets *(awʀ-trə-mā)* The dessert or sweet course.

épaule *(ā-pōl)* Shoulder of mutton, lamb, pork or veal; beef shoulder is called *paleron*.

éperlan *(ā-pair-laʀ)* Sea or river smelt; see also *athérine*.

épice *(ā-pees)* Spice.
  pain d'épice *(paʀ . . .)* Gingerbread.

épicerie *(ā-pees-ree)* Grocer's shop, also called *alimentation*.

épigramme *(ā-pee-gram)* 'Witty remark':
  poitrine d'agneau en *(pwah-treen dan-yō awʀ . . .)* Sliced breast of lamb and a lamb cutlet, both dipped in egg and breadcrumbs, fried or grilled, then served together as a single dish.

épinards *(ā-pee-nahr)* Spinach.

épiphanie *(ā-pee-fa-nee)* Twelfth Night, a holiday feast especially popular with children, and any restaurant worth its salt will celebrate the occasion with an *éphiphanie* cake: a flaky *galette* or sponge ring with tiny king and queen dolls baked inside, which is served decorated with a gold paper crown. Always accompanied by a sweet *sauternes* wine.

équille *(ā-kee-yə)* Sand eel.

escabèche *(es-ka-besh)* Fried fish in a spicy marinade, served cold as a starter.

escalope *(es-ka-lop)* Slice of meat, especially veal, or fish flattened out and lightly fried in butter or fat.

escargot *(es-kar-gō)* Snail.

escarole *(es-ka-rol)* Frizzy salad green similar to *chicorée*.

espadon *(es-pa-dawʀ)* Swordfish; swordfish steak.

espagnole, à l' *(ah les-pan-yol)* Spanish style: with tomatoes, onions, garlic and peppers.
  omelette *(om-let . . .)* Omelette with potatoes, tomatoes and peppers.
Sauce espagnole is a brown sauce made with meat stock, flour and vegetables: an essential of French cooking.

esprot *(es-prō)* Sprat, a

miniature cousin of the herring.

esquinade or **esquinado** *(es-kee-nahd* or *es-kee-nahd-ō)* Spider crab *(araignée de mer).*

estoficado *(es-tō-fee-kah-dō)* See *stocaficada.*

estomac *(es-to-mah)* Stomach of a sheep; beef stomach is called *tripes.*

estouffade or **estouffat** *(es-too-fahd* or *es-too-fah)* Meat stewed very slowly in wine, usually with herbs and vegetables; the Languedoc version is made with pork and haricot beans. Also a name for a clear brown sauce used to dilute thicker sauces, or for basting braised meat.

  estouffat de Noël *(. . . də nō-el)* Beef stewed in Armagnac and wine with shallots.

estragon *(es-tra-gawn)* The herb tarragon.

esturgeon *(es-təər-zhyawn)* Sturgeon.

étoile *(ā-twahl)* Star; star-shaped.

étoffé *(ā-to-fā)* Stuffed; also spelled *étouffé.*

étouffée, à l' *(ah lā-too-fā)* Method of cooking food very slowly in a tightly covered pan with almost no liquid; also spelled *étuvée.*

étourdeau *(ā-tour-dō)* Name for a young capon.

étrangle belle-mère *(ā-trawn-glə bel mair)* 'That which strangles mother-in-law': a colloquial name for the horse mackerel or scad *(saurel).*

étuvée—see *étouffée.*

exocet *(eks-o-set)* Colloquial name for a flying fish (hence the name for the French missile).

express *(eks-pres)* Espresso coffee.

extra *(eks-trah)* Descriptive term meaning exceptional, best-quality or simply very good.

extrait *(eks-trā)* Extract or essence for use in cooking, produced by boiling down the stock of meat, fish, fowl, game or vegetables; even alcoholic beverages are sometimes reduced by boiling to produce *extraits.*

F

façon *(fa-sawn)* Style, manner, fashion.

  à la façon de *(ah lah fa-sawn də)* Prepared in the style of . . .

fagot *(fa-gō)* Meatball.

fagoue *(fa-goo)* General term for sweetbreads.

faim *(fan)* Hunger.

  avoir faim *(a-vwahr . . .)* To be hungry.

faine *(fen)* Beechnut.

faisan *(fə-zawn)* Pheasant; cock pheasant.

faisandé *(fə-zawn-dā)* Gamey or high, applying to game that has been hung.

falculella *(fal-kəə-lā-lah)* Corsican cheese cake.

famille *(fa-mee-yə)* Family-style cooking; simple cooking.

fanchette or **fanchonette** *(fawn-shet, fawn-sho-net)* Cake made of flaky-pastry dough with a cream filling and topped with meringue; also a term for meringue.

fanes *(fan)* Edible tops of certain root vegetables; radish tops are used to make a delicious soup.

fantaisie *(fawn-tā-zee)* 'Passing fancy' or 'whim': a general term for various breads whose price is fixed per loaf rather than by weight; they are usually baked in some fanciful shape, e.g. the 'Picasso', a light egg-bread baked in the shape of an enormous chicken's foot. Also, a descriptive term for any synthetic food product; French law requires the word to appear on the label or package of any such product.

far *(far)* Wheat or buckwheat flour porridge.
  breton *(. . . bre-tawn)* Type of batter pudding usually with raisins and prunes mixed in.
  poitevin *(. . . pwaht-van)* Type of stuffed cabbage (see *poitevine*).

farce *(fars)* 'Trick' or 'practical joke': stuffing or forcemeat. Various minced and seasoned ingredients (frequently pork) used as stuffing.

farcement—see *farçon*.

farci *(far-see)* Stuffed: short for *chou farci*, stuffed cabbage (usually with sausagemeat and vegetables). Also, stuffed breast of veal.

farcidure *(far-see-deer)* Vegetable dumpling, served with soup in central France.

farçon or **farcement** *(far-sawn, far-smawn)* In central France this is a fried sausage-meat and vegetable cake. In the Alps it is a baked dish of potatoes mixed with eggs, sugar, milk, prunes and raisins; one version includes bacon as well.

farée *(fa-rā)* Stuffed cabbage.

farine *(fa-reen)* Flour:
  complète *(. . . kawn-plet)* Wholewheat flour.
  d'avoine *(. . . dav-wahn)* Oatmeal.
  de blé *(. . . de blā)* Wheat; white flour.
  de sarrasin *(. . . de sa-ra-san)* Buckwheat.
  de seigle *(. . .de saig-le)* Rye.
  de son *(. . . de sawn)* Bran flour.
Cornflour is *maïs*. For *soupe à la farine*, see *mehlsuppe*.

fariné(e) *(fa-ree-nā)* Floured; flour-coated.

farineuse or **farineux** *(fa-ree-nez, fa-ree-ne)* Farinaceous or starchy: a general name for farinaceous vegetables—potatoes and pulses—and for cereals.

faséole *(fa-zā-ol)* Type of haricot bean.

fassum or **fassoun** *(fa-seem, fa-soon)* Cabbage stuffed with bacon, sausage-meat, rice, tomatoes, beetroot leaves and onions.

fausse *(fōs)* See *faux*.

fausse daurade *(fōs dō-rahd)* 'Mock daurade': a colloquial name for the red sea bream (*dorade*).

fausse tortue, potage *(pō-tahzh fōs tor-tee)* Mock turtle soup (made with calf's head).

faux *(fō)* 'False': in cooking, 'mock' or 'imitative of'. Also spelled *fausse*.
  faux café *(. . . ka-fā)* Decaffeinated coffee; also called simply *faux*.
  faux-filet *(fō-fee-lā)* Sirloin steak, cut from beside the fillet; also called *contre-filet*.
  faux mousseron *(fō moos-er-on)* Fairy-ring mushroom: small and aromatic, with a pale cap, rings of these fungi appear in October and November.

favart *(fah-var)* Garnish of chicken *quenelles* (little mousses) and tartlets filled with *cèpes* in cream.

faverolles or **favioles** *(fav-rol, fav-yol)* General term used in S France for all varieties of haricot beans (US: shell beans).

favorite, à la *(ah lah fa-vo-reet)* Garnish of braised artichokes, stuffed lettuce, stuffed mushrooms and small *Anna* potato cakes.
  bombe favorite *(bom . . .)* Meringues and cream with kirsch, frozen into a *bombe* shape and served with raspberry purée.

favouille *(fa-voo-yə)* Small spider crab.

fécampoise, sole à la *(sōl ah lah fā-kawн-pwahz)* Sole cooked in a style more commonly called *à la trouvillaise* (see that entry).

fèche *(fesh)* Dish of dried, salted pork liver served with a radish salad.

fechun *(fə-shaн)* Cabbage stuffed with bacon and vegetables.

fécule *(fā-kəəl)* Starch; also, potato-flour.

fenouil *(fən-wee)* Fennel, a vegetable tasting of aniseed, whose bulbous base is eaten raw or braised like celery. Its feathery leaves are also used in a number of dishes.

fenugrec *(fə-nəə-grek)* The herb fenugreek, used in curries.

féouse or **fiouse** *(fā-ooz, fyooz)* A quiche or flan filled with bacon and onions with cream.

féra *(fā-rah)* Highly-prized lake salmon from Savoie in E France.

ferchuse *(fair-shəəz)* Liver, lungs and heart of pork, cooked in pork-fat and red wine with onions, garlic and potatoes.

fermeture *(fair-mə-təər)* Closing; closing day(s).
  annuelle *(. . . an-yoo-wel)* 'On holiday'; yearly closing.
  exceptionelle *(. . . ek-sep-syawн-nel)* Unexpected closing; closed because of illness etc.
  hebdomadaire *(. . . eb-do-ma-dair)* Regular weekly closing day(s).

fermé *(fair-mā)* Closed; closed for business.

fermier *(fairm-yā)* Free-range, natural, farm-made, home-made; local farm produce.

fermière, à la *(ah lah fairm-yair)* 'Farmer's wife style': a garnish for braised meat,

consisting of mixed vegetables stewed very slowly in butter.
  potage *(po-tahzh . . .)* Soup of finely-shredded mixed vegetables with white beans.

Ferté-Macé, tripes de la *(treep də lah fair-tā mah-sā)* Tripe cooked in 'packets' on skewers.

feu *(fə)* Fire; cooking fire; heat.
  feu de bois *(. . . də-bwah)* Wood fire; wood barbecue.

feuillantine *(fə-yawн-teen)* Puff (flaky) pastry rectangles glazed with egg-white and sugar.

feuille *(fə-yə)* Leaf of a tree, plant, vegetable etc; also a page in a book or a sheet of paper.
  pâte feuille *(pat . . .)* Term for flaky or puff pastry; see also *mille-feuille*.

feuilletée *(fəy-tā)* General word for little stuffed puff-pastries.

feuilletté *(fə-yet-tā)* Made of puff-pastry.

feuilleton *(fəy-tawн)* Literally, a serial or serialization (e.g. 'Dallas'): thin, flattened slices of veal or pork spread with stuffing, then stacked on top of each other like a multi-layered sandwich, and braised; served either hot or cold.

fève *(fev)* UK: broad bean; US: shell bean.

févette *(fāv-et)* Tiny, early broad bean.

fiadone *(fee-ya-don)* Brocciu cheese and orange flan from Corsica.

ficelle *(fee-sel)* 'String': a long, thin loaf of white French bread, roughly half the weight of a *baguette*.
  picarde *(. . . pee-kahrd)* Pancake filled with ham and mushrooms, with *béchamel* sauce.

bœuf à la *(bœf ah lah . . .)* Method of cooking beef by first roasting it, then steeping it in stock.

figatelli *(fee-ga-tel-lee)* Corsican spicy pork and pork-liver and herb sausage.

figue *(feeg)* Fig.

figue de barbarie *(feeg də bar-ba-ree)* Prickly pear; the fruit of the prickly pear cactus.

figue de mer *(feeg də mair)* 'Sea fig': a colloquial name for the *violet*, a small, curious-looking sea creature with a fig-like exterior and an edible centre resembling scrambled egg.

filet *(fee-lā)* Fillet: in general terms a tender, boneless cut of meat. Fillet of beef (*. . . de bœuf*) is taken from the underside of the sirloin and divided into five separate cuts: *beefsteak* (the least tender), *chateaubriand, fillet steak, tournedos* and *filet mignon* (the most tender).

Fillet of pork (*porc*), veal (*veau*) and mutton (*mouton*) comes from the fleshy part of the buttocks. Poultry and game fillets are the breasts, cut off from the bone; also called *suprêmes*. Fish fillets are cut lengthwise off the bone.

> **filet d'anvers** *(. . . dawɴ-vair)* Slice of ham or tongue rolled conically and stuffed with one of various fillings; also called *cornet*.

fin or **fine** *(faɴ, feen)* Thin or fine: a descriptive term which may mean thin or thinly-sliced, finely-chopped or best-quality.

financière, à la *(ah lah fee-nawɴ-syair)* 'As the wealthy businessman likes it': this usually refers to meat or poultry served with a garnish of cockscombs, cock's kidneys, *quenelles* (little mousses), lamb's sweetbreads, olives, mushrooms and truffles. The same garnish is used as a filling for a pie or *vol-au-vent, bouchée financière* being a popular version of the latter.

fine—see *fin*.

fine de claire *(feen də klair)* Type of cultivated oyster.

fines herbes *(feenz airb)* A mixture of very finely-chopped herbs—usually parsley, tarragon, chervil and chives—or finely-chopped parsley alone.

fiouse—see *féouse*.

fixe *(feeks)* Fixed, set, unchanging: a menu term referring to fixed-price menus: *prix fixe*.

flageolet *(fla-zhyo-lā)* Flageolet bean; a small, tender haricot bean, which is white or pale green.

flagnarde or **flangnarde** *(flawɴ-nahrd)* Type of sweet batter-pudding with vanilla or grated lemon-rind baked in a deep dish.

flamande, à la *(ah lah fla-mawɴd)* In the Flemish style: a garnish for large cuts of meat, comprising stuffed cabbage, carrots, turnips, potatoes, and sometimes diced pork-belly and sliced sausage.

> **asperges** *(as-pairzh . . .)* Asparagus served hot with hard-boiled egg and melted butter.
> **carbonnade** *(kar-bon-ahd)* Beef and onions braised in beer with herbs.
> **chou rouge** *(shoo roozh . . .)* Red cabbage stewed with apples, sugar and vinegar.
> **salade** *(sah-lahd . . .)* Salad of potato, chicory and onion strips in *vinaigrette*, garnished with fillets of salt herring.

flambée *(flawɴ-bā)* Flamed or flaming: a method of presenting certain dishes by sprinkling them with

spirit, which is set alight just before serving.

flamiche or **flamique** *(fla-meesh, fla-meek)* Leek (or pumpkin) and cheese tart similar to *quiche*, but covered with a thin layer of pastry.

flammekueche *(flam-køø-kø)* Onion, cream, bacon and cream cheese flan; also called *tarte flambée*.

flan *(flawn)* Open pastry tart filled with a sweet or savoury custard and served either hot or cold—as an *hors d'œuvre*, a light main dish or a dessert; roughly equivalent to the US open-faced pie. Also, a colloquial name for *crème caramel*.

flanchet *(flawn-shā)* Flank of beef, used mainly in stews.

flandre *(flawn-drø)* Colloquial name for the flounder *(flet)*.

flangnarde—see *flagnarde*.

flèche *(flesh)* 'Arrow': a flitch of bacon, or a side of cured, salted bacon.

flet or **flétan** *(flā, flā-tawn)* Flounder or halibut—both are flat sea-fish.

fleuron *(flø-rawn)* Crescent-shaped puff pastry used as a garnish or to top a *pâté en croûte*.

flip, consommé à la *(kawn-so-mā ah lah fleep)* Chicken consommé with strips of lettuce, leeks and ham.

flocon *(flo-kawn)* Flake.

florentine, à la *(ah lah florawn-teen)* In the style of Florence in Italy: a dish, usually of eggs or fish, presented on a bed of spinach, which is then coated with *Mornay* sauce, sprinkled with cheese and browned.

floutes *(floot)* Potato *quenelles*—little mousses made of mashed potato.

flûte *(fløøt)* 'Flute': a thin bread-roll, or a flute-shaped biscuit that is served with ice-cream.

foie *(fwah)* Liver of an animal or bird.
  foie gras *(. . . grah)* 'Fat liver': the enlarged liver of a goose or duck which has been force-fed on maize; served in slices or whole, and very rich.

foin, jambon au *(zhawn-bon ŏ fwahn)* Ham boiled with hay or with herbs, in water.

folle *(fol)* 'Silly' or 'crazy': in menu terms it can mean almost anything, and has connotations similar to *surprise* (see that entry).

fond *(fawn)* Bottom, base, centre, heart, depths.
  fond d'artichaut *(. . . dar-tee-shō)* Artichoke heart.

fondant *(fawn-dawn)* 'Melting': a general term for icing. Also the name for a hot *hors d'œuvre* croquette, which can be made from various purées: vegetable, meat, fish, liver etc.

fonds *(fawn)* General term for cooking-stock.

fondu(e) *(fawn-døø)* Melted, or cooked until melted; vegetables reduced to pulp by slow cooking.

fondue *(fawn-døø)* Name for two popular dishes of Swiss invention, in both of which bite-sized portions of food are dipped into a pot at the table:
  fondue au fromage *(. . . ŏ fro-mahzh)* A simmering mixture of melted cheese, white wine, kirsch, and sometimes eggs into which you dip cubes of bread held on skewers.
  fondue bourguignonne *(. . . boor-geen-yon)* Cubes of steak cooked on forks in hot oil, then eaten with various sauces—but not directly from the cooking fork, unless you enjoy blistering your mouth.

fontanelle, asperges à la *(as-pairzh ah lah fawʀ-tawʀ-nel)* Asparagus, with melted butter and soft-boiled eggs into which the asparagus is dipped.

fontanges, potage *(po-tahzh fawʀ-taʀzh)* Soup of puréed peas with sorrel, enriched with cream and egg-yolk.

forestière, à la *(ah lah fo-res-tyair)* Garnish for meat, poultry or game fowl, consisting of potato balls, mushrooms and salt pork sautéed in butter.

fort(e) *(for(t))* Strong or intense; also, concentrated.

fouace, fouasse or **fougasse** *(fwas, fwahs, foo-gas)* General term for cakes and pastries, particularly hearth cakes.

fouée *(fwā)* A bacon and cream flan; also a colloquial term for hearth cake.

fouettée *(fwā-tā)* Whisked or whipped (eggs, cream etc.).

fougasse—see *fouace.*

four *(foor)* Oven.
   au four *(ō . . .)* Baked or roasted in an oven.

fourchette *(foor-shet)* Fork; dinner fork. Also a colloquial word for a wishbone.

fourré(e) *(foo-rā)* Filled or stuffed. Also a name for a soft-centered sweet *(bon-bon)*.

fraîche or **frais** *(frāsh, frā)* Fresh, cool, refreshing. Where food is concerned, it means new, fresh, or in a fresh state: not aged, cured or otherwise preserved.
   crème fraîche *(krem . . .)* is, paradoxically, slightly sour.

fraise *(frez)* Strawberry; also a colourless strawberry *eau-de-vie* (spirit).
   des bois *(. . . dā bwah)* Wild strawberry; also a sweet wild-strawberry liqueur.

framboise *(frawʀ-bwahz)* Raspberry; also a potent colourless spirit *(eau-de-vie)* made from raspberries.

française, à la *(ah lah frawʀ-sez)* 'In the French style', a general descriptive term which varies from region to region around the country. For example, it can signify a garnish of *duchesse* potato-nests fried in egg and breadcrumbs, and filled with diced mixed vegetables; or asparagus tips, braised lettuce and cauliflower florets, in various combinations; or *Anna* potatoes and spinach.
   petits pois *(pe-tee pwah . . .)* Young peas in butter, with lettuce, parsley and baby onions.

franc-comtoise, à la *(ah lah frawʀ-kawʀ-twahz)* In the style of Franche-Comté in central France:
   potée *(po-tā . . .)* Soup-cum-stew of cabbage, potato and pork with sliced sausage.

francillon, salade *(sa-lahd frawʀ-syawʀ)* Salad of mussels, truffles and marinated potato; also called *salade japonaise.*

frangipane *(frawʀ zhee-pan)* A mixture made of egg-yolks, flour, butter and milk for binding poultry and fish forcemeats; also the name of an almond pastry cream or custard that is used as a filling or topping for various dessert pastries.

frappé *(fra-pā)* Iced or chilled; also, served on (or surrounded by) crushed ice.

frascati, à la *(ah lah fras-ka-tee)* Garnish of *foie gras*, truffles and asparagus-filled mushrooms.

fréchure *(frā-shoor)* Pig's lung stew.

fressure *(fra-seer)* Pig or calf's fry, comprising the

heart, liver and lungs, usually stewed.

fretin *(fre-taʀ)* Spawn; young fish, or fry.

friand(e) *(free-yawʀ(d))* 'Fond of . . .': a small, 'lovable' pastry, especially a sausage-roll, or a little almond cake. A *friand* can also be a small potato cake.
   friand de St Flour
   (. . . de saʀ flor)
   Sausage-meat wrapped in
   pastry or leaves.

friandise *(free-yawʀ-deez)* A sweetmeat or titbit: a term for a *petit-four*, sometimes an iced *petit-four*.

fricadelle *(free-ka-del)* Name for various fried cakes or balls made of minced beef or veal, potatoes or bread, plus onions.

fricandeau *(free-kawʀ-dō)* Name for topside (us: rump) of veal; the name can also refer to a dish of braised veal, a slice or fillet of fish braised in fish stock, or pork pâté cooked in a thin slice of pork; also a sausage-meat ball.

fricassée *(free-ka-sā)* Kind of light stew known as a fricassée in English too: it usually consists of white meat or poultry served in a creamy white sauce, often with mushrooms and onions.

frisée *(free-zā)* 'Frizzy': colloquial term for *chicorée*, the frizzy salad green known as chicory in the USA and curly endive in the UK.

fritelle *(free-tel)* Corsican chestnut-flour fritter, served with cheese.

frites *(freet)* Short for *pommes frites*, e.g. fried potatoes; French fries in the USA, chips in Britain.

fritot *(free-tō)* A deep-fried fritter made with small pieces of poultry, lamb or veal sweetbreads, and brains; usually served with tomato sauce. Also a name for various hot *hors d'œuvres* cooked like fritters.

fritter *(free-tair)* Franglais word for *beignet*. The French authorities are currently trying to discourage the use of such intrusions into their language.

frittons *(free-tawʀ)* Pieces of preserved meat mixed with pork or goose bits and cooked in hot fat until crisp.

friture *(free-toor)* Fried food; often a dish of tiny fried fish, which is particularly popular along the Loire.
   à l'italienne *(. . . ah lee-*
   tal-yen) A *fritto-misto* of
   calf's head, brain, marrow, liver, lambs' feet
   and testicles, either deep
   fried in batter or sautéed
   in butter.

frivole *(free-vol)* A colloquial term for a fritter *(beignet)*.

froid(e) *(frwah(d))* Cold, cool or chilled; often used to distinguish a dish which may be served either cold or hot.

fromage *(fro-mahzh)* Cheese: over 400 generally-available kinds are produced in France, and many of them are described in Section Two of this book.
   blanc *(. . . blawʀ)* 'White
   cheese': a mild, soft,
   slightly salty cheese with
   the consistency of
   yoghurt; eaten with fruit
   or sugar for dessert.
   de brebis *(. . . de brā-*
   bee) Ewe's-milk cheese.
   de chèvre *(. . . de shev-*
   re) Goat's-milk cheese.
   à la crème *(. . . ah lah*
   krem) Cream cheese.
   cuit *(. . . kwee)* Fermented cream cheese, which
   is cooked with butter,
   egg-yolk and milk,
   seasoned, and served
   hot.

fondu (. . . fawʀ-dœ)
General name for processed cheese products.

fort (. . . for) Strong, home-made cheese, fermented and often flavoured with spirits.

frais (. . . frā) Similar to fromage blanc, but with a lower fat content and not salty; the French equivalent of light sour cream.

maigre (. . . mā-grœ)
Low-fat cheese.

à tartiner (. . . ah tar-tee-nā) General term for cheese spread.

de vache (. . . dœ vash)
Cow's-milk cheese.

Fromage is also the French word for brawn: cooked, seasoned meat—usually pork—which is pressed in a mould. The word, which derives from fourme, originally meant any moulded foodstuff.

fromagée (fro-mah-zhā)
With cheese; also, shaped in a mould.

froment (fro-mawʀ)
Wheat, wheat-flour.

fruit (frwee) Fruit in general.

confits (. . . kawʀ-fee)
Preserved or crystallized fruit; also, pickled fruit.

de la passion (. . . dœ lah pa-syawʀ) Passion fruit.

rafraîchis (. . . ra-frā-shee) Fruit salad.

fruiterie (frwee-tœ-ree)
Fruit shop, greengrocer's shop.

fruits de mer (frwee dœ mair) Seafood in general, especially refers to shellfish:

plateau de (plah-tō dœ . . .) Large plate piled with various different shellfish such as winkles, clams, mussels, oysters, prawns, cockles, many of which are raw.

fumée (fœ-mā) Smoked or cured.

de moules (. . . dœ mool) Mussels cooked over pine needles; also called éclade.

fumet (fœ-mā) A strong stock used in many sauces to provide flavour; it is made by boiling the bones and trimmings of meat or fish in wine or water. Vegetable fumet is prepared by boiling down the liquid in which various vegetables have been simmered.

G

gaillarde, sauce (sōs gī-yahrd) See gribiche.

gaillette (gī-yet) See caillette.

galabart (ga-la-bar) Large black pudding (boudin).

galantine (ga-lawʀ-teen)
Name for various dishes made from poultry or meat which is first boned and stuffed, then pressed into a symmetrical loaf and cooked in stock; served cold, in slices.

galathée (ga-la-tā) A shellfish similar to the fresh-water crayfish.

galette (ga-let) Large, flat, round cake. The most frequently encountered are made with flaky-pastry dough, unleavened dough (hearth cake) or yeast dough, but the name is applied to a variety of cakes, tarts and brioches, including Twelfth Night cake (see epiphanie).

lyonnaise (. . . lyon-nez)
Cake of puréed potatoes and onions.

de blé noir (. . . dœ blā nwah) Breton buckwheat-flour pancake filled with cheese, meat or fish.

de pommes de terre (. . . dœ pom dœ tair) Small potato cake, sometimes topped with a piece of meat and served as a garnish.

galicien (ga-lee-syeʀ)
Sponge layer-cake filled with pistachio cream, and coated with apricot jam and pistachio icing.

galimafrée *(ga-lee-ma-frā)* A medieval dish; fried chicken or meat stewed in sour grape-juice with ground ginger.

galopiau or **galopin** *(ga-lo-pyō, ga-lo-pan)* Thick pancake made from batter containing crumbled bread or *brioche*.

gamba *(gawn-bah)* Large prawn.

ganse *(gawns)* 'Braid': a kind of sweet fritter.

gantois *(gawn-twah)* Pastry cake made with spices and layered with greengage or plum jam.

garbure *(gar-bøør)* General term for various thick vegetable and meat soups served with slices of bread which have been covered with some savoury spread. These soups are rich, and usually contain bits of preserved goose, duck, pork or turkey. After consuming the meat, vegetables and bread, the soup's life is extended by pouring a glass of wine into the broth remaining in the bowl; the mixture is then drunk. This operation is called the *goudale* or *chabrol*.

garçon *(gar-sawn)* Boy: a vulgar term for 'waiter', included here as a reminder that it should never be used.

gardon *(gar-dawn)* Roach.

garenne *(ga-ren)* Wild rabbit (as opposed to a domestic one).

gargote *(gar-got)* Slang for a poor restaurant.

gargouillau *(gar-gwee-yō)* Pear tart.

garni(e) *(gar-nee)* Garnished. When this word follows a menu entry—e.g. *steak garni*—it means that the dish is accompanied by vegetables and potatoes (often *pommes frites*).

garniture *(gar-nee-tøør)* Garnish.

gascogne *(gas-kon-yø)* Gascony.
    beurre de *(bor dø . . .)* Butter mixed with pounded garlic.

gasconnade *(gas-ko-nahd)* Leg of mutton roasted with garlic and anchovies.

gasconne, à la *(ah lah gas-kon)* In the style of Gascony in SW France:
    agneau *(an-yō)* Boned shoulder of lamb stuffed with minced ham, bread and garlic.
    omelette *(om-let . . .)* Ham, garlic and parsley omelette.

gastrochère *(gas-tro-shair)* Small shellfish *(fistulane)*.

gastronome *(gas-tro-nom)* Gastronome, a connoisseur of fine food.

gâteau *(ga-tō)* General term for cake; may also be used for a savoury tart or loaf.

gaudes *(gōd)* Thick, maize-flour porridge served either hot, or cold in slices, with cream.

gaufre *(gō-frø)* Waffle: pastry cooked in a waffle iron.

gaufrette *(gō-fret)* Latticed potato crisp/chip.

gauloise, à la *(ah lah gōl-wahz)* A garnish of tartlets filled with mushrooms in cream, or with cockscombs and kidneys.
    consommé *(kawn-so-mā . . .)* Chicken consommé with cockscombs and kidneys.
A *gauloise* is an almond cake spread with apricot jam and topped with chopped, roasted almonds.

gayette *(gā-yet)* See *caillette*.

gazeux *(ga-zø)* Carbonated, fizzy.

gebie *(zhø-bee)* A small, white-fleshed shellfish, cooked like shrimps.

gelatine *(zha-la-teen)* Gelatine.

gelée *(zhə-lā)* Jelly, aspic.

gelinotte *(zha-lee-not)* Hazel grouse, a mountain game bird.

gendarme *(zhawn-darm)* 'Policeman': a salted, smoked herring *(hareng saur)*, or a pickled herring. Also a kind of dry, hard Swiss sausage which vaguely resembles a herring or, conceivably, a policeman.

genevoise, sauce *(sōs zhen-vwahz)* Sauce for salmon or trout made of fish stock, red wine, butter and anchovy essence.

genièvre *(zhən-yev-rə)* Juniper berry, also, gin.

génoise, à la *(ah lah zhān-wahz)* In the style of Genoa in Italy: with tomato sauce.
  pâté *(pa-tā . . .)* Genoese cake: sponge cake used as the basis for a wide variety of desserts.

gentilhomme, potage *(po-tahzh zhawн-tee-yom)* Puréed lentil and game soup garnished with game *quenelles* (little mousses).

georgette, pommes *(pom zhor-zhet)* A hot hors-d'œuvre of baked potato filled with a ragoût of freshwater crayfish tails.

germiny, potage *(po-tahzh zhair-mee-nee)* Sorrel soup enriched with cream and egg-yolks.

gibier *(zheeb-yā)* Wild game:
  à plume *(. . . ah plөөm)* Feathered game.
  à poil *(. . . ah pwahl)* Furred game.
  noir *(. . . nwahr)* 'Black game': hided or bristled game, e.g. wild boar.

gigoret or **gigorit** *(zhee-go-rā, zhee-go-ree)* Pig's head cooked in blood and red wine.

gigot *(zhee-gō)* Leg; hind

leg, normally of lamb or mutton.
  d'agneau *(. . . dan-yō)* Roast leg of lamb.

gigue *(zheeg)* Haunch of venison, wild boar, or other game animal.

gingembre *(zhaн-zhawн-brə)* The spice ginger.

girofle *(zhee-rof-lə)* The spice clove.

girolle *(zhee-rol)* Kind of mushroom: see *chanterelle*.

gîte *(zheet)* Shin of beef.
  à la noix *(. . . ah lah nwah)* Topside or silverside of beef; also called *tendre de tranche*.

givrée *(zhee-vrā)* Frosted or frosty: various frosted citrus-fruit *sorbets* served in their skins.

glaçage *(gla-sazh)* A term for several different operations involving the icing, freezing or glazing of foods, which include the process of making ice-creams and sorbets; the glazing of fish, eggs etc. in white sauce; the icing of cakes; the browning or glazing of meat by basting it with stock in a hot oven; and the coating of carrots and onions in a sugary glaze.

glace *(glas)* Ice; also an ice in the sense of an ice-cream, the icing on a cake, and a meat glaze.

glacée *(gla-sā)* Frozen, iced or ice-cold; also denotes the icing on a cake, and glazed fruit.
  biscuit *(bees-kwee . . .)* Ice-cream on sponge-cake, topped with fruit and liqueur.
  jambon *(zham-bawн . . .)* A term for cooking ham.

glaçon *(gla-sawn)* Ice cube.

gnocchi *(nyo-kee)* Dumplings made of *choux* paste or semolina porridge.
  de pommes de terre *(. . . də pom də tair)* Dumplings made from

183

puréed potato mixed with flour.

à la romaine (*. . . ah lah rō-men*) Semolina dumplings sprinkled with grated cheese.

gobie (*go-bee*) Goby, a tiny sea fish that is usually cooked by frying it; also called *goujon de mer*.

godard (*go-dar*) Garnish of *quenelles* (little mousses), cockscombs, kidneys, sweetbreads and truffles, served with poultry or on its own as a second course.

gombaut or **gombo** (*gom-bō*) Okra (hence the thick okra soup called 'gumbo' in the USA); often prepared stewed with tomatoes.

gorenflot (*go-rawн-flō*) A garnish of sausage, potatoes and red cabbage; also the name of a rich, hexagonal pastry made with baba dough.

goudale (*goo-dahl*) Wine added to the broth remaining from a *garbure* to 'extend' it; for details, see under *garbure*.

gouerre or **gouéron** (*gwair, gwā-rawн*) The general name for a group of cakes and tarts made with potatoes and cheese (Burgundy), or with apples or goat's-milk cheese (Berry).

gouffé (*goo-fā*) Garnish of little *duchesse* potato-nests filled with asparagus and mushrooms.

gougelhopf (*goo-gəl-opf*) Sweet *brioche*: see *kougelhopf*.

gougère (*goo-zhair*) Pastry ring made of *choux* paste mixed with *gruyère* cheese.

gougnette (*goon-yet*) Large, sugar-topped fritter or doughnut.

goujon (*goo-zhawн*) Freshwater gudgeon, or *goujonette*. In culinary terms, a *goujon* is a small piece of filleted fish, coated

in flour or egg and bread-crumbs, and fried.

goulasch (*goo-lash*) Hungarian goulash: beef stew with diced onions and paprika, also known as *gulyas*.

gourmand(e) (*goor-mawn(d)*) One who enjoys eating good food.

gourmet (*goor-ma*) A connoisseur of fine food and wine.

gousse d'ail (*goos dī*) Clove of garlic.

goût (*goo*) Taste, in several senses of the word: a flavour, a relish or preference, and a little bite or sample.

goûter (*goo-tā*) To taste, to try (a food, wine etc.).

goyave (*go-yahv*) The tropical fruit guava.

goyère (*go-yair*) A tart filled with a mixture of strong *Maroilles* cheese and cream.

grain (*gran*) Grain, berry or bean.
   grain de raisin (*. . . də rā-zaн*) Grape.
   grains de café (*. . . də ka-fā*) Coffee beans.

graisse (*gres*) Grease, fat, cooking fat, lard or dripping. See also *gras* (fatty).

graisserons (*gres-rawн*) Potted pork meat.

gramolate (*gra-mo-laht*) Water-ice: a sorbet (US: sherbet) made without the inclusion of egg-whites; also called *granité*.

grand(e) (*grawn(d)*) Large, big, great, important.

grand cru (*grawn kroo*) 'Great growth': a top-ranking wine. See the wine notes under Burgundy in Section Two.

grand-duc, œufs (*əf grawн dөk*) Poached eggs in *Mornay* sauce with truffles and asparagus tips.

grand marnier (*grawн*

marn-yā) Much-prized orange liqueur from Cognac in SW France.

grand veneur, sauce *(sōs grawn ve-ner)* Sauce for game based on pepper sauce, to which redcurrant jelly, cream and sometimes hare's blood is added.

granité *(grawn-nee-tā)* A water-ice, usually served sprinkled with sugar; see also *gramolate*.

granvillaise, colin à la *(ko-lan ah lah grawn-vee-yez)* Marinated hake, fried and served with shrimps.

grapiau *(grap-yō)* Name for thick pancakes in central France, some made with potatoes, others sweet; also called *sanciau*.

grappa *(grah-pah)* A colloquial name for *marc* brandy in general; more particularly, it is *marc* flavoured with the evergreen herb rue, a drink originating in N Italy. *Grappa* is also a kind of processed cheese coated with grape pips.

gras or **grasse** *(grah, gras)* Fleshy, fatty, oily or greasy. The term can also be applied to any dish that includes meat; thus, *Mardi-Gras* ('Fat Tuesday', Shrove Tuesday), the last day of Carnival, signals the ending of festivities before Lenten fasting begins.

The same word also denotes the fat content of different foods, especially dairy products, which is expressed as a percentage. So *10% de matières grasses* on the label indicates that the product has a ten per cent fat content.

gras-double *(grah-doo-ble)* Ox tripe.

grasset *(gra-sā)* Thinly-cut flank of beef.

gratin *(gra-tan)* Any dish which is browned in the oven to form a top crust—usually of breadcrumbs and grated cheese—just before it is served.

au gratin *(ō . . .)* Prepared as a *gratin*.

gratinée *(gra-tee-nā)* Cooked *au gratin*: see previous entry. The term is also applied to any soup that is topped with browned, grated cheese, and is a familiar name for traditional French onion soup, which is served on bread and topped with browned, grated cheese.

grattons or **gratterons** *(gra-tawn, grat-rawn)* Bits of 'crackling', made from the residue of the melted fat of pork, goose or turkey; it is salted while still hot, then served cold as an *hors d'œuvre*.

gratuit(e) *(grat-weet)* Free; without charge; complimentary.

grecque, à la *(ah lah grek)* In the Greek style: describes vegetables stewed with oil, coriander and other herbs and served as an *hors-d'œuvre* (often cold); artichokes *(artichauts)* and mushrooms *(champignons)* are often prepared in this way.

grenade *(gre-nahd)* Pomegranate.

grenadier *(gre-nahd-yā)* Sea fish with delicate white flesh, named for the shape of its head which supposedly resembles a French grenadier's cap.

grenadins *(gre-nah-dan)* Small slices of veal fillet cut into triangular or rectangular shapes, interlarded with bacon, and braised; other meat or poultry is sometimes prepared in this way too.

grenoblois, gâteau *(ga-tō gre-nō-blwahz)* Rich walnut cake.

grenouille *(gren-wee-ye)* Frog; also short for frog's leg.

griaudes (*gree-yōd*) See *beursaudes*.

gribiche, sauce (*sōs gree-beesh*) Sauce for fish, composed of hard-boiled egg-yolks pounded with oil and vinegar plus chopped capers, herbs, gherkins and strips of egg-white; also called *sauce gaillarde*.

grignaudes (*green-yod*) Crisply-fried cubes of pork.

grillade (*gree-yahd*) Grilling; food which has been grilled (US: broiled). The word sometimes refers to a mixed grill.

grillé (*gree-yā*) Grilled.
pain (*paʀ . . .*) 'Grilled bread': toast.

grillettes (*gree-yet*) Bits of fatty meat grilled until they are crispy, particularly pork and duck.

grillons (*gree-yawʀ*) Bits of duck, goose or pork meat left over from preserving as *confits*. Sometimes included in 'surprise' salads; see *surprise* and *fantaisie* for comment.

grive (*greev*) Thrush, usually made up into pâtés or terrines, which are frequently—and heart-rendingly—known as *pâté de petit oiseau sauvage* (pâté of little wild bird). Tasty, though.

grondin (*grawʀ-daʀ*) Gurnard, a sea fish with white, flaky flesh.

gros(se) (*grō(s)*) Large or oversized; the large version or variety of something.

gros-blanquet (*grō blawʀ-kā*) Greenish-yellow pear, sweet but with a gritty texture.

groseille (*grō-zā*) Red-currant.
à maquereau (*. . . ah mak-rō*) Gooseberry.

gros sel (*grō sel*) Rock salt; coarse-grained salt.

gruyère (*gree-yair*) Swiss

cheese; see *emmenthal* for details.

gryphée (*gree-fā*) Variety of oyster (*huître*), more commonly called the Portuguese oyster.

guigne (*geen-yə*) Variety of cherry used to make cherry brandy (*guignolet*).

guillaret (*gee-ya-rā*) A kind of sweet pastry.

guitare (*gee-tahr*) Colloquial name for a variety of skate (*raie*) shaped like a flat guitar or violin, which explains its other name: *violon*.

gulyas (*geel-yas*) Hungarian goulash: beef stew with diced onions and paprika; also called *goulasch*.

gymnètre (*zheem-net-rə*) Kind of Mediterranean fish similar in flavour to the cod.

H

haché(e) (*a-shā*) Chopped, minced or ground.
bifteck haché (*biftek . . .*) Hamburger
sauce hachée (*sōs . . .*) Brown sauce with vinegar, tomato puree, chopped ham, mushrooms, capers and gherkins.

hachis (*a-shee*) Hash: a dish based on leftover meat that is chopped or minced and combined with various other ingredients in a sauce.
parmentier (*par-mawn-tyā*) Shepherd's pie.

hachua (*ash-wah*) Bayonne ham (sometimes beef) stewed with peppers and onions.

haddock (*a-dok*) Smoked haddock; fresh haddock is called *aiglefin*.

halicot de mouton (*a-lee-kō də moo-tawʀ*) Mutton stew garnished with turnips, potatoes, onions and sometimes with haricot beans; also called *haricot de mouton*.

hambourgeoise, bifteck à la *(bif-tek ah lah am-boor-zhwahz)* Hamburger.

hareng *(a-rawɴ)* Herring.
  baltique *(bal-teek)* Small Baltic herring.
  blanc *(. . . blawɴ)* Salt herring.
  frais *(. . . frā)* Fresh herring.
  fumé *(. . . fθθ-mā)* Smoked herring.
  pec *(. . . pek)* Freshly-salted herring.
  roulé *(. . . roo-lā)* Roll-mop herring: marinated, spiced herring rolled around a gherkin.
  salé *(. . . sa-lā)* Salt herring.
  saur *(. . . sōr)* Smoked herring.
A kippered herring is the same in French and English: kipper.

haricot *(a-ree-kō)* Bean in general, including both true beans (e.g. kidney beans, lima beans etc.) and edible bean pods (e.g. string beans, French beans etc.).
  blanc *(. . . blawɴ)* White bean, either fresh *(frais)* or dried *(sec)*.
  beurre *(. . . bθr)* Butter bean.
  de Lima *(. . . dθ lee-mah)* Lima bean.
  d'espagne *(. . . des-pan-yθ)* Runner bean.
  de Mouton *(. . . dθ moo-tawɴ)* See *halicot*.
  rouge *(. . . roozh)* Red kidney bean.
  vert *(. . . vair)* French bean or string bean.
Broad or shell beans are described under *fève*, *féverole* and *fevette*.

hâtelette *(at-let)* General name for food cooked on a *hâtelet* (skewer).

hâtereau *(at-rō)* Morsel of food coated in egg and breadcrumbs and fried on a skewer; served coated with sauce as a hot *hors*

d'œuvre or light main course.

haut or **haute** *(ō, ōt)* High; excellent; superior quality.

havraise, lapin à la *(la-ʀah ah lah av-rez)* Rabbit in the style of Le Havre: roast saddle of rabbit, with bacon, served with cream sauce.

hénon *(ā-nawɴ)* Colloquial name for a cockle *(coque)*.

Henri Duvernois *(awʀ-ree dθθ-vair-nwah)* Method of preparing lobster *(homard)* with leeks and mushrooms in a sherry and brandy cream sauce, with rice.

Henri IV *(awʀ-ree kat-rθ)* Garnish of artichoke hearts filled with *béarnaise* sauce, fried potato-balls, truffles and watercress.
  poule au pot *(pool ō pō . . .)* Chicken stuffed with liver and ham and cooked in wine.

herbe *(airb)* Herb; grass.

hérisson *(ā-ree-sawʀ)* Hedgehog, considered a delicacy in some quarters (not mine).

hirondelle *(ee-rawn-del)* Swallow.

hochepot *(osh-pō)* Flemish hotpot: a thick meat soup of oxtail, beef, mutton and various parts of the pig, with cabbage, leeks, potatoes and other vegetables.

hollandaise, sauce *(sōs o-lan-dez)* Tangy sauce made of egg-yolks, butter, vinegar and lemon juice whisked over heat; served warm with eggs, fish and vegetables.

holstein, veau *(vō ol-shtīn)* Sautéed escalope of veal garnished with fried eggs and anchovies.

homard *(ō-mar)* Lobster.

homère, crème d' *(krem dom-air)* Egg custard with honey, wine, cinnamon and lemon.

hongroise, à la *(ah lah oʀ-gwahz)* Hungarian-style: a description of a number of dishes (of eggs, fish and meat) cooked with onions and tomatoes in a cream sauce seasoned with paprika.
    sauce *(sōs . . .)* Creamy white sauce with chopped onions and paprika.

hors d'œuvre *(or-dəv-rə)* Common term for the first course or starter. It may also refer to a selection of hot or cold appetizers served with drinks at table before the first course *(hors d'œuvres à la Russe)*, and to an array of various salads, cold meat dishes and smoked or marinated fish from which you can make your own selection as a first course.

hôte *(ōt)* Curiously enough, this means both host *and* guest.
    table d'hôte *(ta-blə dōt)* Fixed-price menu: see 'In the Restaurant' in Section One.

hôtel *(ō-tel)* Hotel, but also a large town house or public building.
    de ville *(. . . də veel)* City/town hall.
    meublé *(. . . mə-blā)* Lodging house.

hôtelière, à la *(ah lo-təl-yair)* With parsley butter *(beurre maître d'hôtel)* and mushrooms.

hôtellerie *(ō-tel-ree)* Inn or hostelry.

houblon *(oo-blawʀ)* Hops (the kind used in beer-brewing).
    jet d'houblon *(zhā doo-blawʀ)* Hop shoot.

houx *(oo)* Holly.

huile *(weel)* Oil; cooking oil in general.
    d'amande *(. . . dah-mawʀd)* Almond oil.
    d'arachide *(. . . da-ra-sheed)* Peanut oil.
    de maïs *(. . . də ma-ees)* Corn oil.
    de noix *(. . . də nwah)* Walnut oil.

d'olive *(. . . də-leev)* Olive oil.
de soja *(. . . de so-zhah)* Soya bean oil.
de tournesol *(. . . də toorn-sol)* Sunflower oil.

huître *(wee-trə)* Oyster. There are many large oyster beds or 'parks' down the west coast of France. The two main types of oyster eaten are the flat *belons*, considered to be the finest, and the rougher-shelled *creuses* or *portugueses*, which are far more common. There are lots of ways of cooking oysters, but they are usually eaten raw with lemon juice and pepper, brown bread and butter, and copious quantities of chilled white wine.

huîtrier *(wee-tryā)* Oyster-catcher, a marsh bird.

hure de porc *(əer də por)* Pig's head in jelly.

hypocras *(ee-po-kras)* Spiced mulled red wine.

I

igname *(een-yam)* Yam, a type of sweet potato.

île flottante *(eel flo-tawʀt)* 'Floating island': a dessert of whipped poached egg-whites floating in vanilla custard and topped with almonds. Also the name of a dessert consisting of sponge cake slices layered with apricot jam, currants and chopped almonds, which are then steeped in Kirsch, iced with *Chantilly* cream and coated in vanilla custard.

imbrucciate—see *embrucciate*.

impératrice, à l' *(ah laʀ-pair-ah-trees)* 'As the empress likes it': a base for desserts composed of rice mixed with whipped cream, custard and crystallized fruit.

imperiale (*aн-pā-ryal*) A name for several rich garnishes composed variously of cockscombs, truffles, crayfish and soft roes and *foie gras*. Also a type of plum, and a term for a large bottle for wine or spirits holding about four litres.

indienne, à l' (*ah laн-dyen*) East-Indian style: with rice and curry sauces.
  sauce (*sōs . . .*) White sauce containing herbs and curry powder, enriched with cream.
  sole (*sol . . .*) Fillets of sole cooked in a *coulis* of tomatoes and apples in coconut milk and cream flavoured with curry powder.

infusion (*aн-fөө-zyawн*) General term for herb teas and other 'natural' teas which are prepared by steeping the ingredient in question in boiling water to extract its essence.

irlandaise, consommé à l' (*kawн-so-mā ah leer-lawн-dez*) Clear soup with chopped mutton, pearl barley and vegetables.

isard—see *izard*.

italienne, à l' (*ah lee-tal-yen*) Italian style: with *sauce italienne*, or with finely-chopped mushrooms.
  sauce (*sōs . . .*) Brown sauce with chopped mushrooms, ham and tarragon.
  salade (*sa-lahd . . .*) Diced potatoes, carrots, turnips, asparagus tips and peas in mayonnaise with anchovies, salami, tomatoes, olives, capers, and hard-boiled eggs.
  friture (*free-tөөr . . .*) See under *friture*.

izard (*ee-zahr*) Rare Chamois mountain antelope, prepared like roebuck; also spelled *isard*.

izarra (*ee-zah-rah*) Yellow or green liqueur similar to *Chartreuse*.

J

jacque (*zhak*) Apple pancake.

jalousie (*zha-loo-zee*) 'Venetian blind': a small, latticed flaky-pastry cake filled with almond paste and spread with jam.

jambon (*zhawн-boн*) Ham, or leg. Here are the main types of ham:
  blanc (*. . . blawн*) Cooking ham or boiling ham; also called *demi-sel, glacé* and *de Paris*.
  de Bayonne (*. . . de bī-yon*) Lightly-smoked ham eaten raw; also used in various dishes.
  de campagne (*. . . de kawн-pan-ye*) Country ham, smoked and salted according to varying local custom; also called *jambon de montagne* or *de pays*.
  cru (*. . . krөө*) Uncooked ham; raw ham.
  demi-sel (*. . . de-mee sel*) See *blanc* above.
  fumé (*. . . fөө-mā*) Smoked ham.
  glacé (*. . . gla-sā*) See *blanc* above.
  de montagne (*. . . de mawн-tan-ye*) See *de campagne* above.
  de Paris (*. . . de pa-ree*) See *blanc* above.
  de Parme (*. . . de parm*) Parma ham; smoked ham eaten raw in paper-thin slices.
  de pays (*. . . de pā*) See *de campagne* above.
  salé (*. . . sa-lā*) Cured ham
  de York (*. . . de york*) Ready-cooked ham.

There are two main types of *jambon* in the sense of 'leg':
  de porc or **de marcassin** (*. . . de por, de mar-kah-saн*) Leg of pork or wild boar.
  de poulet (*. . . de poo-lā*) Boned, stuffed leg of chicken, usually braised.

jambonneau *(zhawʀ-bo-nō)* Small cooked ham; delicatessen ham, already prepared for eating.

japonaise, à la *(ah lah zha-po-nez)* Japanese style: with Chinese artichoke (called Japanese in French).
  salade *(sa-lahd . . .)* In fact there are two kinds of *salade japonaise*. The first comprises sliced tomato, orange and pineapple sprinkled with lemon juice and sour cream, while the second is a salad of mussels, celery and marinated potatoes with sliced truffles (this is also called *salade francillon*).

jardinière, à la *(ah lah zhardin-yair)* Garnish of several different fresh garden vegetables, which are cooked separately and served in individual groups around the main dish; usually served with roasts, braised meat or pot-roasted poultry.

jarnac *(zhar-nak)* Meringue sponge-cake with jam and cognac; also called *coup de jarnac*.

jarret *(zha-rā)* Shin and/or knuckle of veal or beef.

jau au sang *(zhō ō sawʀ)* Chicken in a blood-thickened sauce.

jaune d'œuf *(zhōn dəf)* Egg-yolk.

jean-doré *(zhawʀ do-rā)* John Dory, a sea fish better-known in France as the *Saint-Pierre*.

Jessica *(zhes-ee-kah)* Garnish of tiny stuffed artichokes, morels and *Anna* potatoes (potato cakes) with a cream sauce; for chicken or veal.

jésuite *(zhā-zweet)* Little flaky-pastry triangles filled with almond paste.

jésus *(zhā-zəə)* Smoked, pork-liver sausage, served hot.

jet de houblon *(zhā də oo-blawʀ)* Hop shoot.

joinville *(zhwaʀ-veel)* Garnish for baked fish, composed of shrimps, mushrooms and truffles in a cream sauce.

joue *(zhoo)* Cheek or jowl of an animal or a fish.

jubilé *(zhoo-bee-lā)* 'Jubilee'.
  potage *(po-tahzh . . .)* Puréed pea soup with chopped vegetables; also called *potage balvet*.
  cerises *(sə-reez . . .)* Poached cherries flamed with kirsch.

juif or **juive** *(zhweef, zhweev)* In the Jewish style.
  carpe *(karp . . .)* Carp braised in white wine, which is served cold in aspic with onion sauce.
  schaleth *(sha-let . . .)* Apple pie made with pasta (noodle paste).

julienne *(zhee-lyen)* Matchstick strips: vegetables, sometimes other ingredients, cut into fine strips for adding to soups, using in garnishes, sauces etc.
  consommé *(kawʀ-so-mā . . .)* Clear soup garnished with thin strips of carrots, leeks, celery, cabbage etc.

jurassienne, à la *(ah lah zhee-ra-syen)* In the style of the Jura, or of Franche-Comté in E France.
  brochette *(bro-shet . . .)* Skewered pieces of cheese wrapped in ham and fried in butter.
  croustade *(kroos-tahd . . .)* Cheese and bacon filled pastries or toasts.
  omelette *(om-let . . .)* Onion and bacon omelette filled with sorrel.

jus *(zhee)* Juice.
  de citron, de tomate etc. *(. . . də see-trawʀ, də tom-art)* Lemon juice, tomato juice . . .
  au jus *(ō . . .)* Roast meat served in its own cooking juice.

K

kaffeekrantz *(ka-fā-krants)* Alsatian raisin-cake, eaten with coffee.

kaki *(ka-kee)* Persimmon.

kalereï *(kal-ra-ee)* Sort of pork brawn with pig's trotters, tail and ears.

kari *(ka-ree)* Curry; also spelled *cari*.

kassler *(kas-lair)* Rolled, smoked fillet of pork.

katoff, poulet *(poo-lā ka-tof)* Chicken split down the back, flattened out and grilled; served on *duchesse* potatoes.

kebab *(kā-bab)* General term for meat cooked on a skewer.

kiev *(kee-ev)* Deep-fried breast of chicken stuffed with herb-and-garlic butter.

kig ha fars *(keeg ah fars)* Breton dish of beef, pork and oxtail slowly cooked with vegetables, served with cabbage and buckwheat dumplings.

kig sal rosten *(keeg sal rosten)* Breton salt-pork roll.

kipper *(kee-pair)* Kippered herring: a large herring, split in half and lightly smoked.

kir *(keer)* Aperitif of dry white wine mixed with the blackcurrant liqueur *crème de cassis*; also called *blanc-cassis*.

kirsch *(keerch)* *Eau-de-vie* or spirit made from the distilled juice of wild black cherries; used extensively in cooking and highly prized by connoisseurs of such things.

kissel *(kee-sel)* Dessert of moulded mixed berries, served hot or cold with double cream; Russian in origin.

knackwurst *(nak-vöörst)* Sausage from the Alsace region, like a frankfurter.

knepfle *(knöp-föl)* Small dumpling, sometimes fried like a fritter; from Alsace.

kokeboterom *(kok-bo-tröm)* Raisin *brioche* (bun).

kougelhopf *(koo-göl-hopf)* Ring-shaped *brioche* cake from Alsace, with raisins, currants and almonds, sometimes steeped in kirsch.

kouign amann *(kween a-man)* Type of Breton puff-pastry cake layered with sugar.

koulibiac *(koo-lee-byak)* See *coulibiac*.

kromesqui *(kro-mes-kee)* See *cromesqui*.

kugelhopf *(kö-gel-hopf)* See *kougelhopf*.

kummel *(köö-mol)* Caraway-seed liqueur.

kumquat *(kööm-kah)* Kumquat: a miniature Chinese orange, which can be eaten raw, used in salads, or made into marmalade.

L

l' and **la** are forms of the French word meaning 'the'.

lache *(lash)* Small, delicate, highly-regarded sea fish similar to the smelt.

laguipière, sauce *(sōs la-gee-pyair)* Creamy white sauce containing chopped truffles and *Madeira*. An older recipe gives it as a reduction of consommé with butter, nutmeg and vinegar.

lait *(lā)* Milk.
  barratté *(. . . ba-ra-tā)* Buttermilk.
  demi-écrémé *(. . . de-mee ā-krā-mā)* Semi-skimmed milk.
  écrémé *(ā-krā-mā)* Skimmed milk.
  entier *(. . . awн-tyā)* Full cream milk.
  ribot *(. . . ree-bō)* Thinned yoghurt.
  stérilizé *(. . . stā-ree-lee-zā)* Long-life milk.

laitages *(lā-tahzh)* Dairy products in general.

laitance or **laite** *(lā-tawʀs, lāt)* Soft roe (of fish).
laitances en sabot *(. . . awʀ sa-bō)* Baked potatoes stuffed with soft herring roes.

laiterie *(lā-tree)* Dairy; dairy shop.

laitier *(lā-tyā)* Made of or with milk; the word also denotes a commercially-made product as opposed to *fermier*, meaning farm- or home-made.

laitue *(lā-tɵɵ)* Lettuce.
batavia *(. . . ba-tav-yah)* Crinkly, bitter Batavia lettuce.
romaine *(. . . ro-men)* Cos lettuce; romaine lettuce.

lamballe, potage *(po-tahzh lawʀ-bal)* Thick soup made of puréed fresh peas and consommé thickened with tapioca.

lambeau *(lawʀ-bō)* A scrap or shred of meat.

lambick *(lawʀ-beek)* Kind of very strong Belgian beer.

lame *(lam)* 'knife-blade': a term meaning a very fine slice.

lamproie *(lawʀ-prwah)* Lamprey or lamprey eel; a fish similar to the true eel *(anguille)*, and caught in estuaries; most frequently prepared by being stewed in wine.

landaise, à la *(ah lah lawʀ-dez)* In the style of the Landes region in W France, where geese are much in evidence; in general, *à la landaise* means that the dish is cooked in goose fat, with garlic and (often) onions, pine nuts and ham.
becfigue or **becfin** *(bek-feeg, bek-faʀ . . .)* Fig-pecker, a tiny bird, which is wrapped in bacon and vine-leaves then spit-roasted or grilled on a skewer; *ortolans* (bunt-ings) are also cooked in this manner.
omelette *(om-let . . .)* Omelette cooked in goose fat with pine nuts and garlic.
ortolan *(or-to-lawʀ . . .)* See *becfigue* above.
pommes *(pom . . .)* Potatoes fried in goose fat, with garlic, chopped onions and ham.

langouste *(lawʀ-goost)* Spiny lobster; crawfish, similar to a lobster but without claws.

langoustine *(lawʀ-goos-teen)* Scampi: the delicate pink shellfish also called the Dublin Bay prawn.

langue *(lawʀg)* Tongue.
de boeuf *(. . . dɵ bɵɵf)* Ox tongue.
de chat *(. . . dɵ sha)* 'Cat's tongue': a small, thin crispy biscuit (named for its shape) served with iced desserts, ice-cream, liqueurs, sweet wines etc. Also used as an ingredient, whole or crumbled, in puddings. Bitter chocolates of a similar shape are also made under this name.
de veau *(. . . dɵ vō)* Calf's tongue.

languedocienne, à la *(ah lah lawʀ-gɵ-dō-syen)* In the style of Languedoc in SW France: with tomatoes, eggplant (aubergine), mushrooms *(cèpes)* and garlic, in various combinations.
escargots *(es-kar-gō . . .)* Snails in a spicy sauce with ham, anchovies, tomatoes and chopped walnuts (also called *lou cagaraulat*).
gratin *(gra-taʀ . . .)* Aubergines layered with tomatoes, topped with parsley, breadcrumbs and grated garlic, then baked until golden.
pâté de pigeon *(pa-tā dɵ pee-zhawʀ . . .)* Pigeon pie with mushrooms, bacon, chicken livers, olives and sautéed salsify.

languier *(lawʀ-gyā)* Smoked pork tongue.

lapereau *(lap-rō)* Young rabbit.

lapin *(la-paʀ)* Rabbit.

lard *(lahr)* Pork fat; larding bacon; a side of bacon. Lard in the English and US sense is rendered, refined pork fat which is called *saindoux* in French.

lardé *(lahr-dā)* Larded, referring to meat which has been threaded or picked with lard before cooking.

lardons *(lahr-dawʀ)* Lardoons: strips of larding fat. Also a name for diced, fried pieces of bacon, that are used in garnishes or as an ingredient in hotpots, *daubes* etc.

lasagnes *(la-zan-ye)* Lasagna: an Italian dish of baked pasta and cheese, with meat sauce.

laurier *(lō-ryā)* Bay: the spice whose leaves are often added to casseroles etc. for flavour.

la varenne *(lah va-ren)* Herb mayonnaise mixed with finely-chopped mushrooms and shallots (*duxelles*).

lavaret *(la-va-rā)* Highly-regarded lake fish of Savoie in E France, which is related to the salmon.

le *(le)* The.

leberknepfen *(lā-bair-knep-fən)* Calf's-liver dumplings or quenelles (tiny poached mousses); Alsatian in origin, and sometimes called *lewerknepfles*.

lèche *(lesh)* 'Lick': a thin slice or sliver.

leckerli *(lā-kair-lee)* Sweet, spicy biscuits with honey, almonds and citrus peel; Swiss in origin.

légumes *(lā-gøøm)* Legumes; vegetables in general but, more specifically, leguminous or pod vegetables.

lentilles *(lawʀ-tee)* Lentils.

les *(lā)* Plural form of the French word meaning 'the'.

letchi or **litchi** *(let-chee, lee-chee)* The oriental fruit lichee.

levadou *(le-va-doo)* Pig's lung stew; also called *frechur*.

levraut *(le-vrō)* Leveret; young hare.

lewerknepfle *(le-vair-knep-fel)* See *leberknepfen*.

liards, pommes en *(pom awʀ lyahr)* Very thin deep-fried potato chips, served with game.

liaison *(lee-ā-zawʀ)* A thickening agent such as arrowroot, or a mixture of egg-yolks and cream, which is added to soups and sauces.

lie *(lee)* Lees or dregs; the sediment left at the bottom of the cask after the wine has been racked (transferred to another cask). *Sur lie* is a term for a wine bottled directly from the cask without first being racked; as a result it can taste very fresh and grapy.

lié(e) *(lee-yā)* From 'liaison'; a term used in sauce-making which means thickened or bound (with some ingredient such as flour).

liégeoise, à la *(ah lah lyā-zhwahz)* In the style of Liège in Belgium: with juniper berries and/or gin.
  café *(ka-fā . . .)* Dessert of iced coffee poured over ice-cream and topped with whipped cream.
  écrevisses *(ek-rev-ees . . .)* Poached crayfish with a whisked-up butter sauce.
  rognons de veau *(ron-yawn də vō . . .)* Calf's kidneys casseroled with juniper berries and gin.

lierwecke *(leer-vek)* Raisin *brioche* (bun) from Alsace.

lièvre *(lyev-rə)* Hare.

limaçon *(lee-ma-sawʀ)* Alternative term for *escargot* (snail).

193

limande *(lee-mawʀd)* Dab, a flatfish similar to sole.
  sole limande *(sol . . .)* Lemon sole.

limon *(lee-mawʀ)* Lime. The French word for lemon is *citron*, but *citron vert* is another name for lime.

limonade *(lee-mo-nahd)* Bottled lemonade; freshly-squeezed lemon juice is *citron pressé*.

limousine, à la *(ah lah lee-moo-zeen)* In the style of Limousin in central France: with red cabbage, chestnuts and *cèpe* mushrooms, in various combinations.
  chou farci *(shoo far-see . . .)* Cabbage stuffed with bacon and chestnuts.
  chou rouge *(shoo roozh . . .)* Red cabbage shredded and stewed with pork fat and chopped chestnuts.

lingue *(laʀg)* Ling; a long, slender relative of the cod.

linot(te) *(lee-nō, lee-not)* Linnet.

liqueur *(lee-ker)* liqueur: the general name for a variety of alcoholic drinks which are made from a mixture of distilled spirits and flavoured syrups, and traditionally taken at the conclusion of a meal or as a nightcap. *Vin de liqueur* is a strong, sweet wine, such as port. See also *ratafia*, which is the French name for a home-made liqueur.

lit *(lee)* Bed. In cooking, the word denotes a 'bed' of one or more ingredients used as a base on which others are served, or the bottom-most layer of a layered dish.

litchi – see *letchi*.

Loire, friture de la *(free-teer də lah lwahr)* Tiny fish, deep-fried and served with lemon.

Longchamp, potage *(po-tazh loʀ-shawʀ)* Thick soup of puréed peas with finely-chopped sorrel, chervil and vermicelli.

longe *(loʀzh)* Loin (of meat).

longuet *(loʀ-gā)* Bread-stick.

longueville, potage *(po-tazh loʀg-veel)* Thick soup made from peas, leeks and lettuce.

lonzo *(loʀ-zō)* Marinated and salted fillet of pork, dried and eaten uncooked as an *hors d'œuvre*, or made into sausages.

lorette, pommes *(pom lo-ret)* Small, crescent-shaped *dauphine* potatoes.

lorgnette *(lorn-yet)* 'Opera-glass': a rolled fish fillet.

lorraine, à la *(ah lah lo-ren)* In the style of Lorraine in NE France: with a garnish of red cabbage cooked in red wine, with horseradish and sautéed potato balls.
  œufs *(ef . . .)* Eggs baked on a bed of bacon and cheese with cream.
  potée *(po-tā . . .)* Hearty soup/stew of pork, bacon, sausage, cabbage and various other vegetables.
  quiche *(keesh . . .)* An open tart with a filling of smoked bacon, eggs, cream and, sometimes, cream cheese.
  tourte *(toort . . .)* Pie filled with pork and veal in cream.

lotte *(lot)* Monkfish: an ugly but highly-regarded sea fish.
  joues de *(zhoo də . . .)* Monkfish cheeks, rightly considered a great delicacy in France.
  des lacs or **de rivière** *(. . . dā lak, do ree-vyair)* Burbot—not a misprint for 'turbot' but an eel-like freshwater fish, highly prized for its flavour.

lou *(loo)* Provençal term for a house or dwelling-place, possibly derived from *lieu*, a location or place; on the menu, *lou* means 'house style', 'speciality' or 'local dish'.

cagaraulat *(. . . ka-ga-rō-lah)* See *languedociene, escargots à la.*

magret *(. . . ma-grā)* See *magret de canard.*

loubine *(loo-been)* The grey mullet.

loukinka *(loo-kaʀ-kah)* Spicy garlic sausage.

loup *(loo)* Wolf; the French don't normally eat wolves, but use *loup* figuratively as a name for sea bass *(bar)*.

de mer *(. . . de mair)* 'Sea wolf': another version of the name for sea bass.

marin *(. . . ma-raʀ)* Also 'sea-wolf': this time it's the tasty wolf fish.

lou trébuc *(loo trā-bøk)* Preserved, potted meat of duck, goose, turkey or pork; usually added to a *garbure.*

lucas, hareng *(a-rawʀ løø-kah)* Smoked herring fillets served cold in a mustard-flavoured mayonnaise garnished with dillweed.

lucullus, œuf *(øf løø-køø-løs)* Poached egg on an artichoke heart, coated in a cream sauce, and garnished with *foie gras* and truffles.

lyonnaise, à la *(ah lah lyoʀ-nez)* In the style of Lyon and its surrounding region: often indicates the presence of onions, or a garnish of braised, stuffed onions and sautéed potatoes.

cervelas *(sair-vø-lah . . .)* Smoked pork sausage sometimes studded with truffles and pistachios and served *en brioche* (wrapped in *brioche* pastry).

gâteau *(ga-tō . . .)* A chocolate and chestnut cake.

gras-double *(grah-doo-ble . . .)* Ox tripe fried with onions and parsley.

gratinée *(grah-tee-nā . . .)* Beef consommé with port and egg (sometimes onions), topped with toasted bread and cheese.

omelette *(om-let . . .)* Omelette filled with onions and parsley.

pommes *(pom . . .)* Sliced potatoes fried with onions.

saladier *(sa-la-dyā . . .)* Calf's head, sheep's and pig's trotters and ox muzzle in a *vinaigrette* dressing with shallots.

sauce *(sōs . . .)* White wine and onion sauce.

M

macaire, pommes *(pom ma-kair)* Baked potatoes mashed with butter, formed into flat cakes, and fried.

macaron *(ma-ka-rawʀ)* Macaroon.

macédoine *(ma-sā-dwahn)* General term for a mixture of vegetables (raw or cooked), or of fruit—i.e. a fruit salad.

macéré(e) *(ma-sā-rā)* Macerated: softened by steeping or soaking, often in alcohol or pickling brine.

mâche *(mash)* Lamb's lettuce: a pale-green, delicately-flavoured salad leaf which is supple rather than crisp.

macis *(ma-see)* The spice mace.

mâconnaise, à la *(ah lah ma-koʀ-nez)* In the style of Mâcon in central France: usually describing meat or fish cooked in *Mâcon* wine.

macreuse *(ma-krøz)* Cut of beef shoulder.

madeleine *(mad-len)* A puffy, bite-sized sponge cake made of flour, butter, eggs and sugar, delicately flavoured with vanilla, orange or lemon, and baked in a shell-shaped mould.

madère *(ma-dair)* The fortified wine *Madeira*, from the Portuguese island of the same name; served as an aperitif and used extensively in cooking.
   sauce madère *(sōs . . .)* Meat stock *(demi-glace)* mixed with *Madeira* wine.

madérisé *(ma-dā-reesā)* Maderized; descriptive of wine that has turned brown and flat through oxidation and old age.

madrilène, à la *(ah lah ma-dree-len)* In the style of Madrid: with tomatoes or tomato juice.
   consommé *(kawн-so-mā . . .)* Chicken consommé with tomato pulp and diced sweet peppers.
   saucisse *(sō-sees . . .)* Ring-shaped sausage of pork and veal forcemeat and sardine fillets.

magistère *(ma-zhee-stair)* A general term for rich, nourishing meat and vegetable soups, invented by Brillat-Savarin.

magnum *(mag-nom)* Magnum: a bottle, normally of champagne, which is twice the size of an ordinary bottle, i.e. holding approximately 1.5 litres.

magret de canard *(ma-grā də kan-ar)* Breast of duck, which is either grilled or fried and often served fairly rare, in thin slices; also known as *maigret* and *lou magret*.

maigre *(mā-gre)* Adjective meaning 'slim', 'lean' or 'low-fat'; see also under *cuisine*. The same word can also refer to vegetable soup, and to the meagre fish.

maigret *(mā-grā)* See *magret*.

maillot *(mī-yō)* 'Vest' or 'swimsuit': a garnish for meat of mixed vegetables with *Madeira* sauce.

maingaux *(maн-gō)* A mixture of whipped cream and *crème fraîche*, which is served with fruit; also spelled *mingaux* or *mingots*.

maintenon, appareil à *(a-pah-rā ah maнt-nawн)* A mixture of puréed onions and shredded mushrooms in thick white sauce, used either as a garnish or as a filling for pastries.
   omelette maintenon *(om-let . . .)* Omelette filled with chicken and mushrooms, covered in a white onion sauce, then sprinkled with cheese and browned.

maïs *(mah-ees)* Maize; corn; sweetcorn; corn-on-the-cob.
   flocons de *(flo-koн də. . .)* Cornflakes.

maison *(mā-zawн)* House; a menu term meaning both 'home-made' and 'the speciality of the house'.
   vin maison *(vaн . . .)* House wine: the wine chosen by a restaurant as its everyday table wine.

maître de chai, entrecôte *(awн-trə-kot me-trə də shā)* Steak 'cellar-master style': either served in a red wine sauce or, more correctly, grilled over vine twigs *(sarments)* or the wood from old wine-barrels.

maître d'hôtel *(me-trə dō-tel)* The head waiter.
   beurre *(bər . . .)* Parsley butter served with grilled meat and fish.

maltaise, sauce *(sōs mal-tez)* *Hollandaise* sauce mixed with the grated peel and juice of blood oranges or of tangerines.

malvoisie, vin de *(vaн də mal-vwah-zee)* Malmsy wine.

mandarine *(mawн-da-reen)* Mandarin orange.

mange-tout *(mawnzh too)* 'Eat everything': the sugar pea, which is eaten shell and all; can be served raw, steamed, par-boiled, or lightly sautéed in butter.

mangue *(mawng)* Mango.

manière, à la *(ah lah man-yair)* 'In the style . . .'.

manouls *(ma-nool)* Sheep's tripe simmered in white wine with tomatoes.

manqué *(mawn-kā)* Moulded sponge-cake topped with praline and crystallized fruit.

maquereau *(ma-krō)* Mackerel, a fairly oily sea-fish often eaten smoked as well as fresh.

maraîchere, à la *(ah lah ma-rā-shair)* 'Market-gardener style': a garnish for roasts and braised meat of mixed vegetables, which vary according to the season.

marasquin *(ma-ras-kan)* Maraschino cherry; also, a liqueur made from Maraschino cherries.

marc *(mar)* The residue of pressed grapes; short for *eau-de-vie de marc*, a clear brandy distilled from the pressed grapes left over from wine-making, including the skins, pips and stalks. It is normally drunk as a *digestif*, or as a pick-me-up with black coffee (*café-marc*) whenever the need strikes. *Marcs* from the better wine-growing regions, notably Burgundy and Champagne, are highly regarded; others are more of an acquired taste.

marcassin *(mar-kah-san)* Young wild boar; yearling.

marchand de vin *(mar-shawn də van)* Wine-merchant.
>   **entrecôte** *(awn-trə-kot . . .)* Entrecote steak served in a sauce or butter made of red wine, shallots and meat stock, often garnished with sliced bone-marrow.

maréchale, à la *(ah lah ma-rā-shal)* 'As the field-marshal likes it': descriptive of sliced meat, poultry or fish fillets fried in a coating of egg and breadcrumbs, and garnished with truffles and asparagus tips.

marengo, poulet or **veau** *(poo-lā, vō ma-rawn-go)* Sautéed chicken or veal cooked with onions, tomatoes and garlic in white wine, garnished with mushrooms, fried croutons and (sometimes) crayfish tails and fried eggs.

marenne *(ma-ren)* An oyster raised in the oyster beds at Marennes, on the west coast of France; usually greenish, and considered particularly fine.

marigny, à la *(ah lah ma-reen-yee)* Garnish of artichokes stuffed with sweetcorn in cream and browned potato balls.
>   **potage** *(po-tahzh . . .)* Pea soup garnished with chopped French beans and fresh peas.

marinade *(ma-ree-nahd)* Marinade, or marinating liquid: usually a mixture of wine, vinegar, seasoning, herbs and spices, oil and sometimes vegetables, in which ingredients are steeped for preserving, flavouring or tenderizing.

mariné(e) *(ma-ree-nā)* Marinated or pickled.

marinière, moules à la *(mool ah lah ma-reen-yair)* Mussels cooked in white wine, with shallots and herbs.

marivaux *(ma-ree-vō)* Garnish of French beans and *duchesse* potato-nests which are filled with finely-chopped carrots, artichoke hearts and mushrooms in *béchamel* sauce, then browned with a topping of parmesan cheese and breadcrumbs.

marjolaine *(mar-zho-len)*
The herb marjoram.

marly, le *(lə mar-lee)*
Rum-soaked *brioche* cake
filled with strawberries and
cream.

marmelade *(mar-mo-lad)*
Thick purée of fruit, or
sweet stewed fruit; what
we would call marmalade
is called in French *confiture
d'oranges.*

marmite *(mar-meet)* A
metal or earthenware cooking-pot for stews, etc., and
a general name for certain
dishes that are cooked in a
marmite.
  petite *(pə-teet . . .)*
  Nourishing clear meat
  soup containing a variety
  of diced vegetables and
  sometimes chicken.

marocaine, à la *(ah lah ma-
ro-ken)* Moroccan-style: a
garnish of diced courgettes
(US: zucchini), peppers,
stuffed with chicken
forcemeat, and saffron rice,
with a tomato-flavoured
sauce; served with lamb.

marquis, le *(lə mar-kee)*
Chocolate sponge cake
with a butter-cream filling.

marron *(ma-rawn)* Chestnut.
  d'Inde *(. . . dand)* Horse-
  chestnut.
  glacé *(. . . gla-sā)* Candied chestnut (very delicious and very
  expensive).

marsala *(mahr-sah-lah)* A
sweet Italian wine similar
to sherry or madeira,
which is drunk as an
aperitif and used in
cooking.

mascotte, à la *(ah lah mas-
cot)* A garnish for small
meat and poultry dishes of
sautéed, sliced artichoke
hearts, browned potato
balls and truffles; a *mascotte* is a hazelnut coffee
cake.

massenet *(ma-sen-ā)*
Garnish of individual *Anna*
potatoes, little artichokes

filled with a bone-marrow
salpicon, and French
beans.
  œufs brouillés *(əf brwee-
  yā . . .)* Scrambled eggs
  with sautéed artichoke
  hearts, *foie gras* and
  asparagus tips.

massepain *(ma-sə-pan)*
Marzipan: a paste of
ground almonds, sugar and
egg-whites made up into
sweets or *petit-fours,* or
used as a topping or filling
in confectionary.

matafan *(ma-ta-fawn)*
Type of thick, heavy
pancake, also spelled
matefaim.

matefaim *(mat-fan)* See
matafan.

matelote *mat-lot)* General
name for stew of fresh-
water fish (usually including eel and pike) cooked in
red or white wine.
Matelote à la Normande is
a sea-fish stew cooked with
cider and *velouté* sauce. The
name *matelote* is also (incor-
rectly) applied to several
veal and poultry dishes
where the ingredients are
stewed in wine.

matignon *(ma-teen-yawn)*
Fondue of mixed veg-
etables (vegetables reduced
to pulp by slow cooking),
sometimes with chopped
ham added, served as a
garnish with a variety of
dishes.

mauve *(mōv)* Mallow, a
salad vegetable.

mayonnaise *(ma-yō-nez)*
Mayonnaise.

mayorquina *(ma-yor-kee-
nah)* A Majorcan cabbage
and tomato soup, made
with garlic, onions, pimentos, leeks and herbs.

mazarin *(ma-za-ran)*
Genoese sponge cake,
hollowed in the centre
and filled with chopped,
crystallized fruit.

méchoui *má-shwee)* North
African term meaning
'roasted': a fat lamb or

sheep is roasted over coals and constantly basted to produce golden-brown crackling, without charring the skin; as the roasting normally occurs out-of-doors and involves a lot of people, the word *mechoui* has become generic in French for a barbecue—but it really refers only to one where a lamb or a sheep is cooked.

médaillon *(mā-dī-yawn)* 'Medallion': a general name for any food that is cut into the shape of a medallion; the word also refers to a round, flat slice of meat, and is a synonym for *tournedos* of beef and veal, and *noisette* of lamb.

médicis, bombe *(bom mā-dee-see)* Ice-cream *bombe* lined with pear ice and filled with iced peach mousse and slivers of kirsch-soaked peach.

megin, tarte au *(tar ō mə-zhan)* Cream cheese tart made with *fremgeye*, a cream cheese home-made in Lorraine; also called *tarte au m'gin* or *mougin*.

mehlsuppe *(mel-sӨӨ-pə)* German leek and onion soup made with flour, butter, stock and cream; also called flour soup (*soupe à la farine*) and sweet-and-sour soup (*soupe aigre-douce*).

mélange *(mā-lawʀzh)* Mixture or blend.

melba *(mel-bah)* Garnish of braised lettuce and little tomatoes filled with finely-diced chicken, mushrooms, and truffles bound in *velouté* sauce, then topped with breadcrumbs and browned.
    pêches *(pesh . . .)* Vanilla ice-cream topped with peaches in syrup and coated in raspberry purée.

melon *(mə-lawʀ)* The general name for all varieties of melon.

d'eau *(. . . dō)* Spanish watermelon; what English-speakers know as watermelon is called *pastèque* by the French.
    sucrin *(. . . sӨӨ-kraʀ)* Honeydew melon.

melsat *(mel-sa)* Type of *boudin blanc*: a large, soft, white pork-sausage.

ménagère, à la *(ah lah mā-nah-zhair)* 'Home-style': with vegetables in general and onions in particular.
    œufs *(Өf . . .)* Fried eggs served on a bed of sautéed vegetables with tomato sauce.
    sole *(sol . . .)* Sole baked on a bed of vegetables, with a red wine sauce.

mendiant *(mawʀ-dyawʀ)* See *quatre mendiants*.

mendole) *(mawʀ-dol)* Picarel, a relative of the sea bream.

menon *(mə-nawʀ)* Roast of kid goat.

menthe *(mawʀt)* Mint.

mentonnaise, à la *(ah lah mawʀ-tawʀ nez)* Garnish of sautéed artichokes, potato 'olives' and courgettes stuffed with rice.

menu *(mə-nӨӨ)* Menu or bill of fare: a course-by-course listing of all the dishes being served at a given meal. Nearly all restaurants will offer two or more menus for both lunch and dinner, each with its own fixed price (*menu prix fixe*), though certain items in a given course may be marked for supplementary charge; see *carte* for further details.

mer *(mair)* Sea or ocean; saltwater.

mercédès *(mair-sā-des)* A garnish of mushrooms, potatoes, lettuce and tomatoes.
    consommé *(kawʀ-so-mā . . .)* Chicken consommé with sherry, sliced cock's kidneys and cockscombs.

mère de sole (*mair də sel*) See *limandelle*.

mère filloux, poularde à la (*poo-lard ah lah mair fee-yoo*) Chicken stuffed with sausage-meat and cooked with sliced truffles under the skin; served in a cream sauce with lamb's sweetbreads.

mère poulard, omelette à la (*om-let ah lah mair poo-lar*) Plain fluffy omelette cooked over an open fire.

meringue (*mə-rang*) Meringue: egg-whites beaten until they are stiff then folded with sugar and cooked in the oven in various ways.

merlan (*mair-lawn*) Whiting, the sea fish; also a colloquial word for hake (*colin*).

merle (*mairl*) Blackbird, usually made into a pâté.

merlus (*mair-lee*) Colloquial names for the hake (*colin*), and, confusingly, for salt cod (*morue*) too; also called *merluzza*.

merluchon (*mair-lee-shawn*) Colloquial name for *colineau* (codling).

merluzza (*mair-lee-za*) See *merlus*.

merveille (*mair-vā*) 'Marvel': a deep-fried sweet fritter topped with vanilla sugar, and sometimes flavoured with brandy.

mesclun (*mes-klan*) Mixed salad greens, including lamb's lettuce, chicory, endive, fennel, wild herbs and even edible weeds: delicious!

méthode (*mā-tod*) Term for preserved pork meat that is sometimes added to *garbure*.

méture (*mā-təər*) Maize-flour fritter with ham and eggs.

meunière, à la (*ah lah mən-yair*) Method of preparing fish by seasoning, flouring lightly and frying in butter, then serving sprinkled with parsley and lemon juice in the hot cooking butter.

meurette (*mə-ret*) A mixture of stock and red wine, bacon, carrots, onions and mushrooms, which is used for poaching fish, meat and eggs; the liquid is then reduced and thickened and served as a sauce with the dish. A speciality of Burgundy, where *meurette* is sometimes synonymous with *matelote*.

mias (*mee-yah*) Also spelled *millat*, this is a type of cherry cake made with batter mixture; similar to *clafoutis*.

miche (*meesh*) Term for a large, round loaf of white bread; also called a *boule*.

mie (*mee*) Crustless bread; the soft centre of a loaf; a crumb.
    pain de mie (*pan də . . .*) Sliced, packaged sandwich loaf.

miel (*myel*) Honey.

migliassis (*meel-ya-sees*) Corsican chestnut-flour cake.

mignardise (*meen-yahr-deez*) Alternative name for a *petit-four* (a sweetmeat often served after a meal).

mignon (*meen-yawn*) 'Dainty' or 'adorable': a small, tender fillet steak (*filet mignon*).

mignonnette (*meen-yawn-net*) A small, round fillet of lamb, also called a *médaillon* or a *noisette*; also a term for coarsely-ground peppercorns (usually white).

mijot (*mee-yō*) Soup of red wine and bread; also spelled *miot*.

milanais (*mee-lah-nā*) Sponge cake laced with aniseed liqueur, spread with apricot jam and topped with aniseed-flavoured icing.

milanaise, à la *(ah lah mee-lah-nez)* In the style of Milan in Italy: a garnish of macaroni tossed in butter and grated cheese with shredded ham, pickled tongue, mushrooms and truffles in a tomato sauce; served with chicken, veal, fried eggs and risotto.

Alternatively, this description may indicate a garnish of little semolina cheese gnocchi, browned.

millas *(mee-ya)* Maize-flour porridge which is eaten either hot with sugar and cream, or left to cool then sliced and fried. Alternatively the mixture may be spread in a flan dish and topped with fruit such as cherries, plums, apples etc. or jam, then sprinkled with crushed macaroons and melted butter and baked in the oven until browned. This concoction is known variously as *millia(ssou), millat, milliat, milliard*, and *millot*.

millat *(mee-yah)* See *mias* and *millas* above.

mille-feuille *(meel føy)* Cake consisting of paper-thin layers of puff-pastry alternating with layers of cream or jam, baked and then decorated with chopped nuts or some other topping. Also a starter, similarly constructed and baked, but layered with fish, vegetables etc. and served with a cream sauce.

millet *(mee-yā)* The cereal grain millet.

millia or **milliard** *(meel-yah)* See *millas*.

milliassou *(meel-yah-soo)* Lemon sponge-cake made with millet; see also *millas*.

milliat *(meel-yah)* See *millas*.

millière *(meel-yair)* Rice and maize porridge.

millot *(mee-yō)* See *millas*.

mimosa *(mee-mo-zah)* Mimosa flower: a bright yellow, edible flower sometimes sprinkled over soups or salads. Also a salad or soup containing chopped, hard-boiled egg-yolk, and a name used in S France for a summer drink of chilled champagne mixed with freshly-squeezed orange juice: sounds much better than Buck's Fizz, and is.

minceur *(man-ser)* Thinness or slimness; see *cuisine* and *nouvelle cuisine*.

minéral(e) *(mee-nā-ral)* 'Mineral': short for mineral water *(eau minérale)*.

minestrone *(mee-nā-stro-nā)* Italian minestrone: thick vegetable soup.

mingaux or **mingots** *(man-gō)* See *maingaux*.

minute *(mee-nøøt)* Minute (i.e. sixty seconds): descriptive of steak or fish (usually sole) grilled or fried quickly and simply, with butter, parsley and sometimes lemon juice.

miot *(mee-yō)* See *mijot*.

mique *(meek)* Maize-flour dumpling eaten as bread or as an accompaniment to soups or stews. They can also be fried then sprinkled with sugar and served as a dessert.

mirabeau, à la *(ah lah mee-ra-bō)* Garnish of anchovy strips criss-crossed on top of a piece of meat, plus olives, tarragon and anchovy butter.

mirabelle *(mee-ra-bel)* Small, golden plum used in confectionary, made into jams and preserves, or distilled into a clear spirit.

mirette, œufs *(øf meer-et)* Tartlet filled with a poached egg-yolk topped with chicken and truffle *salpicon* and coated in a cream sauce.

mirepoix *(meer-pwah)* General term for a mixture of chopped vegetables (usually carrots, onions and celery), slowly simmered, sometimes with diced ham, and used to enhance the flavour of sauces or to accompany certain meat, fish, or shellfish dishes.

mirliton *(meer-lee-tawʀ)* Flaky pastry tartlet with an almond or vanilla cream filling.

miroir, œufs au *(ǝf ō meer-wahr)* Baked eggs, so-called because the cooked egg-white forms a mirror-like surface over the yolk.

miroton de bœuf *(mee-ro-tawʀ dǝ bǝf)* Sliced boiled beef in onion sauce.

missiasoga *(mee-seya-soga)* Dried goat's meat (Corsica).

mississa *(mee-see-sah)* Corsican dish of grilled strips of smoked, marinated pork.

mode, à la *(ah lah mod)* General term meaning 'in the style'.
    bœuf *(bǝf . . .)* Large piece of beef braised in red wine and served hot with onions and carrots; the beef can also be served cold in aspic.

moderne, à la *(ah lah mo-dairn)* Garnish of mixed vegetables with braised stuffed lettuces and little potatoes.

moelle *(m'wel)* Bone-marrow.

mogette or **mojette** *(mo-zhet)* Kind of haricot bean; also spelled *mougette*.

moka *(mo-kah)* Mocha: an Arabian coffee-bean used in making rich, after-dinner coffee, and as a flavouring in cakes, creams and ice-cream.

mokatine *(mo-kah-teen)* Little mocha-flavoured cake or *petit-four*.

mollet or **mollette** *(mo-lā, mo-let)* Soft; soft-boiled.

monaco, consommé *(kawn-so-mā mo-na-kō)* Chicken

consommé thickened with arrow-root and garnished with little cheese-flavoured rounds; also a cream of chicken soup *(crème)* garnished in the same way.

monselet, à la *(ah lah mawʀ-sǝ-lā)* A garnish of truffles, artichoke hearts and fried potatoes.

montagnarde, soupe *(soop mawʀ-tan-yard)* Thick vegetable soup with grated cheese.

montbardoise, truite à la *(trweet ah lah mawʀ-bahr-dwahz)* Trout stuffed with shallots and spinach.

mont-blanc *(mawʀ-blawʀ)* Meringue filled with chestnut purée, topped with a mountain of whipped cream.

mont-bry *(mawʀ-bree)* Garnish of little cheese and spinach cakes and *cèpes* (mushrooms) in cream.

mont-dore, pommes *(pom mawʀ-dor)* Mound of mashed potatoes mixed with cream and cheese, browned in the oven.

monte-cristo *(mawʀt krees-tō)* Sweet flan with an almond filling; also called a *montpensier*.

montmorency *(mawʀ-mo-rawʀ-see)* A type of cherry; also the name given to various tarts, mousses, soufflés, ice-creams and cakes containing cherries and sometimes kirsch or cherry brandy.
    caneton *(kan-tawʀ . . .)* Roast duck with poached cherries in a port sauce.

montpensier *(mawʀ-pawʀ-syā)* A garnish of asparagus tips and truffles in madeira sauce; see also *monte-cristo*.

morceau *(mor-sō)* Morsel, piece, tiny bit or crumb; also a portion or single serving (e.g. of cake or cheese).

morille *(mor-ee)* Morel mushroom: tall and grey

brown, with an egg-shaped cap and honeycomb-like pockets. Found in spring, and highly prized for its flavour.

Mornay, sauce *(sōs mor-nā)* Sauce composed of white *béchamel* sauce and cheese.

mortadelle *(mor-tah-del)* Italian mortadella sausage or *bologna*, served in thin slices on its own, or with other sliced sausages and meats as an *hors d'œuvre*.

morteau, Jésus de *(zhā-zθθ dθ mor-tō)* Large smoked sausage.

morue *(mo-rθθ)* Salt cod, also called *merlu* and *merluche*. Fresh cod is called *cabillaud*.

morvandelle, à la *(ah lah mor-vawʀ-del)* In the style of the Morvan region of Central France:
   jambon *(zhawʀ-boʀ . . .)* Ham in a piquant creamy sauce made with white wine, vinegar, juniper berries, shallots and cream; also called *jambon en saupiquet* and *jambon à la crème*.
   rapée *(ra-pā . . .)* Grated potato mixed with eggs, cream and cheese, baked until it is golden.

muscovite *(mos-ko-veet)* The name is given to various desserts made, supposedly, in the style of Moscow. These are often hexagonal in shape, and include Bavarian cream *(bavarois)*; a vanilla-flavoured iced pudding; a kummel and almond ice-cream *bombe*; and a number of fruit and liqueur jellies covered in a thin layer of frost.

mostèle *(mos-tel)* Rockling, a small sea-fish, found mainly in the Mediterranean.

mou *(moo)* Lights: the lungs of an animal.

mouclade *(moo-klad)* Mussels, cooked in a creamy wine sauce with tumeric and saffron.

mougette *(moo-zhet)* See *mogette*.

mougin *(moo-zhaʀ)* see *m'gin*.

moule *(mool)* Mussel; also, a mould for pastry confectionery.

moulé(e) *(moo-lā)* shaped, moulded or cooked in a mould.
   crème *(krem . . .)* Baked custard dessert.

moulu(e) *(moo-lθθ)* Ground or milled.

mourtaïrol *(moor-tay-rol)* Thick, stew-like soup made with ham, chicken, beef, saffron and selected vegetables.

mousquetaire, sauce *(sōs moos-kθ-tair)* 'Musketeer's sauce, which is made of mayonnaise mixed with a little meat glaze and chopped shallots.

mousse *(moos)* 'Foam': a general term for a cold soufflé or frothy dessert, and also for various savoury purée dishes mixed with whisked egg-white or whipped cream to soufflé consistency.

mousseline *(moos-leen)* A general name for airy, mousse-like dishes containing whipped cream and/or egg-whites, e.g. purées of fish, game, shellfish or poultry mixed with whipped cream and egg-white, which can be poached and served hot in a sauce or served cold in aspic. Also a term used in confectionery for light, frothy cakes and pastries.
   pommes *(pom . . .)* Puréed potatoes mixed with butter, egg-yolks and whipped cream; also the name of a packaged mashed-potato mix.
   sauce *(sōs . . .)* Hollandaise sauce mixed with whipped cream.

mousseron, vrai *(vrā moos-θ-roʀ)* St George's mushroom: has a stubby stalk and a round, bulbous cap whose colour can vary. Grows in spring.

mousseuse or **mousseux** *(moo-sez, moo-se)* 'Frothy' or 'foamy': a general term for sparkling wines of any kind.
  sauce *(sōs . . .)* Softened butter whisked with lemon juice and whipped cream, served cold with fish.

moutarde *(moo-tard)* Mustard.

mouton *(moo-tawʀ)* Sheep or mutton; the principal cuts are:
  baron *(ba-rawʀ)* Saddle and both hind legs.
  carré *(ka-rā)* Best end of neck, crown, rack, rib chops or cutlets.
  collet *(ko-lā)* Neck; scrag end of neck.
  côtes or **côtelettes** *(kot, kot-let)* Loin, loin chops or cutlets.
  côtes de filet *(kot də fee-lā)* Chump chops; mutton chops.
  épaule *(ā-pōl)* Shoulder; rolled shoulder roast.
  gigot *(zhee-gō)* Shank or leg.
  médaillon *(mā-dī-yawʀ)* See *noisette*.
  mignonnette *(meen-yawʀ-net)* see *noisette*.
  noisette *(nwah-zet)* Small, round, boned cutlet; also called *médaillon* and *mignonnette*.
  poitrine *(pwah-treen)* Breast; boneless rolled breast.
  selle *(sel)* Saddle.

mulet *(moo-lā)* The grey mullet: a sizeable and very popular sea fish.

mûre *(meer)* Mulberry.
  sauvage *(. . . sō-vazh)* 'Wild mulberry': blackberry.

murène *(mee-ren)* Moray eel.

muscade *(mees-kahd)* The spice nutmeg.

muscadelle *(mees-ka-del)*

A type of pear *and* a type of grape.

muscat *(mees-kat)* Type of musky aromatic grape.

museau *(mee-zō)* Muzzle: the nose or snout of an animal—particularly ox, pig or beef.

musette, bœuf en *(bœf awʀ mee-zet)* 'Beef in a rucksack' or 'kitbag': a rolled-up piece of beef-shoulder, usually braised; also called *bœuf en ballon*.

mye *(mee)* A type of clam.

myrtille *(meer-tee)* A bilberry or whortleberry.

N

nage, à la *(ah lah nazh)* 'In the swim': a method of cooking small lobsters and freshwater crayfish by poaching them in *court-bouillon* flavoured with herbs.

nancéienne, omelette à la *(om-let ah lah nawʀ-sā-yen)* Onion omelette filled with slices of fried black pudding.

nanette *(na-net)* Garnish of artichokes stuffed with lettuce in cream and mushrooms filled with truffles.

nantais *(nawʀ-tā)* Type of almond biscuit; also a name for a Nantes duckling.

nantaise, à la *(ah lah nawʀ-tez)* In the style of Nantes in Britanny, particularly:
  rouget *(roo-zhā . . .)* Grilled red mullet in a shallot and white wine sauce to which its liver (chopped) is added.

nantua, à la *(ah lah nawʀ-t'wah)* Nantua is noted for crayfish, so in dishes cooked *à la nantua* look for their presence—or their tails, which are often served with:
  poulet *(poo-lā . . .)* Poached chicken with chicken *quenelles*

(mousses) and shrimps in *sauce nantua*.

sauce *(sōs . . .)* White sauce with cream, puréed crayfish and butter.

napolitain *(na-po-lee-tan)* Large almond-pastry cake layered with fruit jams.

napolitaine, à la *(ah lah na-po-lee-ten)* In the style of Naples in Italy: with tomatoes, spaghetti, cheese etc.

sauce *(sōs . . .)* A brown sauce flavoured with horseradish, redcurrant jelly, herbs and *Madeira*, sometimes including chopped ham, sultanas and candied citron; served with beef and game.

tranche *(trawnsh . . .)* Neopolitan ice-cream, composed of alternating layers of ice-cream and iced mousse, shaped like a brick and served in slices *(tranches)*.

narbonnaise, escargots à la *(es-kar-gō ah lah nahr-bo-nez)* Snails in a sauce of mayonnaise mixed with milk and ground almonds.

natte *(nat)* Plaited loaf of bread; see also *fantaisie*.

nature or **au naturel** *(na-tøør, ō na-tøør-el)* Natural, plain, ungarnished, unseasoned or unmixed; with nothing added.

navarin *(na-va-ran)* Ragoût of mutton or lamb cooked with onions and potatoes, or with spring vegetables *(navarin printanier)*.

navet *(na-vā)* Turnip.

nectarine *(nek-ta-reen)* Nectarine: a smooth-skinned peach.

nèfle *(nef-lø)* Medlar, a very tart fruit not unlike a crab apple.

neige *(nezh)* 'Snow' or 'snowy':

œufs à la *(øf ah lah . . .)* Poached egg-white mousses in a thin vanilla custard.

nemrod, consommé *(kawn-so-mā nem-ro)* Game consommé with port, garnished with little game *quenelles* (mousses).

néroli *(nā-ro-lee)* Little orange-flavoured almond cakes.

nesselrode, pouding *(pooding ne-sol-rod)* Ice-cream pudding, containing puréed chestnuts, maraschino liqueur, dried and candied fruit and whipped cream.

neuvic, carpe à la *(karp ah lah nø-veek)* Carp filled with a rich mixture of truffles and *foie gras*, then baked in a wine sauce.

néva, poularde à la *(poo-lard ah lah nā-vah)* Chicken stuffed with chicken forcemeat, *foie gras* and truffles, served cold in *chaud-froid* sauce coated in aspic.

newburg, homard à la *(ō-mar ah lah nø-bøørg)* Lobster newburg: sautéed lobster in a madeira and cream sauce.

niçoise, à la *(ah lah nees-wahz)* In the style of Nice, on the Côte d'Azur: with various combinations of tomatoes or tomato *coulis*, garlic, anchovies, capers, artichokes, olives, new potatoes and courgettes (zucchini); basil and tarragon may well register on the taste buds too.

omelette *(om-let . . .)* Tomato omelette with anchovies.

poulet *(poo-lā . . .)* Roast chicken served with a tomato sauce and braised courgettes, artichokes, new potatoes and olives.

ravioli *(rav-yo-lee . . .)* Ravioli stuffed with minced meat and spinach or Swiss chard, topped with grated cheese and baked; canneloni is also prepared in this way.

salade *(sa-lahd . . .)* Famous salad of which

there are several versions:
the basic ingredients in-
clude lettuce, tomatoes,
hard-boiled eggs, an-
chovies and olives;
French beans, onions,
artichokes, peppers,
capers and tuna are often
added. The dressing is a
garlicky *vinaigrette* made
with olive oil and
seasoned with herbs such
as tarragon, chervil and
basil.
  sauce *(sōs . . .)* Mayonnaise mixed with tomato
purée, tarragon, and
chopped pimentos.

nid *(nee)* Nest: a
hollowed-out 'nest' of some
foodstuff (usually potato)
in which the main in-
gredient of the dish is
served.

nîmoise, à la *(ah lah neem-
wahz)* In the style of
Nîmes in S France:
  carbonnade *(kar-bon-
ard . . .)* Lamb or mut-
ton stewed very slowly
with bacon, potatoes,
garlic, herbs and olive oil.
  escargots *(es-kar-gō . . .)*
Snails in a garlic and herb
sauce containing chopped
ham and anchovies.
  potage de poissons *(po-
tahzh də pwah-sawn . . .)*
Fish and vegetable *bouillon*, thickened with egg
yolks and *aïoli.*.

ninon *(nee-non)* Garnish
of *duchesse* potato-nests
filled with cockscombs and
kidneys, in marrow sauce.

nivernaise, à la *(ah lah
nee-vair-nez)* A garnish of
miscellaneous vegetables
including glazed onions
and carrots.
  omelette *(om-let . . .)*
Omelette filled with ham,
chives and sorrel.

Noël *(no-wel)* Christmas:
  bûche de *(bøøsh de . . .)*
Chocolate Christmas
'log'.
  estouffat de *(es-too-fah
de . . .)* Beef stewed
with shallots in wine and
armagnac.

noir *(nwahr)* Black, dark
or burnt.
  beurre *(bər . . .)* Butter
cooked to a dark-brown
colour, mixed with capers
and parsley.

noisette *(nwah-zet)* Hazelnut or, figuratively, anything small and round—
especially a small, round
piece of meat, normally
lamb or mutton, cut from
the fillet, rib or top leg.
  beurre *(bər . . .)* Butter
cooked to a light hazelnut
brown.
  café *(ka-fā . . .)* Coffee
with the cherry liqueur
kirsch and cream added.
  pommes *(pom . . .)*
Little potato-balls
browned in butter.
  sauce *(sōs . . .)* Hollandaise sauce mixed with
beurre noisette.

noisettine *(nwah-zə-teen)*
Pastry cake filled with
hazelnut cream.

noix *(nwah)* Nut, especially a walnut.

nominoë *(no-mee-nō-wā)*
Puréed chestnut and cream
soup.

nonat *(no-nah)* Tiny
Mediterranean fish used in
omelettes, or deep-fried as
an *hors-d'oeuvre*; see also
poutina.

nonnette *(no-net)* Spiced
gingerbread cake with
icing made in Dijon and
Reims.

noque *(nok)* A type of
quenelle (little dumpling)
used in soups, especially in
Alsace.

normande, à la *(ah lah nor-
mawn)* In the style of
Normandy: a fishy garnish
for fish, consisting of
poached oysters, crayfish,
mussels, shrimps, sliced
mushrooms and truffles.
see *sole* below.
  filet mignon de porc *(fee-
lā meen-yawn də por . . .)*
Pork tenderloin cooked in
cider with apples and
onions, served with
caramelized apple rings.

graisse *(gres . . .)* Mixture of pork and beef fat with herbs, used for cooking.

matelote *(mat-lot . . .)* Sea-fish stew, usually of gurnard, sole and conger eel, with cider and cream.

omelette *(om-let . . .)* Omelette filled either with mushrooms and shrimps, or with apples, cream and *Calvados*.

pommes *(pom . . .)* Sliced potatoes layered with leeks and parsley and baked in stock.

salade *(sa-lahd . . .)* Diced potatoes, celery and ham in a cream dressing.

sauce *(sōs . . .)* Rich white sauce made with fish stock and cream, and often with white wine or cider, too.

sole *(sol . . .)* Originally this dish consisted of sole poached in cider and cream with shrimps; today the sole is poached in white wine and served in *sauce normande* (made with wine) with the elaborate garnish described above.

note *(not)* Note: another name for the bill or check *(l'addition)*.

norvégien *(nor-vā-zhyen)* Rich almond sponge-cake.

norvégienne, à la *(ah lah nor-va-zhyen)* Norwegian-style:
 omelette *(om-let . . .)* Baked Alaska: ice-cream served either in a piping hot pastry cake, or ice-cream on a sponge base coated in hot meringue.
 saumon *(sō-mawʀ . . .)* Salmon served cold in aspic.

nougat *(noo-ga)* Famous soft sweet/candy from Montélimar in Provence, made of almonds or walnuts.

nougatine *(noo-ga-teen)* Vanilla-flavoured sponge cake layered with praline

cream and coated in thick chocolate icing.

nouilles *(n'wee)* Noodles.
 nouillettes *(n'wee-yet)* Small *nouilles*.

nouvelle cuisine *(noo-vel kwee-zeen)* 'The new cooking': a relatively recent reaction in French cooking which rejects the rich sauces, large portions, and heavy, elaborate garnishes of traditional *haute cuisine* cooking. In *nouvelle cuisine* the emphasis is on lighter dishes, smaller portions, the use of only top-quality ingredients—particularly vegetables—and on natural flavours and attractive presentation.

nouzillards au lait *(noo-zee-yar ō lā)* Chestnut and milk soup.

noyau *(no-yō)* Pit or stone of a fruit, sometimes used for flavouring.

nulles *(neel)* Musk-flavoured dessert cream or custard.

O

œuf *(ef)* Egg.
 brouillés *(. . . brwee-yā)* Scrambled eggs.
 en cocotte *(. . . awʀ ko-kot)* Egg baked in an individual ceramic pot with cream, or a purée (sometimes called *en caissette* or *en cassolette*).
 à la coque *(. . . ah lah kok)* Soft-boiled egg in the shell.
 dur *(. . . deer)* Hard-boiled egg.
 frit *(. . . free)* Fried egg.
 mollet *(. . . mo-lā)* Soft-boiled and shelled egg.
 au plat *(. . . ō pla)* Egg cooked in butter, either in the oven or over heat.
 poché *(. . . po-shā)* Poached egg.
 à la poêle *(. . . ah lah pwahl)* Fried egg.

ognon *(on-yon)* Onion; the word is more often spelled *oignon*.

ognonnade *(on-yo-nahd)* Onion stew, more often spelled *oignonade*.

oie *(wah)* Goose.

oignon *(on-yən)* Onion.

oignonade *(on-yo-nahd)* Onion stew.

oiseau *(wah-zō)* Bird.
  sans tête *(. . . sawн tait)* 'Headless bird': a colloquial name for a *paupiette*, a thin slice of beef or veal rolled up and stuffed with one of various possible fillings, and braised.

olive *(o-leev)* Olive.
  en olive *(awн-no-leev)* Foodstuffs (usually meat) which are formed into an olive shape.
  noir *(. . . nwahr)* Black olive.
  picholine *(. . . pee-sho-leen)* Large green olive.
  verte *(. . . vairt)* Green olive.

omble chevalier *(om-blə shə-val-yā)* A species of freshwater salmon similar to the char; found mainly in Savoie, and delicious.

ombre *(om-brə)* Grayling.

ombrine *(om-breen)* Umbrine, a Mediterranean fish prepared like bass.

omelette *(om-let)* Omelette.

onglet *(on-glā)* Flank of beef.

or *(or)* Gold: the colour as well as the metal.
  doré *(do-rā)* Golden; lightly browned.

orange *(o-rawнzh)* Orange: the colour as well as the fruit.
  jus d'orange *(jөө dor-awнzh)* Canned or bottled orange juice.
  givrée *(. . . zhee-vrā)* An orange sorbet served in a hollowed-out orange, often served rock-hard straight from the deep-freeze.
  pressée *(. . . pres-ā)* Freshly-squeezed orange juice.

orangeade *(o-rawn-zhad)* Orangeade.

orangina *(o-rawн-zhee-nah)* Brand-name, now generic, for bottled orangeade.

oreille *(o-rā)* Ear (menu-wise, usually a pig's): see also *oreillette*.
  de mer *(. . . də mair)* 'Ear of the sea': a colloquial name for the ormer or abalone *(ormeau)*: a shellfish with an iridescent, ear-shaped shell.

oreiller de la belle aurore *(o-rā-yā də lah bel ō-ror)* 'Pillow of the beautiful daybreak': an elaborate game pie.

oreillette *(o-rā-yet)* 'Little ear': a preserved pig's ear, a *charcuterie* speciality; also the name of a type of curly sweet fritter flavoured with orange blossom, rum or Armagnac.

orge *(orzh)* Barley.
  perlé *(. . . pair-lā)* Pearl barley.

orientale, à l' *(ah lor-yawн-tahl)* Oriental-style: a general name for vaguely Eastern dishes cooked with tomatoes, flavoured with garlic, or spiced with saffron: more specifically, a garnish of tomatoes stuffed with saffron rice, okra and sweet peppers in tomato sauce.

origan *(o-ree-gawн)* The herb oregano; wild marjoram.

orléans, à la d' *(ah lah dor-lā-yawн)* In the style of the city of Orléans in central France:
  consommé *(kawн-so-mā . . .)* Chicken consommé with *quenelles* (little poached mousses) of minced chicken with cream, tomato purée and pistachios.

orly, à l' *(ah lor-lee)* A method of cooking fish fillets by deep-frying them in batter and serving them with tomato sauce.

ormeau or **ormier** *(or-mō, orm-yā)* The ormer, a shellfish looking something like an ear, which is eaten raw or in soups.

oronge vraie des Césars *(o-rawnzh vrā dā sā-zar)* Caesar's mushroom, a member of the amanite family with a very delicate taste, growing late in the year.

ortie *(or-tee)* Nettle, or stinging-nettle; used in soups.

ortolan *(or-to-lawn)* The ortolan, a kind of bunting common all over Europe, which in the South of France is caught and fattened up, then eaten—usually spit-roasted.

os *(os)* Bone.
   à l'os *(ah los)* On the bone.
   os à moelle *(. . . ah m'wel)* Marrowbone.

oseille *(ō-zā)* Sorrel, a bitter, leafy herb similar to spinach in taste; used in soups, as a filling for omelettes or puréed as an accompaniment for fish and white meat.
   alose à l' *(a-lōz ah l' . . .)* Shad stuffed with sorrel or with sorrel purée.

oublie *(oo-blee)* 'Lost' or 'forgotten': a thin, round wafer.

ouillade *(oo-yahd)* Hearty soup of cabbage and haricot beans with garlic.

ouillat or **ouliat** *(oo-yah, oo-lyah)* Basic onion and garlic soup to which tomatoes, leeks and cheese may be added; also known as *toulia* and *soupe du berger*.

oulade *(oo-lahd)* Soup-cum-stew made from potatoes, cabbage, sausage and salt pork.

oursin *(oor-san)* The sea urchin: a sea creature whose flesh is eaten either raw or mixed into dishes such as scrambled eggs and soups.

outarde *(oo-tahrd)* Bustard: a large scavenging bird which is hunted and served roasted.

ouvert(e) *(oo-vair(t))* Open (shops, restaurants etc.).

oyonnade *(o-yo-nahd)* Goose stewed in wine with its own liver and blood.

P

pacaret *(pa-ka-rā)* With sherry, in general.

paëlla *(pa-yel-ah)* Spanish rice dish which features either mixed seafood, poultry and vegetables or poultry, meat and vegetables, according to the region where it is found.

pagre *(pa-gre)* Species of Mediterranean bream.

paillard, paupiettes de sole *(pō-pyet de sol pī-yahr)* Sole fillets rolled up with a stuffing of fish forcemeat and mushrooms, served in a creamy mushroom sauce.

paillarde de veau *(pī-yahrd de vō)* Veal escalope, grilled.

paille, pommes *(pom pī-ye)* Shredded potatoes, flash-fried.

paillette d'oignon *(pī-yet don-yawn)* Deep-fried onion rings.

pain *(pan)* Bread; a loaf of bread; loaf-shaped.
   azyme *(. . . a-zeem)* Unleavened bread.
   bis *(. . . bees)* Brown bread.
   complet *(. . . com-plā)* Wholemeal bread.
   d'épices *(. . . dā-pees)* Spiced honey gingerbread.
   de froment *(. . . de fro-mawn)* Fine wheat bread.
   grillé *(. . . gree-yā)* Toast.
   de mie *(. . . de mee)* Sliced white bread.
   perdu *(. . . pair-dee)* Sweet fried bread.

de sarrasin *(. . . de sa-ra-zaн)* Buckwheat bread.
de seigle *(. . . de seg-le)* Rye bread.
de son *(. . . de sawн)* Bran bread.
sans sel *(. . . sawн sel)* Salt-free bread.
The same word—*pain*—is also applied to a loaf made of savoury forcemeat (shellfish, fish, chicken, game etc.) bound with a *panade* (see below), which may be served hot or cold; similar to a solid mousse in consistency.

palaille *(pa-lī)* Mixed dish of small sardines and anchovies.

palais de bœuf *(pa-lā de bøf)* Beef palate.

palaise, à la *(ah lah pa-lez)* A garnish of potato balls browned in butter and French beans in cream; also spelled *paloise*.
  sauce *(sōs . . .)* *Béarnaise* sauce with mint instead of tarragon.

paleron *(pal-rawн)* Shoulder cut of beef.

palestine *(pa-lā-steen)* Served with (Jerusalem) artichokes.

palet *(pa-lā)* 'Ice-hockey puck': disc or disc-shaped. A minced beef patty.
  de dames *(. . . de dam)* Thin *petit-four* biscuit decorated with water icing.

palette *(pa-let)* Blade bone, a thin circular cut from the top of the shoulder blade, usually of pork.

palmier *(pal-myā)* 'Palm tree': a flat, palm-shaped puff-pastry sprinkled with icing-sugar; a speciality of Paris.

paloise, à la *(ah lah pal-wahz)* See *palaise*.

palombe *(pa-lomb)* Wild pigeon; wood pigeon.

palourde *(pa-loord)* Carpet shell, a type of clam; also the name of a variety of squash.

pamplemousse *(pawн-ple-moos)* Grapefruit.

panaché *(pa-na-shā)* Mixed or mixed together; used of vegetables, salads, fruit salads etc. and to mixed drinks such as shandy.

panada or **panade** *(pa-na-dah, pa-nad)* A paste of milk, butter, flour and water that is used for binding forcemeat or stuffing; also a simple soup made of butter, bread, stock and water or milk.

panais *(pa-nā)* Parsnip.

pan bagnat *(pan ban-ya)* Sandwich containing onions, lettuce, anchovies, black olives, green peppers, tomatoes and often hard-boiled eggs, in a *vinaigrette* sauce, served in a long loaf or large bun which is split in half and brushed with olive oil before filling; a café and restaurant speciality in S France, and delicious for lunch or a picnic.

panetière *(pa-ne-tyair)* General term for a kind of *croustade* in which a pastry or bread shell is filled with pre-cooked food and then baked until it is golden brown.
  sole à la *(sol ah lah . . .)* Round toast topped with a sautéed fillet of sole curled round a *ragoût* of mushrooms.

panier *(pan-yā)* 'Wicker-basket'; a name for various pastry or potato dishes that are shaped like a basket.
  en sucre tiré *(. . . awн søø-kre teer-rā)* Spun sugar basket for fruit and ices.

panisse or **panisso** *(pa-nees, pa-nee-sō)* Fried cake made of chick-peas or maize sprinkled with sugar.

panizze *(pa-neez)* Corsican chestnut-flour cake.

pannequet *(pan-kā)* Pancake: another name for a

crêpe or galette, except that a *pannequet* will always be spread with some sweet or savoury mixture, rolled or folded in four, then topped with sugar, or crushed nuts, grated cheese, breadcrumbs, etc., and browned in a hot oven before serving.

panoufle *(pa-noo-flə)* Cut of meat from the lower part of the top of a beef sirloin.

pantin *(pawн-taн)* Small pastry filled with fine pork forcemeat.

panure *(pa-nөөr)* A coating of breadcrumbs.

papayer *(pa-pā-yā)* The tropical fruit papaya or pawpaw.

papillote *(pa-pee-yot)* 'Curl-paper': paper frills decorating the end bones of chops, cutlets etc.; also a small cut of meat (usually veal) baked inside a case made of oiled paper.

paprika *(pa-pree-kah)* Paprika; Hungarian sweet red pepper.

Pâques *(pak)* Easter.
  œuf de *(ef də . . .)* Easter-egg.
  pâté de *(pa-ta de . . .)* Pie filled with pork, chicken or rabbit mixed with chopped hard-boiled eggs.

parfait *(par-fā)* 'Perfect': an iced mousse. Ice-cream, originally made with coffee cream only, but now variously flavoured; the name is also used to describe a fish, meat or vegetable mousse or terrine.

parfum *(par-faн)* Flavour or aroma, particularly of desserts such as ice-creams, mousses and sorbets.

Paris *(pa-ree)* Paris.
  jambon de Paris *(zhawн-bawн de . . .)* Cooking or boiling ham, normally unsmoked, sometimes lightly smoked; it is sometimes boned. Also called *jambon blanc, demi-sel* or *glacé*.

Paris-Brest *(pa-ree brest)* Large, crown-shaped *choux* pastry filled with praline butter cream and topped with chopped almonds.

parisienne, à la *(ah lah pa-ree-zyen)* In the style of Paris: with a garnish of braised lettuce or artichokes and *pommes parisienne*, the last being one of many dishes bearing this description. Others include:
  bœuf bouilli froid *(bөf bwee-yee fwah . . .)* Sliced cold beef with sliced potatoes and beans in *vinaigrette* with onion rings and chopped herbs.
  consommé *(kawн-so-mā . . .)* Chicken consommé with diced mixed vegetables and chervil.
  gâteau *(ga-tō . . .)* Meringue-covered sponge cake layered with frangipane cream.
  homard *(o-mar . . .)* Cold lobster in mayonnaise with truffles and a vegetable salad in jelly.
  omelette *(om-let . . .)* Onion and mushroom omelette covered with chipolata sausages.
  pommes *(pom . . .)* Tiny browned potato-balls tossed in concentrated meat glaze with parsley.
  poulet *(poo-lā . . .)* Sautéed chicken with *duchesse* potatoes in a white wine sauce.
  salade *(sa-lahd . . .)* Vegetable salad embelished with crayfish and truffles in mayonnaise.
  sauce *(sōs . . .)* Cold sauce for asparagus, made of cream cheese beaten with oil and lemon juice, paprika and chervil.

parme, jambon de *(zhawн-boн de parm)* Parma ham.

parmentier *(par-mawн-tyā)* In general, garnished, filled or made with potatoes.

bœuf, bouilli sauté *(bœf boo-yee sō-tā . . .)* Diced boiled beef and potatoes sautéed together.

pommes *(pom . . .)* Potato cubes cooked in butter with parsley.

poulet sauté *(poo-lā sō-tā . . .)* Chicken sautéed with diced potatoes, served in a white wine sauce.

parmesane, à la *(ah lah par-mā-zan)* Descriptive of dishes containing parmesan cheese.

pascal, œufs en cocotte *(œf awн ko-kot pas-kal)* Baked eggs covered in a mustard and cream sauce with herbs.

pasta frolla *(pahs-tah fro-lah)* Delicate, sweet pastry, like savarin pastry.

pastèque *(pas-tek)* Watermelon.

pastille *(pas-tee-yə)* Small, round, hard, sweet/candy of flavoured sugar; cough drops and similar medications are also called *pastilles*.

pastis *(pas-tees)* Popular licorice-flavoured aperitif, usually mixed with water; also an orange and brandy flavoured yeast cake.

    landaise *(. . . lawн-dez)* Pastry filled with prunes.

pastissoun *(pas-tee-soon)* Orange-flavoured pastry.

patate *(pa-tat)* Sweet potato or yam.

pâte *(pat)* Dough, pastry, paste or batter, including moist pastes such as those made from tomatoes or almonds, and dried ones in the form of pasta or noodles.

    à brioche *(. . . ah bree-osh)* Rich yeast dough used mainly for cakes and buns.

    à chou *(. . . ah shoo)* *Choux* pastry.

    brisé *(. . . bree-zā)* Short crust pastry.

    feuilletée *(fœy-tā)* Flaky or puff pastry.

    sucrée *(sœk-ra)* Sweet short crust pastry.

pâté *(pa-tā)* Pâté: meat paste. Also a pie, pasty or patty: a pastry case filled with a mixture of meat, game, fish or vegetables, baked in the oven, and served cold or hot. A *pâté* is usually richer than a conventional pie or pasty, however, and is often baked in a mould rather than a pie-dish.

    en croûte *(. . . awн kroot)* A rich preparation of meat, game, fowl or fish baked in a rectangular pastry case and served cold, in slices.

    de petit oiseau sauvage— see *grive*.

    en terrine *(. . . awн-tai-reen)* A rich mixture of meat, game, fowl or fish baked in a bacon-lined pottery dish called a *terrine*, and always served cold. This is the starting dish known familiarly as *pâté* or *terrine*. In English and American usage, *pâté* is thought of as being quite smooth in texture, rather like a thick spread, while *terrine* is considered rougher, with largish bits of the ingredients present.

patelle *(pa-tel)* Limpet.

pâtisserie *(pa-tees-ree)* A general term for pastries, and for the shop where they are sold. More generally, the word embraces the whole art or craft of pastry-making.

pâtissier or **pâtissière** *(pa-tees-ya(ir))* A pastry-cook.

    crème *(krem . . .)* A custard of eggs, sugar, flour, milk and vanilla or other flavouring used as a pastry filling.

    noix *(nwah . . .)* Colloquial terms for the topside or chump end of the loin of veal.

patranque *(pa-trawнk)* Thick puréed mixture of crumbled bread simmered in milk with butter and cheese, eaten as a first course; sometimes the mixture is left to cool and solidify, then cut into rounds and fried. Also called *aligot au pain*.

patron *(pa-trawʀ)* Proprietor, manager or boss.

pauchouse *(pō-shooz)* See *pochouse*.

paupiette *(pō-pyet)* Beef or veal olive: a thin slice of beef or veal or fish which is stuffed and rolled up, then braised, also called *oiseau sans tête*.

pauvre homme, sauce *(sōs pōv-rom)* 'Poor man's sauce': made of stock and vinegar with chopped shallots, parsley and fried breadcrumbs.

pavé *(pa-vā)* 'Paving-stone': a term for various thick and/or square items including thickly-sliced beefsteak and a number of square or rectangular cakes and spiced breads; also various cold savoury preparations, usually mousses, made in square or rectangular moulds, and often coated in aspic.

pays *(pā)* Land: a country or nation in the English sense, but in French also a region, a district, the soil or the countryside; rural as opposed to urban.
  jambon de pays *(zhawʀ-bawʀ də . . .)* Country ham, salted and smoked according to local custom.
  vin de pays *(vaʀ də . . .)* Local or regional table wine; see the section on wine for details.

paysanne, à la *(ah lah pā-zan)* Country- or peasant-style: meat served with onions, carrots, turnips, celery, potatoes and bacon.
  omelette *(om-let . . .)* Potato, sorrel and herb omelette.
  pommes *(pom . . .)* Sliced potatoes layered with sorrel, garlic and herbs and baked in stock.

potage *(po-tahzh . . .)* Mixed vegetable soup.
sole *(sol . . .)* Sole poached with mixed vegetables, served with concentrated vegetable *bouillon*.

peau *(pō)* The skin of an animal.

pebronata de bœuf *(pā-bro-nah-tah də bəf)* Corsican beef stew with a spicy sauce of wine, tomatoes, onions, garlic and peppers.

pec, hareng *(ar-awʀ pek)* Freshly salted, unsmoked herring.

pêche *(pesh)* Peach.

perche *(pairsh)* Perch.

perche de mer *(pairsh də mair)* Sea bass, more usually called *bar*.

perchette *(pair-shet)* Baby perch, usually deep-fried.

perdreau *(pair-drō)* Young partridge.

perdrix *(pair-dree)* Partridge.

père tranquil, potage du *(po-tahzh dəə pair trawʀ-kee)* Puréed lettuce soup.

périgourdine à la *(ah lah pā-ree-goor-deen)* In the style of Périgord in SW France: accompanied by, with a sauce of, or stuffed with truffles and often *foie gras*.
  ballottine de lièvre *(ba-lo-teen də lyev-re . . .)* Boned hare stuffed with rabbit, veal or pork, *foie-gras* and truffles.
  cassoulet périgourdin *(ka-səə-lā pā-ree-goor-daʀ)* Stew of haricot beans, mutton, garlic sausage and stuffed goose neck.
  cèpes *(sep . . .)* Cèpes (fleshy mushrooms) cooked with bacon, parsley, garlic and *verjus* (unripe grape juice).
  tourain or **tourin** *(too-raʀ . . .)* Onion soup with tomatoes, egg-yolks and sometimes cheese.

213

périgueux, sauce *(sōs pā-ree-gǝ)* Demi-glace (brown) sauce with *Madeira* and chopped truffles.

pernod *(pair-nō)* Popular brand of the liquorice-flavoured aperitif *pastis*.

pernollet, salade *(sa-lahd pair-no-lā)* Salad of truffles and crayfish mixed with mayonnaise, served in a large lettuce leaf.

perrier *(pair-ryā)* Brand of sparkling mineral water, probably France's best-known and most widely-available.

persane, à la *(ah lah pair-san)* A garnish of sliced fried aubergine (eggplant) and onion rings, sweet peppers and tomato pulp; served with lamb cutlets.

persil *(pair-see)* Parsley.

persillade *(pair-see-yahd)* Finely-chopped parsley and shallots (or garlic) used as flavouring in a wide variety of dishes
   de bœuf *(. . . dǝ bǝf)* Sautéed beef sprinkled with *persillade*.

persillée *(pair-see-yā)* Seasoned with parsley; also a word applied to the veining in certain blue cheeses.

pet de nonne *(pā-dǝ-non)* 'Nun's fart': an unlikely name for a light puffy fritter *(soufflé beignet)*.

peteram or **pétéran** *(pait-ram, pā-tā-rawn)* Stew of ham, sheep's tripe and sheep's trotters with wine.

petit(e) *(pǝ-tee(t))* Small or delicate; a diminutive version of . . .

petit beurre *(pǝ-tee bǝr)* Popular tea-biscuit made with butter.

petit déjeuner *(pǝ-tee dā-zhe-nā)* Breakfast.
   complet *(. . . kawn-plā)* Continental breakfast: coffee or tea plus croissants and/or bread, butter and jam.

petite marmite *(pǝ-teet mar-meet)* See *marmite*.

petites fondues à la bourguignonne *(pǝ-teet fawn-dǝǝ ah lah boor-geen-yon)* Fried cheese squares, served as a first course.

petit-four *(pǝ-tee foor)* General term for small biscuits, chocolates, cakes, candied fruit and other sweetmeats served after lunch or dinner with coffee. Also called *mign-ardises* and *friandises*.

petit gris *(pǝ-tee gree)* Little (grey) snail.

petit pain *(pǝ-tee pan)* Bread roll or savoury loaf.

petit pâté *(pǝ-tee pa-tā)* Small pastry-roll filled with pâté.
   de Pézenas or **de Béziers** *(. . . dǝ pā-zen-a, dǝ bā-zyā)* Little pastry-rolls with a sweet or savoury filling, but traditionally with sweetened mutton forcemeat.

petits pois *(pǝ-te pwah)* Little green peas: the implication is that they are young and fresh, but peas are nearly always called *petits pois* in shops and restaurants.

petit pot de chocolat *(pǝ-tee pō dǝ sho-ko-lah)* Rich chocolate mousse served in a little pot.

petit poussin *(pǝ-tee poo-san)* Young chicken, usually presented as a whole bird for one person to eat.

petit salé *(pǝ-tee sa-lā)* Salt-pork: a general term for dishes made with salt pork, but may also be roasted salt-pork prepared by a *charcutier*, often as a salt-pork roll.

petit-suisse *(pǝ-tee swees)* A soft fresh cheese made of milk and cream, which is eaten with sugar as an accompaniment for fruit.

pétoncle *(pā-tawn-klǝ)* A queen scallop, which is smaller than a *coquille*

Saint-Jacques.

pflutten *(p'flee-ten)* Semolina and potato gnocchi fried in squares; Alsatian in origin.

piballes *(pee-bahl)* Colloquial term for baby eels, also called *civelles.*

pibronata *(pee-bro-nah-tah)* Spicy tomato and pepper sauce; a Corsican speciality.

picarde, ficelle à la *(fee-sel ah lah pee-kahrd)* Pancake filled with ham and mushrooms, coated in *béchamel* sauce.

picaut *(pee-kō)* Normandy name for *dindon* (turkey).

pichet *(pee-shā)* Pitcher, jug, pot or decanter. House wine is often served decanted into a *pichet* (one litre), a *demi-pichet* (half-litre), or a *quart* (quarter-litre).

pièce de bœuf *(pyes de bef)* Large cut of beef from the top of the rump.

pied *(pyā)* Foot, trotter or hoof.

pieds et paquets *(pyā ā pa-kā)* Sheep's or calf's trotters and stuffed rolled tripe 'packages' with tomato and white wine sauce.

piémontaise, à la *(ah lah pyā-mawn-tez)* In the style of Piedmont in N Italy: a garnish of little croquettes, or *timbales,* made of rice mixed with shredded truffles, mushrooms, ham and pickled tongue; served in tomato sauce with meat or poultry.
　sauce *(sōs . . .)* White sauce containing chopped onions, truffles, pine kernels and garlic, served with chicken.

pigeon *(pee-zhawn)* Pigeon.

pigeonneau *(pee-zhon-nō)* Young pigeon; squab.

pignon *(peen-yon)* Pine nut, pine kernel.

pilaf or **pilau** *(pee-laf, pee-*

lō) Savoury rice (Indian in origin), which is first stewed in butter then cooked in stock and popularly mixed with other ingredients such as lamb's or sheep's sweetbreads, chicken's liver, kidneys, shellfish (mussels, shrimps, lobster) and white meat.

pilchard *(peel-shahr)* Small fish similar to the sardine, usually tinned in spiced oil.

piment *(pee-mawn)* Red pepper or pimento; a general name for cayenne pepper, chilli powder and paprika.
　doux *(. . . doo)* Sweet red or green pepper, also called *poivron.*
　fort rouge *(. . . for roozh)* Hot red chilli pepper.

pimentée *(pee-mawn-tā)* Hot, peppery or spicy.

pimprenelle *(pan-pre-nel)* Salad burnet, a somewhat bitter-tasting salad green.

pince *(pans)* Claw or pincer of a crab, lobster etc.

pintade *(pan-tahd)* Guinea-fowl.

pintadeau *(pan-ta-dō)* Young guinea-fowl.

pipérade *(pee-pā-rahd)* Popular Basque country dish: fluffy omelette or scrambled eggs mixed with tomatoes, onions, garlic, peppers and Bayonne ham.

piquant(e) *(pee-kawnt)* Spicy, hot or indeed piquant.
　sauce piquante *(sōs. . .)* Brown spicy sauce (based on *sauce diable*) with vinegar, chopped capers and gherkins, herbs and spices.

pique-nique *(peek-neek)* Picnic.

pirozhki or **pirogui** *(pee-rosh-kee, pee-rō-gee)* Little pies or pastries filled with a vegetable *salpicon,* meat or fish forcemeat, or cream cheese; Russian in origin.

215

piron, rable de lièvre à la *(rahb-lə do lyev-rə ah lah pee-rawn)* Saddle of hare marinated in *marc*, roasted, and served with grapes and shallots in a peppery cream sauce.

pissala *(pee-sa-lah)* Purée of tiny fish such as anchovies.

pissaladière *(pee-sa-la-dyair)* Flan similar to a pizza, which is topped with puréed onions, anchovies, black olives and sometimes tomatoes.

pissenlit *(pee-sawn-lee)* 'Wet-the-bed': a colloquial name for the dandelion *(dente-de-lion)*, renowned as a diuretic.
  salade de *(sa-lahd də . . .)* Dandelion leaf salad with cubes of fried bacon and fried bread.

pistache *(pee-stash)* Pistachio nut.
  en pistache *(awn . . .)* Method of braising mutton or partridge in wine with vegetables and 50 cloves of garlic.

pistou *(pees-too)* Sauce of basil and garlic (and sometimes pine nuts, cheese and grilled tomatoes), pounded into a paste and mixed with oil; similar to the Italian *pesto*. Also a name used in S France for *basilic* (the herb basil).
  soupe au *(soop ō . . .)* Vegetable and pasta soup similar to minestrone, served with *pistou* sauce.

pithiviers *(pee-tee-vyā)*
  gâteau de *(ga-tō də . . .)* Puff-pastry filled with rum and almond cream.
  pâté de *(pa-tā də . . .)* Lark pâté wrapped in pastry.

pivarunata *(pee-vair-oo-nah-tah)* Corsican goat and sweet-pepper stew.

plaisir *(plā-zeer)* 'Pleasure': a small wafer rolled into a cone.

plat *(pla)* Dish, both literally and in the sense of a course or particular item on the menu. The *plat du jour* is the dish of the day, or today's special. A plate, in the more literal sense, is an *assiette*.

plat-de-côtes *(pla də cot)* Rib chops; short ribs; a flank cut of beef or pork.

plateau *(pla-tō)* Platter, tray or large serving-dish.
  de fruits de mer *(. . . də fwee də mair)* Large plate of various shellfish (some raw such as oysters and little clams) usually including shrimps, prawns, mussels, winkles and cockles and perhaps some local salt-water fish.

plie franche *(plee frawnsh)* Plaice, a flatfish also called *carrelet*.

pluvier *(pləə-vyā)* Plover.

pochard *(po-shahr)* Variety of wild marsh duck.

poché(e) *(po-shā)* Poached.

pocheteau *(posh-tō)* Skate: a large flatfish.

pochouse *(po-shooz)* Stew of lake and river fish containing—principally—eel, carp, trout, pike, burbot and bream, with white wine and garlic.

poêle *(pwahl)* Stove or oven; also a frying-pan or cooking-pot.

poêlé(e) *(pwah-lā)* Pot-roasted.

pogne *(pon-yə)* Brioche cake filled with fruit or jam.

pognon *(pon-yawn)* Burgundian flat cake.

point, à *(ah pwan)* 'To the precise point': in the nick of time, or just right. Ripe or ready to eat—the perfect moment for consuming a given product, particularly fruit or cheese. Also a term describing a steak cooked until it just stops bleeding: roughly 'medium rare'.

poirat *(pwah-ra)* Pear tart.

poire *(pwahr)* Pear.

poiré *(pwah-rā)* Perry: sparkling pear wine.

poireau *(pwah-rō)* Leek.

poire william *(pwahr weel-yam)* Famous colourless pear *eau-de-vie* or spirit, made in Alsace (also known as *poire guillaume*).

pois *(pwah)* Pea or peas; green peas.
  cassés *(. . . ka-sā)* Split peas.
  chiches *(. . . sheesh)* Chick-peas.
  chinois *(. . . sheen-wah)* 'Chinese peas': a colloquial name for soya beans.
  secs *(. . . sek)* Dried peas.
  petits pois *(pə-tee . . .)* Little garden peas.

poison *(pwah-zawʀ)* Poison.

poisson *(pwah-sawʀ)* Fish:
  d'eau douce *(. . . dō doos)* Freshwater fish.
  de lac *(. . . də lak)* Lake fish.
  de mer *(. . . də mair)* Sea fish.
  de rivière *(. . . də reev-yair)* River fish.
  de roche *(. . . də rosh)* Rock fish.
  pilote *(. . . pee-lot)* Pilot fish, similar to the mackerel.
  volant *(. . . vō-lawʀ)* Flying fish.

poissonnaille *(pwah-sawʀ-nā-yə)* Small fish, or fry.

poissonnerie *(pwah-son-ree)* A fishmonger's.

poitevin, far(ci) *(fahr(see) pwaht-vaʀ)* Cabbage stuffed with onions, bacon, herbs and other vegetables bound with cream and eggs, cooked with salt pork

in *court-bouillon*.

poitrine *(pwah-treen)* Breast cut of veal, pork, lamb or mutton; also, brisket of beef.
  fumée *(. . . føø-mā)* A side of cured bacon, from which slices are cut.

poivrade, sauce *(sōs pwahv-rahd)* Brown sauce *(espagnole)* generously seasoned with pepper, served with game or beef.

poivre *(pwahv-rə)* Pepper.
  blanc *(. . . blawʀ)* White pepper.
  de Cayenne *(. . . də kah-yen)* Red pepper; cayenne pepper.
  en grains *(. . . awʀ graʀ)* Peppercorns.
  gris *(. . . gree)* Black pepper, also called *poivre noir*.
  de la Jamaïque *(. . . də lah zha-mā-yeek)* Allspice.
  moulu *(. . . mool-yøø)* Ground pepper, also called *poivre en poudre*.
  noir *(. . . nwahr)* See *p. gris*.
  en poudre *(. . . awʀ poo-drə)* See *moulu*.
  rose or **rouge** *(. . . roz, roozh)* Red pepper.
  vert *(. . . vair)* Green peppercorns.

poivré(e) *(pwah-vrā)* Peppery or spicy.

poivre, steak au *(stek ō pwahv-rə)* Fillet steak with pepper sauce.

poivre d'âne *(pwahv dan)* Name for the bitter herb savoury *(sarriette)*.

poivron *(pwahv-rawʀ)* Sweet pepper (either green or red).

pojarski *(po-zahr-skee)* Fish or meat minced and formed into the shape of a chop, then fried.

polenta *(po-len-tah)* Maize or corn-meal porridge which, when cooled and solidified, is cut into little squares that are fried in butter until golden brown, and sprinkled with cheese.

polonaise, à la *(ah lah po-lo-nez)* In the style of Poland:

  asperges *(as-pairzh . . .)* Asparagus sprinkled with *beurre noisette*, fried breadcrumbs and chopped hard-boiled egg-yolks. Cauliflower *(chou-fleur)* is similarly prepared.
  carpe *(karp . . .)* Stuffed carp in red wine sauce with browned almonds.

pomme *(pom)* Apple. Also a potato, abbreviated from *pomme de terre*.

pomme de terre *(pom də tair)* Potato ('apple of the earth'), often shortened to *pomme* in menu entries (and in this book) when there is no confusion with apples.

pompe aux grattons *(ponp ō gra-tawn)* Pastry combining morsels of pork and pork fat, fried to crackling.

pompe de Noël *(ponp də nō-el)* Traditional Christmas Eve cake eaten in Provence; also called *gibassier*.

pomponette *(pom-po-net)* Little stuffed pastry pouches, served as an *hors-d'œuvre*.

porc *(por)* Pork, pork-meat or pig. The principal cuts are:

  carré *(ka-rā)* Loin roast.
  côte *(kot)* Loin chop.
  échine *(ā-sheen)* Shoulder; UK: spare rib.
  filet *(fee-lā)* Fillet or tenderloin.
  jambon *(zhawn-bawn)* Ham.
  jamboneau *(zhawn-bo-nō)* Knuckle.
  palette *(pa-let)* US: shoulder butt; UK: blade bone.
  pied *(pyā)* Foot or trotter.
  plat de côte *(pla-də-kot)* Picnic shoulder or boneless shoulder; US: spare ribs; UK: hand.
  poitrine *(pwah-treen)* Bacon or belly.

porcelet *(pors-lā)* Piglet; sucking pig.

portefeuille *(por-tə-fey)* 'Wallet': where food is concerned, this means 'wrapped' or 'enclosed in . . .'.

porto *(por-tō)* Port wine, used extensively in cooking.

port-royal, salade *(sa-lahd por-ro-yal)* Salad of apples, French beans and potatoes in mayonnaise with hard-boiled eggs.

portugaise *(por-tœ-gez)* Type of oyster *(huître)*.

portugaise, à la *(ah lah por-tœ-gez)* In the Portuguese-style: a garnish of tomatoes (sometimes stuffed), garlicky tomato pulp *(fondue)* and/or *sauce portugaise*.

  potage *(po-tahzh . . .)* Thick soup made with rice, onion, bacon, tomatoes and garlic.
  sauce *(sōs . . .)* Rich tomato sauce with onions and herbs.

potable *(po-ta-blə)* Drinkable; suitable for drinking.
  eau *(ō . . .)* Drinking water.

potage *(po-tahzh)* Thick soup (as opposed to *consommé*, which is clear), made basically in one of three forms: puréed soup usually of vegetables such as carrots, peas, lettuce, leeks and potatoes, etc.; cream soup, based on *béchamel* sauce (made with milk) with cream added; and *velouté* soup, based on creamy white *velouté* sauce (made with white stock) often with eggs and cream added.

pot-au-crème *(pot-ō-krem)* Little pot filled with a cold creamy egg custard, variously flavoured.

pot-au-feu *(pot-ō-fə)* Method of cooking meat and vegetables in stock, with bread, pasta or rice; very similar to *petite marmite* and providing a nourishing meal of soup, meat and vegetables. Beef and chicken with root vegetables, leeks, cabbage, potatoes, etc. are traditional ingredients; regional variations include pork, veal, garlic sausage, lamb, goose—almost anything, in fact.

potée *(po-tā)* Any concoction of meat and vegetables cooked in an earthenware pot, but this generally means a hearty soup based on pork, cabbage and potatoes with as many variations as a *pot-au-feu*.

potiron *(po-tee-rawʀ)* Name for pumpkin, also called *citrouille* and *courge*.

potje flesh or **vleesch** *(pozh flesh or vleesh)* Rabbit, veal and chicken terrine (Flanders).

pouding *(poo-ding)* Pudding; English pudding: a term applying to a large number of preparations both savoury and sweet. See also *boudin*.

poudre *(poo-drə)* Powder; granules.
  en poudre *(awʀ . . .)* Powdered, granulated, crushed or ground.

poularde *(poo-lahrd)* Chicken or hen.

poule *(pool)* Hen.

  au pot *(. . . ō pō)* Kind of *pot-au-feu* made with beef and a stuffed chicken.

poulet *(poo-lā)* Young chicken or pullet; a general name for chicken. *Poulet fermier, poulet de grain* and *poulet jaune* are all terms for free-range chickens, the last being maize-fed.

poulette, à la *(à lah poo-let)* Method of preparing various cooked meats (particularly offal) and mushrooms in *sauce poulette* with a garnish of little onions and mushrooms.
  sauce *(sōs . . .)* White *(velouté)* sauce mixed with egg-yolk, lemon

juice and chopped parsley. *Poulette* is another name for a young chicken *(poulet)*.

poulpe *(poolp)* Octopus.

pountari *(poon-ta-ree)* Cabbage leaves variously stuffed with bacon, sausage-meat or pork-fat mince.

pounti *(poon-tee)* Soufflé made with Swiss chard or spinach, plus bacon and (often) prunes.

poupeton *(poop-tawʀ)* Meat roll made by wrapping one piece of meat inside another.

poussin *(poo-saʀ)* small chicken.

poutargue *(poo-targ)* A salty paste, made from the roes of tuna or mullet mashed up in olive oil; also called *boutargue*.

poutina et nonnats *(poo-tee-nah ā no-nah)* Mixture of baby seafish such as sardines and anchovies, which is used principally in *fritures*, omelettes, and to make paste.

praire *(prair)* Name for a small clam.

pralin(e) *(pra-leen)* Blend of crushed nuts (esp. almonds) and caramel, used in confectionary as a filling or topping; also the name of a sweet or candy consisting of a caramel-coated almond.

praliné *(pra-lee-nā)* Containing or coated with praline, or almonds; also the name of a sponge-cake layered and coated with praline butter-cream and sprinkled with chopped almonds.

pré-salé *(prā sa-lā)* Salt-meadow or salt-marsh.
  agneau de *(an-yo də . . .)* Lamb raised on salt-meadows, rendering their flesh particularly delicious.

pressé(e) *(pres-sā)* Squeezed or pressed: see *citron* and *orange*.

pression (pres-syawʀ) Pressure or compression: slang term for draft beer.

primeur (pree-mər) First, earliest, new or young; the term usually refers to early fruit and vegetables, and also to new wine.

princesse, à la (ah lah praʀ-ses) A garnish, mainly for fish (e.g. sole), chicken or sweetbreads, consisting of truffles, asparagus tips and white sauce.
    consommé (kawʀ-so-mā . . .) Chicken consommé garnished with tiny chicken *quenelles* (mousses) and asparagus tips.

printanière, à la (ah lah praʀ-tawn-yair) A garnish of early spring vegetables such as baby carrots and turnips, for meat dishes and soups.
    beurre (bər . . .) Butter pounded with cooked peas, beans, asparagus and other vegetables; used in soups, sauces and *hors-d'œuvres*.

prisultre (pree-zœl-trə) Corsican term for raw ham; the name, also spelled *prisutte* and *prizzutu*, comes from the Italian word *prosciutto*.

prix (pree) Price, charge or cost.

prix fixe (pree feeks) Fixed-price (menu).

prizzutu—see *prisultre*.

profiteroles (pro-fee-tə-rol) Little *choux*-pastry balls filled either with savoury purées of game or cheese, or with sweet custard pastry-cream (*crème pâtissière*), whipped cream or jam.

propriétaire (pro-pryā-taire) Proprietor, owner or manager; see also *patron*.

provençale, à la (ah lah pro-vawʀ-sal) In the style of Provence, S France: cooked and served with tomatoes and garlic, and often with onions, olives, anchovies and eggplant (aubergine) too.
    fenouil (fen-wee . . .) Fennel bases stewed with onions, tomatoes and garlic.
    gratin (gra-taʀ . . .) Sliced potato baked in layers with onions, tomatoes and garlic.
    morue (mo-rœə . . .) Flaked poached salt cod simmered in tomato pulp (*fondue*) with garlic and parsley.
    tomates (to-mart . . .) Baked tomato halves topped with breadcrumbs, herbs and garlic.

prune (prœn) Plum.

pruneau (prœ-nō) Dried plum: prune.

puit d'amour (pwee da-moor) 'Source of love': flaky-pastry crowns filled with pastry-cream *crème patissière*) or thick gooseberry jelly.

pulenta (pœə-len-tah) Corsican chestnut-flour bread.

purée (pœə-rā) Purée: a preparation obtained by mashing and sieving almost any foodstuff, or by liquidizing it in a blender.

Q

quart (kar) Quarter: one-fourth part.
    quart de vin (. . . də vaʀ) A quarter of a litre of wine, normally served in a pitcher, pot or flask.

quartier (kar-tyā) 'Quarter' in the sense of the hindquarters of a beast; loosely, any portion, chunk or segment.

quasi de veau (ka-zee də vō) UK: chump end of loin of veal; US: standing rump of veal.

quatre-épices (ka-trā-pees) 'Four spices': a blend of ground ginger, nutmeg, white pepper and cloves.

quatre mendiants *(kat mawn-dyawn)* 'Four friars', the colours of whose habits are echoed by the components of this dessert: figs, almonds, raisins and hazelnuts.

quenelle *(kə-nel)* Little poached mousse or very light dumpling made from meat, fish, game or fowl, which is pounded in a mortar to a paste-like consistency before being moulded and poached.
   quenelles de brochet *(. . . də bro-shā)* Small pike mousses served hot in a cream sauce.

quetsche *(kwetch)* A type of plum; also the name of a clear brandy or *eau-de-vie* made from these plums.

queue *(kə)* Tail.
   de bœuf *(. . . də-bəf)* Oxtail.
   d'écrivisses, gratin de *(gra-tan də kə dek-rə-vees)* Crayfish tails in a creamy white wine and brandy sauce topped with breadcrumbs and baked till golden.
   quiche *(keesh)* An open pastry tart filled with a variety of ingredients, usually savoury, such as bacon, ham, vegetables, cheese etc., mixed with eggs and cream to form a custard, then baked and served hot or cold.
   lorraine *(. . . lo-ren)* See under *lorraine*.

quimper, maquereau à la façon de *(mak-air-ō ah lah fa-sawn də kam-pā)* Cold, poached mackerel with a sauce made of eggs, butter and herbs.

R

rabes *(rab)* Salted cod's roes.

rabiole *(rab-yol)* A kind of turnip.

râble *(rahb-lə)* Saddle of hare or rabbit.

rabot(t)e *(ra-bot)* Kind of fruit dumpling in which a whole apple or pear is baked inside a shortcrust-pastry case; also called a *talibur*.

Rachel *(ra-shel)* Garnish of artichoke hearts and sliced bone-marrow with wine sauce.
   consommé *(kawn-so-mā . . .)* Chicken consommé garnished with tiny chicken *quenelles* (mousses) and small lettuce-rolls stuffed with puréed chicken.

racine *(ra-seen)* Root of a plant; a root vegetable.

raclette *(ra-klet)* Famous Savoyard cheese fondue dish prepared by turning a large piece of cheese before an open flame, scraping off the melting surface, and eating it while it is still hot with bites of baked potato. In the restaurants of Savoie, the melting and scraping operation is conducted for you at the table using an ingenious Heath Robinson machine, leaving you free to concentrate on eating.

radis *(ra-dee)* Radish.

rafraîchi(e) *(ra-frā-shee)* Cooled, chilled or fresh.
   fruits *(fwee . . .)* Fresh-fruit salad.

ragoût *(ra-goo)* Ragoût: a stew made from pieces of meat, fowl or fish which are first browned or sautéed, and then cooked slowly in a covered pan in meat juice or stock, either alone or with vegetables.
   Ragoûts of vegetables are also made in much the same way; they are usually served as a garnish, or bound in a thick sauce as a filling for pastries, bread *croûtes* etc.

raie *(rā)* Ray or skate: a large flat fish.

raifort *(rā-for)* Horse-radish.

raïoles *(rah-yol)* Name used in S France for ravioli.

raisin *(rā-zaʀ)* Grape.
  de Corinthe *(. . . də koʀaʀt)* Currant (dried).
  de Smyrne *(. . . də smeeʀn)* Sultana.
  sec *(. . . sek)* Raisin.

raisiné *(rā-zee-nā)* Jam or jelly made with grapes, often containing other fruits too.

raïto *(rī-tō)* Sauce for fish, made of red wine, tomatoes, garlic and ground walnuts; also known as *rayte*.

ramequin *(ram-kaʀ)* Ramekin: an individual earthenware baking or serving dish. Also a name for various cheesy dishes: small cheese-flavoured *choux* pastries, cheese fondue with wine, mustard and garlic, and hot cheese tartlets, some not unlike Welsh rarebit.

ramereau *(ram-rō)* Young pigeon; ring dove.

ramier *(ram-yā)* Wood-pigeon.

râpé *(rah-pā)* Grated or scraped; short for *fromage râpé*: grated cheese.
  morvandelle *(. . . morvawʀ-del)* Baked dish of grated potatoes mixed with cream, eggs and cheese.

raphael, salade *(sa-lahd raf-el)* A salad of lettuce mixed with paprika mayonnaise covered with sliced cucumber, asparagus tips, tomatoes and radishes in *vinaigrette*.

rascasse *(ras-kas)* Scorpion fish.

ratafia *(ra-ta-fyah)* Home-made liqueur, prepared by steeping fruit (or sometimes nuts) in distilled spirits or wine. Restaurants sometimes make their own *ratafia* and serve it as a speciality of the house,

usually as an aperitif; *vin d'orange*, made with orange segments steeped in white wine, is a typical —and particularly delicious—one. *Ratafia* is also a kind of macaroon popular in S France.

ratatouille *(ra-ta-twee-yə)* Renowned Provençal dish comprising tomatoes, aubergine (eggplant), onions, sweet peppers, courgettes and garlic, stewed in olive oil and served either hot or cold.

ravigote *(ra-vee-got)* 'Reviver':
  beurre *(bər . . .)* Butter pounded with shallots, tarragon, salad burnet, chervil and other herbs; also called *beurre chivry*.
  sauce *(sōs . . .)* Thick vinaigrette mixed with chopped gherkins, capers, tarragon, chervil and other herbs.

ravioles *(rav-yol)* Pastries flavoured with goat's cheese.

ravioli *(rav-yo-lee)* Ravioli.

rayon de miel *(ra-yawʀ də myel)* Honeycomb.

rayte—See *raïto*.

recette *(rə-set)* Recipe.

réchauffé(e) *(rā-shō-fā)* 'Reheated': any dish made with ingredients which have already been cooked.

récolte *(rā-kolt)* Harvest, gathering or grape-picking.

régence *(rā-zhawʀs)* A rich garnish of truffles, *quenelles* (little mousses), *foie gras*, mushrooms and cockscombs.
  sauce *(sōs . . .)* Brown sauce blended with puréed onions and flavoured with ham; served with sweetbreads or chicken.

régime *(rā-zheem)* Diet; slimming diet; health diet. Also, oddly enough, a bunch of bananas.

réglisse *(rā-glees)* Liquorice.

reguigneu (rə-geen-yə) Fried slices of country ham (*jambon cru* or *jambon de campagne*).

reine (ren) 'Queen': a category of chicken whose size or weight falls between that of a young chicken (*poulet*) and a fattened roasting hen (*poularde*).

reine, à la (ah lah ren) 'As the queen likes it': with chicken or puréed chicken.
  bouchée (boo-shā . . .) Little puff-pastry cases (*vol-au-vent*) filled with chicken and mushrooms in a creamy sauce (see also *vol-au-vent*).
  poulet (poo-lā . . .) Poached chicken stuffed with seasoned chicken forcemeat served in a white sauce (*allemande*) with little chicken pastries. Another version of *poulet à la reine* is very like our *Chicken à la King*!—finely-diced chicken mixed with mushrooms in a rich white sauce.

reine-claude (ren-klōd) Greengage.

reine-jeanne, consommé à la (kawʀ-so-mā ah lah ren zhe-an) Chicken consommé garnished with tiny chicken *quenelles* (mousses) and chervil leaves.

reine pédauque (ren pā-dōk)
  omelette (om-let . . .) Two almond omelettes sandwiched with apple purée and cream, and topped with meringue.
  salade (sa-lahd . . .) Salad of quartered lettuces in a cream dressing topped with cherries and orange peel.

reinette (ren-et) General term for a family of French dessert apples, roughly equivalent to the pippin family.

relais (rə-lā) Inn, hostelry or stopping-place.
  relais routier (. . . roo-tyā) Transport café or restaurant serving reasonably-priced meals, and once rather romantically renowned for the quality of their food and their ambience, some still live up to that reputation, others don't.

religieuse (rə-leezh-yəz) 'Nun': an elaborate cake made of éclairs or *profiteroles* filled with coffee, chocolate or vanilla cream, which are erected in a pyramid to resemble a nun in her habit. Also the name for an apple and apricot jam tart with a latticed pastry top—the barred windows of a nunnery?

rémoulade, sauce (sōs rā-moo-lahd) A sort of piquant mayonnaise made with a paste of hard-boiled egg-yolks mixed with oil and vinegar, chopped herbs, capers, gherkins and mustard.

renaissance, à la (ah lah rə-nā-sawʀs) Garnish for roasts, consisting of little mounds of young vegetables.

repas (rə-pa) General term for a meal or repast.

restaurant (rais-to-rawʀ) Restaurant: any public eating-place, from the word 'restore'.

réveillon (rā-vā-yawʀ) Traditional Christmas Eve or New Year's Eve feast, celebrated by the French in restaurants rather than at home. If you wish to join them, book well ahead.

rhubarbe (rəə-barb) Rhubarb.

rhum (rom) Rum.

ribot, lait (lā ree-bō) Drinking yoghurt.

riche (reesh) Rich; rich food.
  sauce (sōs . . .) Creamy sauce enriched with lobster butter and diced truffles; also called *sauce diplomate*.

sole *(sol . . .)* Poached sole fillets in *sauce riche* with a garnish of sliced lobsters and truffles.

Richelieu *(ree-shə-lyə)* Large almond pastry gâteau filled with apricot jam and frangipane (almond) cream.

Richelieu, à la *(ah lah ree-shə-lyə)* 'As Cardinal R. liked it' (one presumes): with potatoes, lightly roasted in butter, braised lettuce and stuffed tomatoes.

    sole *(sol . . .)* Fillets of sole coated with egg and breadcrumbs, cooked in butter, then served with truffles and *maitre d'hotel* (parsley) butter.

rigodon *(ree-go-dawʀ)* A Burgundy flan which comes in two forms: as a savoury *brioche* pastry flan filled with diced bacon or ham, and as a sweet flan filled with fruit or nuts.

rillauds *(ree-yō)* Bits of pork cooked in seasoned lard and preserved in jars; also called *rillons*.

rillettes *(ree-yet)* Bits of pork or goose meat which are first prepared as *rillauds* (see above), then pounded to a paste in a mortar and preserved in stoneware pots.

rillons *(ree-yawʀ)* See *rillauds*.

ris *(ree)* Sweetbreads: of a calf *(ris de veau)*, or a lamb *(ris d'agneau)*. NOTE: don't confuse *ris* with *riz* (rice) when ordering, or you'll be in for a shock.

risotto *(ree-zo-tō)* Rice cooked in meat stock, then mixed with other ingredients such as diced meat, shellfish, vegetables, cheese, mushrooms, truffles etc.; also spelled *rizotto*.

rissole *(ree-sol)* Small deep-fried puff-pastry rolls filled with various forcemeats; like the British

sausage-roll.

rissolé(e) *(ree-so-lā)* Fried or sautéed.

rivoli, poulet *(poo-lā ree-vo-lee)* Sautéed chicken with truffles, sautéed potatoes and sherry sauce.

riz *(ree)* Rice (but see note under *ris* above).
    brun or **complet** *(. . . braʀ, kom-plā)* Brown rice.

rizotto—see *risotto*.

Robert, sauce *(sōs ro-bair)* Brown *(demi-glace)* sauce, seasoned with vinegar, chopped onions and mustard.

rochelaise, à la *(ah lah rosh-lez)* In the style of La Rochelle in Charentes:
    chaudrée *(shō-drā . . .)* Soup-cum-stew of tiny seafish in wine.

rognon *(ron-yawʀ)* Kidney; on a menu, *rognon* normally means lamb's or calf's kidney, less frequently pig's. CAUTION: *rognon blanc* ('white kidney') is a term for testicle, which *is* eaten in France.

rognonnade de veau *(ron-yawʀ-nahd də vō)* Saddle of veal with the kidney included.

rois, galette des *(ga-let dā rwah)* Twelfth-Night cake: see *épiphanie*.

romaine, laitue *(lā-tœ ro-men)* Romaine or cos lettuce.

romaine, à la *(ah lah ro-men)* A garnish of moulded spinach mousses *(timbales)* with anchovies, and *Anna* potato cakes with tomato sauce.
    sauce *(sōs . . .)* Spicy brown sauce, slightly sweet-tasting, with currants, sultanas and pine nuts.

romanov *(ro-ma-nof)* A garnish of cucumber stuffed with chopped mushrooms *(duxelles)* and *duchesse* potato nests filled with a *salpicon* of celeriac and mushrooms with horseradish.

romarin *(ro-ma-raн)* The herb rosemary.

romsteck *(rom-stek)* Franglais for rumpsteak.

rond de gigot *(rawн də zhee-gō)* Thick slice of mutton taken straight through the leg, bone included.

Roquefort *(rok-for)* Blue-veined cheese made from ewe's milk. In 1411 the inhabitants of Roquefort-sur-Soulzon were granted the exclusive right to cure their famous cheese in the caves nearby, and although nowadays some of the milk is imported from elsewhere, the cheeses are still cured in those caves and sold with an official label affirming their authenticity. Beware of imitations!

rosbif *(roz-beef)* Franglais for roast beef. English-style.

rosé *(ro-zā)* Rosy; rose-coloured; short for *rosé* wine.

rosette *(ro-zet)* Dry pork sausage, served in slices like salami; the *rosette de Lyon* is particularly well known.

rossini *(ro-see-nee)* A garnish of truffles and sliced *foie gras*, served, in particular, with *tournedos* and with eggs (*œufs*)).

rôti *(rō-tee)* Roast; a meat-roast.

rôtie *(rō-tee)* A slice of bread which is toasted or baked; also the name for a *canapé* spread with forcemeat, served with roast game or fowl.

rôtisserie *(rō-tis-ree)* 'Roasting-spit': a restaurant specialising in roast, grilled and fried meat.

rouelle *(roo-wel)* A thick slice of veal cut across the leg.

rouennaise, à la *(ah lah roo-awн-nez)* In the style of Rouen in Normandy:
  caneton *(kan-tawн. . .)* Roast duckling stuffed with its own liver, served in a blood-thickened sauce.
  pieds de mouton *(pyā də moo-tawн . . .)* Stuffed sheep's trotters, grilled or fried.
  sauce *(sōs . . .)* Red wine and shallot sauce enriched with liver; served with duck, and with poached eggs.

rouge *(roozh)* Red: short for red wine.
  de rivière *(. . . də reev-yair)* 'The red one of the river': the shoveller duck.

rouget *(roo-zhā)* The red mullet.

rouille *(roo-yə)* Fiery sauce to go with fish soups, made by blending hot red peppers and garlic with a mayonnaise-like paste of pounded bread.

rouilleuse, poulet *(poo-lā roo-yəz)* Chicken in a blood-thickened wine and garlic sauce.

roulade *(roo-lahd)* Menu term for various rolled meat or fish dishes, which may be either plain or stuffed; the name can also apply to a rolled omelette or rolled-up vegetable soufflé or mousse.

roulé(e) *(roo-lā)* Rolled; a general name for savoury or sweet pastry rolls, Swiss roll, etc.
  hareng *(a-rawн . . .)* Rollmop herring, see *hareng*.

roussette *(roo-set)* Dog-fish, a small shark sometimes served under the pleasanter name of rock salmon; also the name for a brandy-flavoured fritter with sugar topping.

routier *(roo-tyā)* see *relais*.

royale *(ro-yal)* Various

225

savoury, moulded custards used to garnish clear soups. The basic ingredients for a plain *royale* are eggs and consommé beaten together; to this mixture fish, meat and vegetable purées are added.

royale, à la (*ah lah ro-yal*) 'In the royal style': various poultry and fish dishes in which the principal ingredient is first poached then coated with cream-thickened *velouté* sauce, and finished off with truffles and other garnishes.
  consommé (*kawn-so-mā . . .*) Chicken *consommé* garnished with diced *royale* (see above).
  lièvre (*lee-evr . . .*) Boned hare stuffed with veal and bacon, braised in brandy and red wine, then served with sliced truffles.
  sauce (*sōs . . .*) White sauce based on chicken stock enriched with cream, butter, sieved truffles and sherry.

royan (*ro-yawn*) A kind of large sardine.

rumsteak (*rom-stek*) Franglais for rumpsteak.

russe, à la (*ah lah rooss*) 'In the Russian style':
  salade (*sa-lahd . . .*) Mixed diced vegetable salad in mayonnaise with pickled tongue, sausage, lobster and truffles garnished with anchovies, capers and gherkins.
  sauce (*sōs . . .*) White sauce seasoned with mustard, herbs, sugar and lemon juice.
  sole (*sol . . .*) This sole dish is described under its alternative name, *à la paysanne*.

Charlotte russe is Bavarian cream custard in a mould lined with sponge fingers.

S

sabayon (*za-ba-yawn*) Whipped-up wine and egg-yolks, served as a frothy sauce or eaten on its own as a dessert.

sablé (*sa-blā*) Sort of crumbly shortbread biscuit or cookie.

sabodet (*sa-bo-dā*) Sausage made of pig's head, served hot in thick slices.

sabot—see *laitances*

safran (*sa-fran*) The spice saffron.

sagan (*sa-gawn*) A garnish of rice (risotto) and mushrooms stuffed with puréed brain.

sagou (*sa-goo*) Sago: edible starch from the pith of certain palm trees; used for thickening soups etc.

saignant (*sen-yawn*) 'Bloody': a rare steak, cooked slightly longer than *bleu*, which is very rare indeed. A *saignant* steak is removed from the heat just as it starts to bleed.

saindoux (*san-doo*) Lard or pork-fat, used for frying etc.

saint-cloud, potage (*po-tahzh san kloo*) Thick soup of puréed peas and lettuce, garnished with croutons.

Sainte-Menehould (*sant men-ə-hood*) A piquant brown sauce with mustard, chopped shallots, gherkins and vinegar; served with pig's trotters.
  pieds de porc (*pee-ā də por . . .*) Pig's trotters cooked slowly for a long time so that the bones become soft enough to eat.

Saint-Flour (*san floor*)
  friand de (*free-awn də . . .*) Sausage meat

wrapped in pastry or leaves.

pommes *(pom . . .)*
Sliced potatoes baked with diced bacon on a bed of cabbage leaves.

Saint-Germain, à la *(ah lah saʀ zhair-maʀ)* A garnish of peas or of thick pea purée with sautéed artichokes.

potage *(po-tahzh . . .)*
Puréed pea soup enriched with butter.

Saint-Honoré *(saʀ tō-no-rā)*
Little round *choux* pastry-puffs iced with sugar and set around a large, cream-filled pastry ring to form a 'jewelled' crown.

Saint-Jacques, coquille *(ko-kee saʀ zhak)* Scallop, shellfish with white flesh and a coral 'tongue'.

Saint Malo, sauce *(sōs saʀ ma-lō)* White sauce seasoned with onions, mushrooms, mustard, anchovy essence and herbs, served with fish.

Saint-Pierre *(saʀ-pyair)*
The sea fish John Dory.

Saint-Saëns *(saʀ sawʀ)*
Truffle and *foie-gras* fritters, cock's kidneys and asparagus tips, served as a garnish for chicken *suprêmes* (breasts).

saison *(sā-zawn)* Season; in season.

saisonnier *(sā-zon-yā)*
Seasonal.

salade *(sa-lahd)* Salad.

saladier *(sa-la-dyā)*
General term for a large, mixed salad; also, a salad-bowl. See also *lyonnaise*.

salaison *(sal-lā-zawʀ)* Salting: a general term for salted fish and meat.

salambo *(sa-lawʀ-bō)*
Small, iced *choux* pastry cake filled with kirsch-flavoured cream.

salamis *(sa-la-mee)*
Salami.

salda *(sal-dah)* Rich soup made from sausage and

bacon with various vegetables.

salé *(sa-lā)* Salted, salty or pickled.

salmigondis *(sal-mee-gawʀ-dee)* Ragôut of various pre-cooked meats.

salmis *(sal-mee)* General term for various game-fowl dishes in which the whole bird is first partly roasted, then divided into joints and skinned, and finally simmered in wine sauce.

salon de thé *(sa-lawn də tā)* Tea-room.

salpicon *(sal-pee-kawʀ)*
French culinary mainstay: an all-purpose preparation of diced meat, fish and vegetables, which is bound in a sauce and used as a stuffing, garnish, pastry filling or *hors-d'œuvre* spread.

salsifis *(sal-see-fee)* Salsify, also called the oyster plant; served hot with a butter or cream sauce, or raw in salads.

sanciau *(sawʀ-syō)*
General term for a thick pancake, either sweet or savoury.

sandre *(sawʀ-drə)* Pike-perch, a freshwater fish regarded as something of a delicacy.

sandwich *(sawʀd-weesh)*
Sandwich; French sandwiches are usually made with the long *baguette* loaf which is slit horizontally and stuffed with all kinds of good things.

sang *(sawʀ)* Blood.
-cuit *(. . . kwee)* Cooked blood, used in a wide variety of sauces and as an ingredient in black puddings; also known as a *sanguette* or *sanquette*.

sanglier *(sawʀ-lyā)* Wild boar.

sangria *(sawʀ-gree-yah)*
Spanish drink of wine and lemonade, served with orange or lemon peel

sangue *(sawʀg)* Corsican

black pudding, sometimes incorporating grapes.

sanguette *(sawn-gete)* See *sang-cuit*.

sanguine *(sawn-geen)* Blood orange; also a type of pancake made of chopped onions cooked in chicken's blood; also called *sanguette* (see *sang-cuit*).

sansiot *(sawn-syō)* Head of a calf.

santé *(sawn-tā)* Health: the customary French drinking toast, short for *à votre santé* ('to your health').

    potage *(po-tahzh . . .)* Thick soup made of puréed potatoes and leeks plus shredded sorrel, enriched with butter, cream and egg-yolk.

sarcelle *(sar-sel)* Teal, a species of wild duck.

sarde, à la *(ah lah sahrd)* Sardinian style: with a garnish of French beans, cheesy rice croquettes, mushrooms and tomato sauce

sardine *(sar-deen)* Sardine or pilchard.

sarladaise, à la *(ah lah sarlah-dez)* With truffles.

    cajasse *(ka-zhas . . .)* Rum-laced cake or pastry.

    mique *(meek . . .)* Maize flour dumpling served with stews.

    pommes *(pom . . .)* Potatoes layered with truffles and baked in a casserole, sometimes with *foie-gras*.

sarments *(sar-mawn)* Vine twigs, used for grilling steak in Bordeaux.

sarrasin *(sa-ra-san)* Buckwheat; buckwheat flour.

sarrasine, à la *(ah lah sa-raseen)* (A garnish of little buckwheat cakes and rice tartlets filled with tomato and sweet pepper pulp *(fondue)*).

sarriette *(sar-yet)* The bitter herb savoury, also called *poivre d'âne*.

sauce *(sōs)* Sauce: a liquid or semi-liquid dressing for food, and a notable feature of French cooking. See under their individual names for details of the many French sauces.

sauciau *(sō-syō)* See *sanciau*.

saucisse *(sō-sees)* Sausage; fresh sausage (as opposed to dry); any sausage which must be cooked in some way before eating it.

saucisson *(sō-see-sawn)* Dry sausage; prepared or smoked sausage; any ready-to-eat sausage. In certain recipes, *saucisson* may be cooked (or recooked) as well, e.g. the sliced salami on a pizza.

sauge *(sōzh)* Sage (herb).

saumon *(sō-mawn)* Salmon.

    fumé *(. . . foo-mā)* Smoked salmon.

Saumonette *(sō-mawn-net)* Sea eel, or dogfish.

saumuré *(sō-moo-rā)* General term for any food which has been salted or pickled in brine.

saupiquet *(sō-pee-kā)* Piquant sauce of wine vinegar, cream, juniper berries and shallots.

saur *(sōr)* Salted, smoked herring *(hareng saur)*; also called *sauret*.

saurel *(sō-rel)* The horse mackerel.

sauret *(sō-rā)* See *saur*.

sausson or **saussoun** *(sōsawn* or *sō-soon)* Paste of anchovies, almonds, olive oil and mint, spread on bread as an *hors d'œuvre*; also called *sauce aux amandes*.

sauté *(sō-tā)* Sautéed: lightly fried or browned (usually in butter) over a high heat while shaking the pan. A *sauté* (noun) is a dish of something that has been sautéed.

sauterelle *(sō-trel)* Colloquial name for the mantis

shrimp (*squille*), and also for the common shrimp (*crevette grise*).

sauvage (*sō-vahzh*) Wild or natural, as opposed to domestic or cultivated.

savarin (*sa-va-raɴ*) Doughnut shaped yeast cake flavoured with rum or kirsch.

savoy, biscuits de (*biskweeh də sav-wahr*) Savoy sponge cake.

savoyarde, gratin (*gra-taɴ sa-vo-yar*) Thinly sliced potatoes baked in stock with cheese.

savoyarde, à la (*ah lah sa-vo-yahrd*) In the style of Savoie in E France: often with cheese and potatoes.
　omelette (*om-let . . .*) Omelette with fried potatoes and cheese.
　soupe (*soop . . .*) Thick vegetable soup with grated cheese.

scarole (*ska-rol*) Escarole, not unlike the salad green *chicorée*.

schaleth (*sha-let*) See *juif*.

schifela (*shee-fə-lah*) Smoked shoulder of pork with a salad of potatoes and onions, or with pickled turnip.

schnitzen (*shnit-zən*) Garnish of dried pears and apples, served with game.

schwarzwurst (*shvartsveerst*) Smoked pork and onion sausage, from Alsace.

scorpion (*skor-pyawɴ*) 'Scorpion' or 'scorpionfish': a colloquial name for *rascasse*.

sec or **sèche** (*sek, sesh*) Dry or dried.

sèche or **seiche** (*sesh*) Cuttlefish.

seigle (*se-gle*) Rye; ryeflour; rye-bread.

sel (*sel*) Salt.
　sel marin (*. . . ma-raɴ*) Sea salt.
　gros sel (*grō . . .*) Rock salt; coarse salt.

selle (*sel*) Saddle or back: a cut of meat—particularly of lamb, mutton and rabbit —comprising the hindquarters, from the last rib to the legs.

seltz (*selts*) Short for *eau de seltz*: soda water or seltzer.

semoule (*sə-mool*) Semolina: coarse-ground wheat-flour.

sépiole (*sā-pyol*) Small cuttlefish (*seiche*).

service (*sair-vees*) Service, service charge or tip. The normal service charge in France is 15 per cent of the total bill.
　service compris (*. . . kompree*) Service charge included (in which case a further tip may be left at your discretion).
　service non compris (*. . . nawɴ kom-pree*) Service charge not included, also written *service en sus*. If you are uncertain whether or not service has been included in your bill, always ask.
En deux services refers to a dish—especially duck—that is presented in two stages: first the breast is served, then the legs, usually boned and garnished with a salad.

serviette (*sair-vyet*) Napkin (also means a towel).
　à la serviette means 'served in a napkin'; truffles are sometimes presented like this.

sétoise, langouste à la (*lawɴ-goost ah lah sāt-wahz*) Crawfish in a spicy sauce with tomatoes, garlic and brandy; named after Sète, a port on the Mediterranean, the dish is remarkably similar to *homard* (or *langouste*) *à l'américaine*.

sicilienne, potage de grenouilles à la (*po-tahzh də gren-wee-ye ah lah see-seel-yen*) Soup of pounded frog's legs blended with white (*velouté*) sauce, thickened with cream, egg-yolks and pistachio butter.

simple *(san-plə)* Simple, plain, unmixed; by itself.

sirop *(see-rō)* Syrup.

sobronade *(so-bro-nahd)* Thick soup of pork, ham, white beans, turnips, onions, probably carrots, celery, leeks, along with garlic and herbs.

socca *(so-kah)* Flat cake or pancake made of chick-pea flour.

soja *(so-zhah)* Soya; soya bean.

soissonaise, à la *(ah lah swah-so-nez)* With white kidney-beans ((haricots blancs).

sole *(sol)* Dover sole, considered the most delicate-tasting of all flatfish.

solette *(so-let)* Slip, small sole.

solférino, potage *(po-tahzh sol-fā-ree-nō)* Thick soup of puréed tomatoes, carrots, leeks and potatoes, seasoned with garlic and enriched with butter.

solognote, à la *(ah lah so-lon-yot)* In the style of Sologne, a wooded area south of the Loire.
  feuilletée *(fəy-tā . . .)* A puff-pastry with a game stuffing.
  lièvre *(lee-evr . . .)* Hare braised in wine with herbs, served cold with prunes.

sommelier *(so-mel-yā)* Person in charge of the wine cellar; the wine-waiter.

sorbet *(sor-bā)* Sorbet or water-ice (US: sherbet).

soubise *(soo-beez)* A purée of onions and rice, served as an accompaniment to meat.
  sauce *(sōs . . .)* Rich white onion sauce.

sou-fassum *(soo-fa-səm)* Boiled cabbage stuffed with rice and sausage meat; also called *capoun* and *fassum*.

soufflé *(soo-flā)* Various sweet or savoury dishes made of puréed ingredients with egg-yolks and stiffly-beaten egg-whites which puff up when baked. The name also covers dishes that are firmer, more mousse-like in texture, which are generally served cold whereas a true soufflé is eaten straight from the oven.

soupe *(soop)* Soup; the word *soupe* generally indicates a thick country-style broth containing pieces of meat and vegetables, as opposed to smooth *velouté* and cream soups and *potages* where the ingredients are usually puréed. An exception is the puréed *soupe de poissons* of Provence.

souper *(soo-pā)* Supper, to eat supper; late dinner.

soupir de nonne *(soo-peer də non)* 'Nun's sigh': soufflé fritter, also called *pet de nonne*.

sous-noix de veau *(soo nwah də vō)* The underpart of silverside of veal.

souvaroff or **souvarov, à la** *(ah lah soo-va-rof, soo-va-rov)* Method of cooking poultry and game in a sealed casserole with truffles, brandy and *foie-gras*. A *souvarov* is also a *petit-four* layered with apricot jam and covered with icing sugar.

spaetzle *(spāt-zle)* Sort of noodle-dumplings either poached with melted butter or fried; also spelled *spätsel* and *spetzli*.

spätzel—see *spaetzle*.

spécial *(spā-syal)* Special.

spécialité *(spā-syal-ee-tā)* Speciality.

spetzli—see *spätzle*.

squinado *(skee-nah-do)* Colloquial name for the spider crab *(araignée de mer)*.

stanley, poulet *(poo-lá stan-lee)* Sautéed chicken

coated in a creamy onion and curry sauce, garnished with truffles.

steak or **steack** *(stek)* Steak or beefsteak. To specify how you want your steak cooked, you can ask for it:
   à point *(ah pwaн)* Medium: cooked until it just stops bleeding.
   bien cuit *(bee-aн kwee)* Well-done.
   bleu *(blə)* Ultra-rare: cooked for the shortest possible time.
   saignant *(sen-yawн)* Very rare: cooked for very slightly longer than *bleu*.

steak tartare *(stek tar-tar)* Raw minced beef mixed with chopped onions, capers, parsley and worcester sauce, served with a raw egg.

stocaficada *(sto-ka-fee-kah-dah)* Dried cod which has been split open and flattened. Popular in S France, especially Nice, where it is stewed with onions, tomatoes, garlic and basil. Also called *estoficada, morue plate* and *stockfish*.

stockfish *(stok-feesh)* See previous entry.

Strasbourg *(straz-boor)* Town in Alsace, NE France.
   salamis de *(sa-la-mee-də . . .)* Sausage made from smoked pork and beef.
   saucisse de *(sō-sees də . . .)* Frankfurter sausage, again of smoked pork and beef.

strasbourgeoise, à la *(ah lah straz-boorzh-wahz)* In the style of Strasbourg: with sauerkraut, *foie gras* and salt pork or sausage.
   consommé *(kawн-so-mã . . .)* Thickened consommé flavoured with juniper berries, garnished with strips *(julienne)* of red cabbage, sliced Strasbourg sausage and horseradish.

stuffatu *(stoo-fa-too)* Corsican meat sauce made of tomatoes, onions and wine and mixed with pasta.

subric *(soo-breek)* General term for a little ball or croquette made of ground or puréed meat, fish or vegetables bound with a thick sauce and fried in butter; served as an *hors d'œuvre*.

suc de viande *(seek də vee-awнd)* Meat juice.

suçarelle, escargots à la *(es-kar-gō ah lah soo-sa-rel)* Snails prepared with tomatoes, garlic, sausage and white wine, which are traditionally sucked, rather than picked, from their shells.

sucée *(soo-sã)* Crunchy *petit-four* containing finely-chopped candied fruit.

sucette *(soo-set)* Lollipop.

sucre *(soo-krə)* Sugar:
   brun *(. . . braн)* Brown sugar.
   cristallisé *(. . . krees-ta-lee-zã)* Granulated sugar.
   en morceaux *(. . . awн mor-sō)* Cube or lump sugar.
   en poudre *(. . . awн poo-drə)* Caster (powdered) sugar.
   glace *(. . . glas)* Icing sugar.
   roux *(. . . roo)* Demerara sugar.

sucre de pommes *(soo-krə də pom)* Apple sugar sticks.

sucrée *(soo-krã)* Sweet, sweetened or sugary; with sugar.

sucrin *(soo-kraн)* Sweet melon.

suédoise *(swãd-wahz)* Dish of poached fruit set in jelly.

sultane, à la *(ah lah sool-tan)* 'As the sultan likes it': with pistachio nuts or pistachio butter, or with an elaborate garnish of tartlets filled with puréed truffles and pistachio nuts, cocks-combs and little *canapés* of minced chicken, which is served with chicken *suprême*.

Also a general term applied to certain sweets and pastries for no reason except that the name perhaps sounds inviting.

supioun or **suppion** *(see-pyoon, see-pyawn)* Colloquial name for a small cuttlefish *(sépiole)*.

suprême *(see-praim)* Short for *suprême de volaille*: breast and wing fillets of poultry (usually chicken) or, in some recipes, of game fowl.

    sauce *(sōs . . .)* Creamy white sauce.

surprise *(seer-preez)* Surprise: a mystery dish. This is a menu term meaning nothing in particular except that whatever the dish is, the chef probably made it up at the last minute, quite possibly out of desperation. A *surprise* dish is often concocted from left-overs, and if it contains seafood the surprise may be that you don't feel very well after eating it. Best approached with caution, except for the following:

    melon *(me-lawn . . .)* Chilled melon filled with fruit and sprinkled with liqueur.

    omelette *(om-let . . .)* Baked Alaska: sponge cake filled with ice cream, covered with meringue and eaten hot; also called *omelette norvégienne*.

sus, en *(awn see)* In addition: and additional or extra charge.

suzette, crêpe *(kraip see-zet)* Thin pancake flamed with orange liqueur at the table, and served with orange butter sauce.

sylvette, sole *(sol sil-vet)* Fillets of sole sautéed with shredded vegetables and sherry, served with truffles

and little tomatoes stuffed with fish purée.

table *(ta-ble)* Table.

table d'hôte *(ta-ble-dōt)* Term for a fixed-price meal of several courses.

tablette *(ta-blet)* Tablet or bar (of chocolate etc.).

tablier de sapeur *(ta-blyā de sa-per)* Ox tripe coated in egg and breadcrumbs, then grilled and served with *Béarnaise* or *tartare* sauce.

tagliarini *(tal-yah-ree-nee)* Thin flat strips of pasta (Corsica).

talibur *(ta-lee-beer)* See *rabot(t)e*.

talleyrand *(tal-lā-rawn)* A great 17th-century gourmet after whom a number of elaborate dishes have been named, including a garnish of truffles, mushrooms, goose liver and cream sauce with macaroni and/or parmesan cheese.

    omelette *(om-let . . .)* Onion omelette seasoned with curry powder, garnished with fried sweetbreads.

    sauce *(sōs . . .)* Rich cream sauce with madeira and finely diced truffles and pickled tongue.

tapenade *(ta-pa-nahd)* Thick paste made of tuna, capers and olives pounded with anchovies; spread on toast.

tapioca *(tap-yō-kah)* Tapioca: starch of the cassava or manioc plant, used in puddings and to thicken soup.

tartare, sauce *(sōs tar-tar)* Cold sauce of mayonnaise made with pounded hard-boiled egg-yolks and containing chopped onions, mustard, gherkins, capers and herbs. See also *steak tartare*.

tarte *(tart)* Tart or flan; a pastry shell filled with fruit, jam, custard, or some similar mixture, usually but not always sweet. Like a US open-faced pie, baked either in a pie dish or a flan ring.

tarte flambé—see *flammekueche*.

tarte tatin *(tart ta-taʀ)* Upside-down apple tart.

tartelette *(tart-let)* Small, open tart with either a sweet or a savoury filling.

tartine *(tar-teen)* A slice of bread and butter, eaten either on its own or spread with jam, jelly, or almost anything else that won't fall off; equivalent to the US open-faced sandwich.
 swisse *(. . . swees)* Rectangular flaky-pastry filled with vanilla cream.

tartiner *(tar-tee-nā)* To spread something on something else.
 fromage à tartiner *(fro-mahzh ah . . .)* Cheese spread.

tartouffe *(tar-toof)* Old-fashioned term for a potato.

tartouillat *(tar-twee-yah)* Burgundian apple tart.

tasse *(tas)* Cup; a coffee or tea cup.

tastevin *(tas-tə-vaʀ)* Wine-tasting cup.

tatin—see *tarte*.

taupe *(tōp)* Porbeagle: a kind of edible shark.

tendre de tranche *(tawʀ-dre də trawʀsh)* UK: topside of beef; US: rumpsteak.

tendron de veau *(tawʀ-drawʀ də vō)* Veal rib roast.

terée de moules *(tair-rā də mool)* Mussels cooked over pine-needles; also called *éclade*.

tergoule or **tord-goule** *(tair-gool, tor-gool)* Rice and cinnamon pudding.

terrine *(tai-reen)* A rectangular earthenware cooking-dish with a cover; also the name of a type of coarse pâté—see under *pâté* for details.

terriné(e) *(tai-ree-nā)* Baked in a terrine.
 de porc *(. . . də por)* Pork chops layered in a casserole with sliced potatoes and ham, and baked with white wine, garlic and juniper berries.

tête *(tait)* Head; the head of an animal.

tête d'aloyau *(tait dal-wah-yə)* Rump cut of beef taken from just beside the sirloin.

tétras *(tā-tra)* Grouse.

thé *(tā)* Tea:
 au citron *(. . . ō see-trawʀ)* Lemon tea.
 au lait *(. . . ō lā)* Tea with milk.
 nature *(. . . na-təər)* Black tea.

thermidor, homard *(ō-mar tair-mee-dor)* Classic lobster dish consisting of sautéed lobster served in the shell in a creamy white wine sauce topped with parmesan cheese and browned.

thon *(tawʀ)* Tuna; tunny fish.

thonne *(ton)* Veal marinated in oil, lemon juice and herbs, then cooked with tuna fish.

thourins *(too-raʀ)* Milk-and-onion soup, sometimes with cheese, served over sliced bread; also spelled *tourain* and *tourin*.

thym *(taʀ)* The herb thyme.

tian *(tyaʀ)* Shallow earthenware cooking-dish. Also refers to preparations cooked in a *tian*, such as the mixed vegetable *gratins* of Provence.

tiède *(tyed)* Tepid or warm.

tilleul *(tee-yəl)* Lime tree;

233

its dried flowers are used to make a delicious and healthful herb tea.

timbale *(tan-bahl)* Drum-shaped mould used for baking various dishes. The name has also come to mean the actual food that is baked in this mould (then turned out onto a dish). The classic *timbale* is encased in a pastry shell. Increasingly, the term covers small fish or vegetable mousses or jellies that are turned out of their mould and served as an *hors d'œuvre* or garnish.

tioro *(tyor-ō)* Fish, tomato, onion and garlic stew, also called *ttoro*.

tisane *(tee-zahn)* Herbal tea of any kind.

tomate *(to-mat)* Tomato.

tomate de mer *(to-mat də mair)* Red sea anemone, used in fish soups.

topinabour *(tō-peen-a bor)* Jerusalem artichoke.

tord-goule—see *tergoule*.

torta castagnina *(tor-tah kas-tan-yee-nah)* (Corsican chestnut-flour tart with raisins, almonds, walnuts and pine kernels laced with rum.

torte *(tort)* A general name for a variety of sweet flans, mostly German or Alsatian in origin, and for rich layer cakes, usually with cream.

tortue *(tor-tœ)* Tortoise or turtle of any kind, land or marine; it is usually the flipper *(nageoire)* that is eaten.
   consommé *(kawn-so-mā . . .)* Turtle consommé with madeira and pieces of turtle.
   sauce *(sōs . . .)* Brown sauce flavoured with tomatoes and herbs mixed with madeira.
The name is also given to a garnish of *quenelles* (small mousses), truffles, mushrooms, olives, crayfish, brains and gherkins in *sauce tortue (en tortue)*, served with veal.

toscane, à la *(ah lah tos-kan)* In the style of Tuscany in N Italy: a garnish of macaroni mixed with puréed *foie gras* and diced truffles, served with veal, sweetbreads or chicken sautéed in a coating of breadcrumbs and parmesan.

totelots *(tōt-lō)* Hot noodle salad with hard-boiled eggs.

tôt-fait *(tō fã)* 'Quickly-made': plain but rich sponge cake flavoured with lemon.

touffe *(toof)* Bunch; stalks tied together, e.g. a bunch of parsley or chives.

toulia *(tool-yah)* Onion soup with tomatoes, leeks, cheese and garlic; also called *ouliat, tourri* and *soupe du berger*.

toulouse *(too-looz)* Type of large *saucisse* (a sausage that requires cooking) renowned for its flavour; traditionally served with puréed onions.

toulousaine, à la *(ah lah too-loo-zain)* In the style of Toulouse in SW France: with a garnish of truffles, sweetbreads, chicken *quenelles* (little mousses), kidneys and cockscombs in white sauce.
   aillade *(ī-yard . . .)* Aïoli (garlic mayonnaise) mixed with pounded walnuts.
   dindonneau *(dan-do-nō . . .)* Turkey stuffed with chestnuts, minced pork and *cèpes* (mushrooms).
   foie gras *(fwah-grah . . .)* Garlic-spiked *foie gras* wrapped in a pastry case.
   pommes *(pom . . .)* Quartered potatoes sautéed in goose fat, then cooked with stock and garlic.

toupin *(too-pan)* Fat-bodied, narrow-necked earthenware cooking-pot, used especially for *daubes* and *garbures*. The name also applies to various dishes cooked in a *toupin*.

tourain—see *thourins*.

tourangelle, à la *(ah lah toor-awн-zehl)* In the style of Touraine in central France: often with prunes.

tourin—see *thourins*.

tournedos *(toor-nə-do)* Small, round fillet steaks of beef.

tournesol *(toor-nə-sol)* Sunflower.
  grain de *(graн də . . .)* Sunflower seed.
  huile de *(weel də . . .)* Sunflower oil.

touron *(too-rawн)* A sweet or candy of almond paste with pistachios, hazelnuts, and crystallized fruit; also spelled *ttouron*.

tourri *(too-ree)* See *toulia*.

tourte *(toort)* Covered pie or covered tart, similar to the English meat or meat-and-vegetable pie. There are also sweet *tourtes*, filled with fruit or pastry cream.

tourteau *(toor-tō)* Oilcake or hearthcake; also the name of a type of large crab.
  tourteau fromagé *(. . . from-arzhā)* Kind of cheesecake made with goat's milk round Poitou.

tourtereau or **tourterelle** *(toort-rō, toor-tə-rel)* Turtle dove.

tourtière *(toor-tyair)* Pie tin or flan mould, or the food cooked in it: in particular chicken and salsify pie (Périgord).

toute-épice *(too-tā-pees)* Allspice: ground myrtle seed, also called *poivre de la Jamaïque*.

train *(traн)* Hindquarters of an animal.

traiteur *(trā-tər)* Caterer; delicatessen.

tranche *(trawнsh)* A slice, portion or serving (of bread, cheese etc.); a slice, rasher or cut (of meat).

trébuc *(trā-bөөk)* Potted, preserved meat of goose, duck, turkey or pork, sometimes added to *garbure*; also called *tromblon*.

treize desserts de Noël *(trez dā-sair də nō-wel)* 'Thirteen Christmas desserts', served traditionally on Christmas Eve in Provence: a mixture of fresh, dried and candied fruits, plus nuts, little cakes and mixed sweets.

trénels or **trénouls** *(trā-nel, trā-nool)* Lamb's tripe cooked with tomatoes, ham and white wine; also called *manouls*.

treuffe *(trөf)* Slang word for potato *(pomme de terre)*.

tripe, à la *(ah lah treep)* Hard-boiled eggs covered with *sauce soubise* (onion sauce).

tripes *(treep)* Tripe: the stomach of a ruminant animal, notably pig, sheep, calf and ox.

tripettes *(tree-pet)* Corsican term for sheep's tripe.
  à la mode de Corse *(. . . ah lah mod də kors)* Fried tripe with tomato sauce.

tripotchka *(tree-poch-kah)* Spicy black pudding made of mutton and veal.

tripous or **tripoux** *(tree-poo)* Stuffed, highly-seasoned sheep's feet.

tromblon *(trom-blawн)* See *trébuc*.

trompette de la mort *(trom-pet də lah mor)* 'Trumpet of death': mushroom also known by the more appetizing name *corne d'abondance*.

tronçon *(trawн-sawн)* Thick slice of meat or fish; chunk.

trouffe *(troof)* Slang word

235

for potato (*pomme de terre*).

trouvillaise, à la *(ah lah troo-vee-yez)* In the style of Trouville in Normandy: with shrimps, mussels and mushrooms.
  sole *(sol . . .)* Poached sole with mussels, shrimps and mushrooms in a white cream sauce enriched with shrimp butter.

truche *(treesh)* Colloquial term for potato *(pomme de terre)*.

truffade or **truffado** *(treefahd, tree-fa-dō)* Fried potato cake mixed with cheese, bacon and garlic; alternatively a dish of mashed potatoes mixed with cheese then baked.

truffe *(treef)* Truffle: the highly-esteemed brown/black fungus found growing underground among oak or hazel tree roots, notably in the Périgord and Quercy region. The same name applies to a chocolate sweet with a dark, buttery centre.

truffé *(troo-fá)* Garnished, stuffed or otherwise accompanied by truffles.

truffiat *(troo-fyah)* Also known as *bourre chrétien*; this comes in two forms: as a potato-cake, and as a potato wrapped in pastry.

truite *(trweet)* Trout.
  arc-en-ciel *(. . . ar-kawʀsyel)* Rainbow trout.
  de lac *(. . . de lak)* Lake trout.
  de rivière *(. . . de reevyair)* River trout.
  saumonée *(. . . sō-monā)* Salmon trout.

truite de mer *(trweet de mair)* Alternative name for the sea trout or salmon trout *(truite saumonée)*.

ttoro *(to-rō)* See *tioro*.

ttouron *(too-rawʀ)* See *touron*.

tuile *(tweel)* 'Roof tile': an almond biscuit shaped like a curved roof tile.

turbot *(teer-bō)* Turbot: a large, white sea fish, very flat in shape, with a subtle flavour.

V

vache *(vash)* Cow; also a general name for cow's-milk cheese.

vacherin *(vash-raʀ)* An elaborate dessert of stacked meringue rings filled with whipped cream or ice-cream, and decorated with strawberries. In some versions the rings are made of almond paste rather than meringue. This is also a name given to certain cow's-milk cheeses, such as *Vacherin Mont d'Or*, *Vacherin d'Abondance* etc.

vairon *(vai-rawʀ)* Minnow: a small freshwater fish.

valence *(va-lawʀs)* Spanish orange.

valenciennes, à la *(ah lah va-lawʀ-syen)* With a garnish of rice and pimentos in a white wine or tomato sauce.
  langue de Valenciennes Lucullus *(lawʀg de . . . lee-kee-lee)* Smoked tongue with *foie gras*.
  lapin *(la-paʀ . . .)* Rabbit stewed with raisins and prunes.

vallée d'auge, poulet *(poolā va-lā dōzh)* Chicken cooked with *calvados*, cider, apples and cream; veal *(veau)* is prepared in the same way.

vanille *(va-nee-yə)*
Vanilla.

vanneau *(va-nō)* Lapwing, a bird related to the plover.

vapeur *(va-per)* Steam or vapour.
  pomme *(pom . . .)*
  Steam or boiled potatoes.

varié *(var-yā)* Varied, assorted or mixed: a menu term referring usually to mixed *hors d'œuvres*, shell-fish, side-dishes of vegetables and so on.

vauclusienne, truite à la *(trweet ah lah vō-klœz-yen)* Trout fried in olive oil, served with a little of the oil mixed with lemon juice.

veau *(vō)* Veal. The principal cuts are:
  carré *(ka-rā)* Middle neck; UK: best end of neck; US: rib roast or shoulder.
  collet *(ko-lā)* UK: scrag end; US: 'city chicken'.
  côtelettes *(kot-let)* Rib chops or escalope.
  crosse *(kros)* Ankle or lower end of leg.
  cuisseau *(kwee-sō)* Also called *noix*. UK: fillet, fillet steak; US: round roast, round steak, rump roast.
  épaule *(ā-pōl)* Shoulder.
  escalope *(es-ka-lōp)* Thin slice taken from the *cuisseau*.
  jarret *(zha-rā)* Leg; UK: knuckle.
  longe *(lawᴚzh)* Loin or loin chop.
  noix *(nwah)* See *cuisseau*.
  poitrine *(pwah-treen)* Breast.
  quasi *(ka-zee)* UK: chump; US loin steak.
  rouelles *(roo-wel)* Fillet.
  tendron *(tawᴚ-drawᴚ)* Breast.

velouté *(vel-oo-tā)* Basic creamy white sauce made from veal or chicken stock thickened with flour and butter; also the name of many soups based on *velouté* sauce.

venaison *(və-nā-sawᴚ)*

Venison; also called *chevreuil*.

vendanges *(vawᴚ-dawᴚzh)* Grape-harvest.
  soupe des *(soop dā . . .)* Soup made from beef, veal and vegetables, which is traditionally ladled out to the grape-pickers.

vendéen *(vawᴚ-dā-aᴚ)*
  fressure *(frā-seer . . .)* Pig's liver, heart, lungs and spleen cooked in blood and served cold.
  pâté *(pa-tā . . .)* Pork and rabbit pâté.

ventre *(vawᴚ-trə)* The belly, breast or stomach of an animal.

ventrèche *(vawᴚ-tresh)* Smoked or salted breast of pork.

vénus *(vā-nəəs)* Cockle, the edible sea mollusc.

verdi *(vair-dee)* A garnish of truffles and macaroni.
  suprêmes de volaille *(səə-praim də vo-lā . . .)* Sautéed chicken suprêmes in a pastry case with macaroni, *foie gras* and sliced truffles.

verdurette *(vair-dəə-ret)* Vinaigrette sauce with chives, chervil, tarragon and chopped hard-boiled egg-yolks.

verdurière, omelette à la *(om-let ah lah vair-dəər-yair)* Omelette with lettuce, sorrel, tarragon, chervil and parsley mixed in with the eggs.

verjus *(vair-zhəə)* The juice of unripe grapes.

vermicelle *(vair-mee-sel)* Vermicelli: fine threads of pasta, used mainly in soups.

verni *(vair-nee)* Venus shell, a type of clam.

véronique *(vā-rawᴚ-neek)* With grapes, in general.
  bombe *(bom . . .)* Pistachio nut and chocolate ice-cream *bombe*.
  poularde *(poo-lard . . .)*

Poached chicken served with a cream sauce and grapes; sole is also prepared in this way.

verre *(vair)* Glass: and drinking glass or wine glass.

vert(e) *(vair(t))* Green: the colour and also in the sense of 'new', in some cases.

> **anguille au vert** *(awн-gee ō . . .)* Eel served cold with *sauce verte*.
> **sauce verte** *(sōs . . .)* Green mayonnaise mixed with a paste of pounded tarragon, watercress, parsley and spinach.
> **vertes de Marennes** *(. . . də ma-ren)* Greenish oyster raised in the Marennes oyster parks.

vert-pré *(vair-prā)* A garnish of matchstick potatoes, watercress and parsley butter for red-meat dishes.

verveine *(vair-ven)* The herb verbena; also a popular herbal tea *(infusion)* made with verbena.

vessie *(vai-see)* Pig's bladder.

> **poularde en** *(poo-lard awн. . .)* Stuffed chicken poached in a pig's bladder with vegetables.

viande *(vee-yawнd)* Meat in general.

vichy *(vee-shee)* A popular mineral-water, slightly fizzy, which comes from the town of the same name.

> **carottes à la** *(ka-rot ah lah . . .)* Glazed young carrots, sliced.

vichyssoise, crème à la *(krem ah lah vee-shee-swahz)* Famous leek and potato soup, served either hot or cold.

Victoria *(veek-tor-yah)* Queen Victoria was apparently the inspiration for the following: a garnish of tomatoes stuffed with mushroom purée and quartered artichokes cooked in butter.

> **sauce** *(sōs . . .)* Brown *(espagnole)* sauce mixed with port and redcurrant jelly, and spiced with cinnamon and cloves; served with venison.
> **sole** *(sol . . .)* Poached sole garnished with a *salpicon* of crawfish and truffles in a creamy lobster sauce.

The name *Victoria* is also given to a rich fruit and nut cake laced with rum.

vieille *(vyā)* Sea wrasse.

viennoise, à la *(ah lah vyen-wahz)* Food fried in a coating of egg and breadcrumbs; also, with a garnish of olives, capers, lemons, anchovies and chopped hard-boiled eggs.

vierge *(vyairzh)* 'Virgin': a term for the best-quality olive oil, from the first pressing of the olives; also a name for butter whipped with lemon to a froth, which is served with asparagus.

vigne *(veen-ye)* Vine, grape-vine or vineyard.

vigneronne, à la *(ah lah veen-yə-ron)* 'Winegrower's style': with grapes, vine-leaves, wine or *marc*.

> **cagouilles** *(ka-goo-yə . . .)* Snails cooked in white wine with garlic or shallots, and parsley.

vignoble *(vee-no-blə)* Vineyard; a wine-producing region.

villeroi *(veel-rwah)* Dishes which are deep-fried in a coating of egg, breadcrumbs and white sauce.

vin *(vaн)* Wine:

> **blanc** *(. . . blawн)* White wine.
> **maison** *(. . . mā-zawн)* House wine; see also *maison*.
> **mousseux** *(. . . moo-sə)* Sparkling wine.
> **ordinaire** *(. . . or-dee-nair)* 'Ordinary wine';

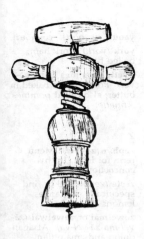

table wine.

rosé *(. . . ro-zā)* Rosé wine.

rouge *(. . . roozh)* Red wine.

rouge de Bordeaux *(. . . roozh də bor-dō)* Red Bordeaux wine, called claret in the UK (but not in France).

de table *(. . . də ta-blə)* Table wine.

vinaigre *(vee-nā-grə)* Vinegar.

vinaigrette *(vee-nā-gret)* Traditional oil-and-vinegar dressing for salads, widely used in French cooking as a base for other sauces and as a dressing for other dishes, often with added ingredients.

vincent *(vaʀ-sawʀ)* Variant of *sauce vert*: green mayonnaise sauce with herbs and chopped egg-yolks.

violet *(vyō-lā)* See *figue de mer*.

violette *(vyō-let)* Violet: its petals are crystallized (a speciality of Toulouse).

violon *(vyō-lawʀ)* 'Violin': a violin-shaped fish related to the skate; also called *guitare*.

viveur *(vee-vər)* Term for dishes which are liberally seasoned with cayenne or paprika.

omelette *(om-let . . .)* Omelette made with a mixture of sautéed diced beef, celeriac and artichoke hearts.

vladimir *(vla-dee-meer)* Garnish of sautéed cucumbers and courgettes with a sauce made from sour cream, horseradish and paprika.

voisin, pommes *(pom vwah-zaʀ)* Potato-cake made of sliced potato and grated cheese.

volailles *(vol-ī)* General term for poultry and fowl.

vol-au-vent *(vol-ō-vawʀ)* A light puff-pastry case shaped like a little pot, with a tasty filling—there are lots of kinds—and a tiny pastry lid; served hot. Perhaps the most familiar kind of *vol-au-vent* is *bouchée à la reine*, which has a filling of savoury creamed chicken.

vosgienne, à la *(ah lah vō-zhyen)*

côtes *(kot . . .)* Pork chops cooked with plums in a vinegar and white wine sauce.

hogue *(hōg . . .)* Plum cake made with rye-flour.

vras *(vras)* Colloquial name for the wrasse *(vieille)*.

W

waffelpasteta *(va-fəl-pas-tā-tah)* Truffled *foie gras* baked in pastry.

waldorf, salade *(sa-lahd val-dorf)* Salad of apples, celery and walnuts in mayonnaise.

walewska, sole *(sol va-lev-skah)* Poached sole with truffles and lobster, coated in cheese sauce with lobster butter then browned in an oven.

239

waterzooi or **waterzootje** *(va-tair-zoo-yə)* Freshwater fish or chicken stewed with vegetables in a creamy sauce.

whisky *(wis-kee)* Whisky— specifically, scotch whisky.

william *(weel-yam)* Kind of sweet autumn pear; also a pear-based drink: see *poire*.

winterthur, langouste à la *(lawn-goost ah lah veen-tair-tøer)* Spiny lobster or crawfish sliced and mixed with shrimps and mushrooms, served hot in the shell with *béchamel* sauce blended with lobster butter, topped with cheese and browned.

X

xavier, potage *(po-tahzh g'zav-yā)* Creamy rice soup with egg-yolks, butter and cream, garnished with diced chicken *royale*.

xérès *(k'sā-res)* Sherry.

Y

yaourt *(ya-oort)* Yoghourt.

york *(york)* York ham; boiled ham.

Yvette, pommes *(pom ee-vet)* Potato strips baked in butter; also called *pommes Annette*.

Z

zephyr *(ze-feer)* Menu term for light, frothy concoctions.

zeste *(zest)* Peel or rind, specifically of oranges, lemons or limes.

zewelmai or **zewelwai** *(zā-vel-mā zā-vel-vā)* Alsatian onion-and-cream flan.

ziminu *(see-mee-nøø)* Corsican fish soup similar to *bouillabaisse*.

zingara, à la *(ah lah zan-ga-rah)* 'Gypsy-style': with tomato sauce, or with a garnish of ham, truffles, tongue and mushrooms, plus tomato sauce.

zucchini *(zøø-kee-nee)* Italian marrow; courgette.

ACKNOWLEDGEMENTS

The authors and publishers would like to express their thanks to the following for inspiration, advice and practical assistance during the writing and production of this book: Michel Guérard, of Les Prés d'Eugénie; Jean-Claude Drai, of La Renaissance; A. Bonnet, of Au Pouilly-Fuissé; Marc Meneau of L'Espérance; Food and Wine from France, and The French Government Tourist Office; Technical Art Services, who prepared the maps; Evelyne du Boisson; Ilse Krist; Louisa Gosling; Lucy Evans; Margaret Hallam; and Nicky Colville.